D0142831

Restoration England

CONFERENCE ON BRITISH STUDIES
BIBLIOGRAPHICAL HANDBOOKS

Editor: J. JEAN HECHT

Consultant Editor: G. R. ELTON

Restoration England 1660-1689

WILLIAM L. SACHSE
UNIVERSITY OF WISCONSIN

CAMBRIDGE
for the Conference on British Studies
AT THE UNIVERSITY PRESS
1971

Published by the Syndics of the Cambridge University Press
Bentley House, 200 Euston Road, London N.W.1
American Branch: 32 East 57th Street, New York, N.Y.10022

Library of Congress Catalogue Card Number: 72–152640

ISBN: 0 521 08171 8

Printed in Great Britain
at the University Printing House, Cambridge
(Brooke Crutchley, University Printer)

CONTENTS

PREFACE

This handbook is designed to provide as comprehensive a general bibliography of Restoration England as can be managed within the compass of some two thousand items. The period here covered runs from the spring of 1660, when Charles II gained the throne, to the winter of 1688–9, when it passed to William and Mary.

The categorical arrangements are those which have been adopted for the series as a whole. These apply, essentially, to the national history of England in its political, economic, social and intellectual aspects. A few works dealing with Wales, Scotland and Ireland have been included, but their selection has been governed by the major objective. It will be noticed that no attempt has been made to provide systematic listings of works in the fields of Local History, Colonial History or Literary History. But some works in these categories have been included, in various sections, when they tend to illustrate the main currents of English life. For example, references to works on Local History may be found under Constitutional or Political History, while some works dealing with the colonies may be found there, and others under Economic History. As for Literary History, a few items of importance will be found under Intellectual History, and, to the extent that they illustrate various aspects of the English scene, in other sections.

In a bibliography such as this, the problem of selection is, of course, the thorniest one. Since it is intended primarily for advanced students and mature scholars, few works of a 'popular' character have been included. But there are some books and a few articles, without the paraphernalia of scholarship, which deserve to be listed. In determining the inclusion of such works, the criteria adopted are the absence or rarity of more academic treatment as well as certain qualities – informativeness, readability, point of view – which make them interesting. An attempt has been made to exclude obsolete works. But it is difficult, even dangerous, in many instances to pass judgment here. In a sense no historical work is ever obsolete. It may be deemed out of date with regard to its substantive content, and still be of value because of the approach and interpretations which it embodies.

A second problem is the location of individual items within the framework of the fourteen established categories. It need hardly be said that certain works may justifiably be placed in more than one. Thus certain items may be labelled either Social or Economic, Political or Constitutional, Religious or Intellectual. No work has been entered more than once in the listing. The reader should, therefore, in some instances, extend his searches beyond a given section. He will gain some assistance through cross-references – by item number alone where the same author is cited, and by author's name as well as number where a different writer is involved.

To most items some comment has been appended, conveying the compiler's opinion of the value of the work, or serving to elucidate its character when this is not obvious from the title. The relevance of works not confined to the period (which always refers to the years 1660–89) is particularly noted. Evaluations in most instances represent a consensus of the findings of scholars. Controversial works of any importance are so labelled. Useful works on common topics are frequently linked together in the commentary. Here the predilections of the compiler probably loom larger than elsewhere.

When compiling any bibliography, a chronological cut-off point must be established if the work is ever to go to the printer. This handbook represents a systematic search for items in print on 1 January 1969. Some useful works of later imprint, however, have been included.

I am indebted to Dr J. Jean Hecht, the General Editor, for his useful counsel on many questions which have arisen during the preparation of this book, and for his careful reading and checking of the manuscript. I also wish to thank Professor Paul H. Hardacre, of Vanderbilt University, for his preliminary critical review of the manuscript, and Professor Douglas Lacey, of the United States Naval Academy, for criticizing the section on Religious History. Some of my graduate students at the University of Wisconsin have also been helpful, particularly John Campbell, who assisted me with much of the preliminary searching, and Margaret Steneck and Stephen Beaumont, who made valuable suggestions for the Science and Technology and Military and Naval sections. Financial and other assistance from the University of Wisconsin is also gratefully acknowledged.

WILLIAM L. SACHSE

Madison, Wisconsin
April 1971

ABBREVIATIONS

AgHR	*Agricultural History Review*
AHR	*American Historical Review*
Ann. Sci.	*Annals of Science*
BHM	*Bulletin of the History of Medicine*
BIHR	*Bulletin of the Institute of Historical Research*
Cam. Hist. J.	*Cambridge Historical Journal*
CMH	*The Cambridge Modern History*, ed. Lord Acton *et al.*, Cambridge, 1902–26
Church Hist.	*Church History*
CQR	*Church Quarterly Review*
Ec. Hist.	*Economic History*
EcHR	*Economic History Review*
EHR	*English Historical Review*
Hist.	*History*
Hist. J.	*Historical Journal*
Hist. T.	*History Today*
HLQ	*Huntington Library Quarterly*
Hug. Soc. Proc.	*Proceedings of the Huguenot Society of London*
JEH	*Journal of Ecclesiastical History*
JFHS	*Journal of the Friends' Historical Society*
JHI	*Journal of the History of Ideas*
JMH	*Journal of Modern History*
JSAHR	*Journal of the Society for Army Historical Research*
Lib.	*Library*
LQR	*Law Quarterly Review*
MM	*Mariner's Mirror*
Mod. Phil.	*Modern Philology*
N. R. Roy. Soc.	*Notes and Records of the Royal Society*
PP	*Past and Present*
TRHS	*Transactions of the Royal Historical Society*

EXPLANATORY NOTES

Where no place of publication is given, it is London. Where there is more than one place of publication, the London edition is usually cited, except in a few instances where it was not available to the compiler.

Works are entered under the name of author rather than editor. This is the case whether or not they were published during the lifetime of the author. For example, the Wheatley edition of Pepys's diary is entered under Pepys, not Wheatley.

For printed sources where no author's name occurs, editors' names generally precede titles of works. But where works have been published by official agencies of the United Kingdom the opposite course has been taken.

I BIBLIOGRAPHIES

1 *Annual bibliography of the history of British art.* Cambridge, 1936–. Begins with publications of 1934; very detailed.

2 *Annual bulletin of historical literature.* 1912–. Begins with publications of 1911; published by the Historical Association. Sections are devoted to the seventeenth century.

3 Bateson, Frederick W. (ed.). *The Cambridge bibliography of English literature.* Cambridge, 1940–57. Vol. II covers 1660–1800. Contents include sections on education, social history, historians, and antiquaries. A new edition of the entire work is being prepared. A supplement to 1955, ed. George Watson, appeared in 1966.

4 Baxter, Stephen B. 'Recent writings on William III', *JMH*, **38** (Sept. 1966), 256–66.

5 Bellot, H. Hale and A. Taylor Milne. *Writings on British history, 1901–1933* (Royal Historical Society). 1968–, 5 vols. in 7 parts. Includes books and articles published between these years. Vol. I deals with auxiliary sciences and general works, vol. III with the Tudor–Stuart era. An elaborate and valuable compilation, but without annotation.

6 Berkowitz, David S. *Bibliotheca bibliographica Britannica, or bibliographies in British history.* Waltham, Mass., 1963–. In progress.

7 Besterman, Theodore. *A world bibliography of bibliographies.* 4th ed., Lausanne, 1965–6, 5 vols.

8 *A bibliography of parliamentary debates of Great Britain* (House of Commons Library, document no. 2). 1956. The best guide for the subject.

9 Bland, Desmond S. *A bibliography of the inns of court and chancery* (Selden Society, supplementary ser., III). 1965.

10 Callender, Geoffrey A. R. (ed.). *Bibliography of naval history*, part 1 (Historical Association Leaflets, no. 58). 1924.

11 Caron, Pierre and Marc Jaryc (eds.). *World list of historical periodicals and bibliographies.* Oxford, 1939.

12 Chaloner, William H. 'Bibliography of recent work on enclosure, the open fields, and related topics', *AgHR*, **2** (1954), 48–52.

13 Chappell, Edwin. *Bibliographia Pepysiana.* Blackheath, 1933. A short-title list, chiefly of the compiler's books.

14 Chrimes, Stanley B. and I. A. Roots (eds.). *English constitutional history: a select bibliography* (Helps for Students of History, no. 58). 1958.

15 Christophersen, Halfdan O. *Bibliographical introduction to the study of John Locke* (Skrifter utgitt av det Norske Videnskaps-Akademi i Oslo). Hist.-fil. Klasse, no. 8. Oslo, 1930.

16 Chubb, Thomas. *The printed maps in the atlases of Great Britain and Ireland: a bibliography, 1579–1870.* 1927. Contains biographical notes on map makers, engravers, and publishers.

17 Clark, George N. *List of authorities on British relations with the Dutch, 1603–1713.* 1920.

18 Cordeaux, Edward H. and D. H. Merry. *A bibliography of printed works relating to the University of Oxford.* Oxford, 1968. Nearly 9000 items in all, with elaborate categorization.

19 Cowley, John D. *A bibliography of abridgements, digests, dictionaries, and indexes of English law to the year 1800.* 1932.

20 Crane, Ronald S. *et al.* (eds.). 'English literature of the Restoration and eighteenth century', published annually in *Philological Quarterly*, 1926–. Very useful for students of social and intellectual history. The bibliographies from 1926 to 1950 have been republished in two vols., ed. Louis A. Landa and Arthur Friedman (Princeton, 1950–2); those from 1951 to 1960 in two vols., ed. Gwin J. Kolb and Curt A. Zimansky (1962).

21 Davies, Godfrey (ed.). *Bibliography of British history, Stuart period, 1603–1714.* Oxford, 1928. The standard bibliography for the Stuart period as a whole. 2nd ed., rev., by Mary F. Keeler (1970).

22 Day, Cyrus L. and Eleanore B. Murrie. *English song-books, 1651–1702: a bibliography with a first-line index of songs.* 1941.

23 Dexter, Henry M. *Congregationalism of the last three hundred years as seen in its literature.* New York, 1880. Lectures, with a bibliographical appendix of over 7000 titles, covering 1546–1879.

24 Ford, Wyn K. *Music in England before 1800: a select bibliography.* 1967. A substantial, detailed work.

25 Frewer, Louis B. (ed.). *Bibliography of historical writings published in Great Britain and the Empire, 1940–1945.* Oxford, 1947.

26 Fussell, George E. 'Agriculture from the Restoration to Anne', *EcHR*, **9** (Nov. 1938), 68–74. A bibliographical essay devoted to various works on agriculture.

27 —— 'English printed books on agriculture: part 4, 1651–1700', *Bookman's Journal*, **14** (Sept.–Oct. 1926), 160–7; **16** (no. 6, 1928), 306–16.

28 —— *Exploration of England: a select bibliography of travel and topography, 1570–1815.* 1935.

29 —— and V. G. B. Atwater. 'Travel and topography in seventeenth-century England: a bibliography of sources for social and economic history'. *Lib.*, 4th ser., **13** (Dec. 1932), 292–311.

30 Gerould, James T. (ed.). *Sources of English history of the seventeenth century, 1603–1689, in the University of Minnesota library, with a selection of secondary material* (Research Publications of the University of Minnesota, bibliographical series, no. 1). Minneapolis, 1921.

31 Gray, George J. *Bibliography of the works of Sir Isaac Newton, together with a list of books illustrating his life and works.* 2nd ed., rev. and enlarged, Cambridge, 1907.

32 Grose, Clyde L. *A select bibliography of British history, 1660–1760.* Chicago, 1939, repr. 1967. Indispensable; detailed and well-organized, with considerable comment.

33 —— 'Studies of 1931–40 on British history, 1660–1760', *JMH*, **12** (Dec. 1940), 515–34. A bibliographical article.

34 —— 'Thirty years' study of a formerly neglected century of British history, 1660–1760', *JMH*, **2** (Sept. 1930), 448–71. A bibliographical article.

35 Gross, Charles. *A bibliography of British municipal history, including gilds and parliamentary representation.* 2nd ed., Leicester, 1966. A reprint of the 1897 ed., with a preface by G. H. Martin.

36 Howard-Hill, Trevor H. *Bibliography of British literary bibliographies.* Oxford, 1969. Useful for students of intellectual and social history.

37 Humphreys, Arthur L. *A handbook to county bibliography, being a bibliography of bibliographies relating to the counties and towns of Great Britain and Ireland.* 1917.

38 *International bibliography of historical sciences.* Paris, 1930–.

39 Jacobs, Joseph and Lucien Wolf. *Bibliotheca Anglo-Judaica: a bibliographical guide to Anglo-Jewish history.* 1888.

40 Jacobs, Phyllis M. 'Registers of the universities, colleges, and schools of Great Britain and Ireland', *BIHR*, **37** (Nov. 1964), 185–232.

41 Jenkins, Rhys T. and William Rees (eds.). *Bibliography of the history of Wales.* 2nd ed., Cardiff, 1962. The basic guide.

42 Kahl, William F. *The development of London livery companies: an historical essay and a select bibliography* (Kress Library of Business and Economics, pub. no. 15). Boston, Mass., 1960. Lengthy bibliography, supplemented by Kahl in *Guildhall Miscellany*, **2** (Apr. 1962), 99–126.

43 Kellaway, William (ed.). *Bibliography of historical works issued in the United Kingdom, 1957–1960* (Institute of Historical Research). 1962. This and the following work are excellent compilations, but lack annotation.

44 —— *Bibliography of historical works issued in the United Kingdom, 1961–1965* (Institute of Historical Research). 1967.

45 Keynes, Geoffrey L. *John Evelyn: a study in bibliophily and a bibliography of his writings.* Cambridge, 1937.

46 Lancaster, Joan C. (ed.). *Bibliography of historical works issued in the United Kingdom, 1946–1956* (Institute of Historical Research). 1957. Excellent compilation, without annotation.

47 MacPike, E. F. 'English, Scottish, and Irish diaries, journals, and commonplace books, etc., 1500–1900: a bibliographical guide to selected material', *Bulletin of Bibliography*, **17** (Sept.–Dec. 1942, Jan.–Apr. 1943), 183–5, 213–15.

48 Madan, Falconer. *Oxford books: a bibliography of printed works relating to the university and city of Oxford or printed or published there*, vol. III. Oxford, 1931. Extends to 1680.

49 Manwaring, George E. (ed.). *A bibliography of British naval history: a bibliographical and historical guide to printed and manuscript sources*. 1930. Printed sources include articles but not books.

50 Matthews, Arnold G. *The works of Richard Baxter: an annotated list*. Oxted, 1932.

51 Matthews, William (comp.). *British autobiographies: an annotated bibliography of British autobiographies published or written before 1951*. Berkeley, 1955.

52 —— *British diaries: an annotated bibliography of British diaries written between 1442 and 1942*. Berkeley, 1950. A very useful work; brief descriptions of diaries are given. Some unpublished diaries are included.

53 Maxwell, William H. and Leslie F. (eds.). *A legal bibliography of the British Commonwealth of Nations*, I, *English law to 1800*. 2nd ed., 1955.

54 Milne, A. Taylor (ed.). *Writings on British history*. 1937–60, 8 vols. Includes books and articles published from 1934 to 1945; an admirable work, virtually comprehensive but not annotated.

55 Mogg, W. Rees. 'Some reflections on the bibliography of Burnet', *Lib.*, 5th ser., **4** (Sept. 1949), 100–13.

56 Mollat, Michel. *Les sources de l'histoire maritime en Europe du moyen âge au XVIIIe siècle*. Paris, 1962.

57 Murphy, Gwendolen. *A bibliography of English character-books, 1608–1700*. 1925.

58 Noyes, Gertrude E. *Bibliography of courtesy and conduct books in seventeenth-century England*. New Haven, 1937. Nearly 500 items, many from the period.

59 Ogden, Henry V. S. and Margaret S. Ogden. 'Bibliography of seventeenth-century writings on the pictorial arts in English', *Art Bulletin*, **29** (Sept. 1947), 196–201.

60 Pollen, John H. (ed.). *Sources for the history of Roman Catholics in England, Ireland, and Scotland from the Reformation period to that of emancipation, 1533 to 1795* (Helps for Students of History, no. 39). 1921.

61 Smith, Joseph. *Bibliotheca anti-quakeriana, or a catalogue of books adverse to the Society of Friends...with biographical notices of the authors*, etc. 1873. This and the following retain considerable value.

62 —— *A descriptive catalogue of Friends' books, or books written by members of the Society of Friends...from their first rise to the present time*. 1867, 2 vols. A third, supplementary volume was published in 1893.

63 Starr, Edward C. (ed.). *A Baptist bibliography, being a register of printed material by and about Baptists, including works written against the Baptists*. Philadelphia, etc., 1947–, 13 vols. In progress; an elaborate compilation, now through 'Layton'.

64 Stride, Edward E. 'A bibliography of works relating to the Huguenot refugees: whence they came and where they settled', *Hug. Soc. Proc.*, **1** (1887), 130–49.

65 Upcott, William. *Bibliographical account of the principal works relative to English topography*. 1818, 3 vols. A useful guide to seventeenth- and eighteenth-century works.

66 Walcott, Robert. 'The later Stuarts (1660–1714): significant work of the past twenty years (1939–1959)', *AHR*, **68** (Jan. 1962), 353–70. Useful in bringing Davies (21) and Grose (32) up to date.

67 —— *The Tudor–Stuart period of English history (1485–1714): a review of changing interpretations* (Service Center for Teachers of History, no. 58). New York, 1964. A lucid and well-balanced treatment, providing useful appraisals of various important and controversial works.

68 Wallis, Peter J. *Histories of old schools: a revised list for England and Wales*. Newcastle-upon-Tyne, 1966. Deals with schools before 1700; arrangement is by counties.

69 Weed, Katherine K. and Richmond P. Bond. *Studies of British newspapers and periodicals from their beginning to 1800: a bibliography* (University of North Carolina Studies in Philology, extra ser., no. 2). Chapel Hill, 1946.

70 White, Arthur S. *A bibliography of regimental histories of the British army* (Society for Army Historical Research). 1965.

71 Whitley, William T. (ed.). *A Baptist bibliography, being a register of the chief materials for Baptist history, whether in manuscript or in print.* 1916–22, 2 vols. Vol. I covers 1526–1776; valuable, but being superseded by Starr (63).

72 Whitney, James P. *A bibliography of church history* (Historical Association Leaflets, no. 55). 1923.

II CATALOGUES, GUIDES, AND HANDBOOKS

73 Adair, Edward R. *The sources for the history of the council in the sixteenth and seventeenth centuries* (Helps for Students of History, no. 51). 1924.

74 American Theological Library Association. *Index to religious periodical literature.* Chicago *et al.*, 1953–.

75 Arber, Edward. *The term catalogues, 1668–1709, with a number for Easter term, 1711.* 1903–6, 3 vols. Classified lists of works from contemporary booksellers' quarterly catalogues. More valuable than Eyre's *Transcript* (107).

76 Atkinson, Christopher T. 'Material for military history in the reports of the Historical Manuscripts Commission', *JSAHR*, **21** (Spring 1942), 17–34.

77 Barnes, George R. *A list of books printed in Cambridge at the University Press, 1521–1800.* Cambridge, 1935.

78 Bittner, Ludwig and Lothar Gross. *Repertorium der diplomatischen Vertreter aller Länder seit dem Westfälischen Frieden*, vol. I, *1648–1715* (International Committee of Historical Sciences). 1936.

79 Bodleian Library. *Catalogi codicum manuscriptorum bibliothecae Bodleianae*, Oxford, 1845–1930, 20 vols. Includes such important collections as the Ashmolean, Tanner, and Rawlinson MSS.

80 —— *Summary catalogue of western manuscripts*, ed. Falconer Madan and Herbert H. E. Craster. Oxford, 1895–1953, 7 vols. in 8.

81 Bond, Maurice F. *The records of Parliament: a guide for genealogists and local historians.* Canterbury, 1964.

82 Brendon, John A. *A dictionary of British history.* 1937.

83 *British humanities index* (The Library Association). 1963–. Quarterly; indexes many local and special journals.

84 British Museum. *The catalogues of the manuscript collections.* 1962. Lists the major collections of the Museum, and their catalogues.

85 —— *General catalogue of printed books.* 1959–66, 263 vols. The photolithographic ed., going to 1955. The importance of the Museum's holdings makes this an indispensable work.

86 —— *General catalogue of printed books: ten-year supplement, 1956–65.* 1968, 50 vols.

87 —— *Subject index of modern books.* 1902–. Covers books acquired 1881–1960, except for years 1951–5.

88 *The British national bibliography: a subject list of new books published in Great Britain.* 1950–. Appears annually; index vols. published periodically.

89 *The bulletins of the National Register of Archives.* 1948–. Particularly useful for information on local collections.

90 *A catalogue of the manuscripts preserved in the library of the University of Cambridge.* Cambridge, 1861–7, 5 vols.

91 Cheney, Christopher R. (ed.). *Handbook of dates for students of English history* (Royal Historical Society guides and handbooks, no. 4). 1945. A basic chronological guide.

92 Clark, G. Kitson and Geoffrey R. Elton (eds.). *Guide to the research facilities in history in the universities of Great Britain and Ireland*. 2nd ed., Cambridge, 1965.

93 Cokayne, George E. (ed.). *Complete baronetage, 1611–1800*. Exeter, 1900–6, 5 vols.

94 —— *The complete peerage of England, Scotland, Ireland, Great Britain, and the United Kingdom*. New ed., revised and enlarged by Vicary Gibbs *et al.*, 1910–59, 13 vols. The definitive biographical compilation.

95 Collins, Arthur. *The peerage of England*, ed. Egerton Brydges. 1812, 9 vols. First published 1709; still useful.

96 Cox, John C. *Churchwardens' accounts from the fourteenth century to the close of the seventeenth century*. 1913. Provides a chronological list of accounts.

97 Crane, Ronald S. and Frederick B. Kaye. *A census of British newspapers and periodicals, 1620–1800* (University of North Carolina Studies in Philology, vol. XXIV, no. 1). Chapel Hill, 1927. Includes location of individual items.

98 Crawford and Balcarres, James L. Lindsay, earl of (ed.). *Catalogue of a collection of English ballads of the seventeenth and eighteenth centuries* (Bibliotheca Lindesiana). Aberdeen, 1890; also New York, 1961, 2 vols. Mainly 1660–89. An index to the main collection of state poems and ballads, 1660–1702, is in *Notes and Queries*, 5th ser., **6** (1876), 401–533 *passim*.

99 —— *Catalogue of English broadsides, 1505–1897* (Bibliotheca Lindesiana). Aberdeen, 1898.

100 —— *Catalogue of English newspapers, 1641–66* (Bibliotheca Lindesiana). Aberdeen, 1901.

101 Croft-Murray, Edward and Paul Hulton. *Catalogue of British drawings*, vol. I. 1960. British Museum collection. Covers sixteenth and seventeenth centuries.

102 Davenport, Francis G. (ed.). 'Materials for English diplomatic history, 1509–1783, calendared in the reports of the Historical Manuscripts Commission, with reference to similar materials in the British Museum', Historical Manuscripts Commission, 18th Report, 1917, pt. 2, pp. 357–402. A useful guide to the more readily available sources.

103 Davies, Godfrey. *A student's guide to the manuscripts relating to English history in the seventeenth century in the Bodleian Library* (Helps for Students of History, no. 47). 1922. A brief guide.

104 Dr Williams's Library. *Early nonconformity, 1566–1800: a catalogue of books in Dr Williams's Library, London*. Boston, Mass., 1968, 5 vols. An author catalogue.

105 Ekwall, B. O. Eilert. *Concise Oxford dictionary of English place-names*. 4th ed., Oxford, 1960.

106 Esdaile, Arundell J. K. *A dictionary of the printers and booksellers who were at work in England, Scotland, and Ireland from 1668 to 1725*. 1922. Contains brief notices; cf. Plomer (147).

107 [Eyre, G. E. Briscoe]. *A transcript of the registers of the worshipful Company of Stationers from 1640–1708 A.D.* 1913–14, 3 vols.

108 Fordham, Herbert G. *The road-books and itineraries of Great Britain, 1570 to 1850*. Cambridge, 1924. Useful for social history; includes bibliography.

109 Fortescue, George K. (ed.). *Catalogue of the pamphlets, books, newspapers, and manuscripts relating to the Civil War, the Commonwealth, and Restoration, collected by George Thomason, 1640–1661*. 1908, 2 vols. Known as Thomason Tracts. An invaluable collection in the British Museum.

110 Fowler, Robert C. (ed.). *Episcopal registers of England and Wales* (Helps for Students of History, no. 1). 1918. A brief guide to episcopal records.

111 Francis, Frank (ed.). *Narcissus Luttrell's Popish Plot catalogues* (Luttrell Society reprints, no. 15). Oxford, 1956. A photographic reprint of the 1680 ed.

112 Fry, Mary Isabel and Godfrey Davies, 'Supplements to the *Short-title catalogue 1641–1700*', *HLQ*, **16** (Aug. 1953), 393–436. Items not listed in Wing (173).

113 Gabler, Anthony J. 'Check list of English newspapers and periodicals before 1801 in the Huntington Library', *Huntington Library Bulletin*, **2** (Nov. 1931), 1–66.

114 Gee, Edward A. *A catalogue of all the discourses published against popery during the reign of King James II.* 1689. Authors include Church of England men and dissenters.

115 Gillett, Charles R. *Catalogue of the McAlpin collection of British history and theology.* New York, 1927–30, 5 vols. An important collection in Union Theological Seminary, New York. Vols. III and IV cover 1653–1700.

116 Giuseppi, Montague S. (ed.). *A guide to the manuscripts preserved in the Public Record Office.* 1923–4, 2 vols. Still of some use, though superseded by (117).

117 *Guide to the contents of the Public Record Office.* 1963, 2 vols. Vol. I describes legal records, vol. II state papers and departmental records. Replaces Giuseppi (116).

118 Hall, Hubert (ed.). *List and index of the publications of the Royal Historical Society, 1871–1924, and of the Camden Society, 1840–1897.* 1925.

119 Hardacre, Paul H. 'County record offices in England and Wales: a list of guides and references', *American Archivist*, **25** (Oct. 1962), 477–83. Useful for local records; arrangement by counties.

120 HMSO. *Publications of the Royal Commission on Historical Manuscripts* (Sectional List, no. 17). Issued annually.

121 —— *Record publications* (Sectional List, no. 24). Issued annually; guide to the publications of the PRO, etc.

122 Hicks, Frederick C. *Materials and methods of legal research.* 3rd ed., rev., Rochester, N.Y., 1942.

123 Historical Manuscripts Commission. *A guide to the reports...issued by the Royal Commissioners for Historical Manuscripts*, part 1: *Topographical.* 1914.

124 —— *Guide to the reports of the Royal Commission on Historical Manuscripts, 1870–1911*, part 2: *Index of persons*, ed. Francis Bickley. 1935–8, 2 vols.

125 —— *Guide to the reports of the Royal Commission on Historical Manuscripts, 1911–1957*, part 2: *Index of persons*, ed. A. C. S. Hall. 1966, 3 vols.

126 —— *Record repositories in Great Britain.* 2nd ed., 1966. An informative guide, arranged under places and regions.

127 Jenkins, Claude. *Ecclesiastical records: three lectures* (Helps for Students of History, no. 18). 1920. More specialized than Whitney (72).

128 Jones, Philip E. and Raymond Smith. *A guide to the records in the Corporation of London Records Office and the Guildhall Library Muniment Room.* 1951.

129 Jones, Thomas (ed.). *A catalogue of the collection of tracts for and against popery (published in or about the reign of James II) in the Manchester library founded by Humphrey Chetham* (Chetham Society, XLVIII, LXIV). 1859–65.

130 Kennedy, W. P. M. 'List of visitation articles and injunctions, 1604–1715', *EHR*, **40** (Oct. 1925), 586–92.

131 Kunitz, Stanley J. and Howard Haycraft. *British authors before 1800: a biographical dictionary.* New York, 1952.

132 Library of Congress. *The national union catalog of manuscript collections.* Ann Arbor, Mich., 1962. Describes holdings of various U.S. repositories.

133 —— *The national union catalog: pre-1956 imprints.* 1968–. 129 vols. to date (to 'Curschmann'). For other Library of Congress catalogues, see vol. I, vii–x.

134 Lloyd, John Edward and Rhys T. Jenkins (eds.). *The dictionary of Welsh biography down to 1940.* 1959.

135 Long, Philip. *A summary catalogue of the Lovelace collection of the papers of John Locke in the Bodleian Library, Oxford* (Oxford Bibliographical Society Publications, new ser., VIII). Oxford, 1959. A collection of marked importance.

136 McCulloch, John R. *The literature of political economy: a classified catalogue of select publications...with historical, critical, and biographical notices.* 1845; also New York, 1964.

137 Milford, Robert T. and Donald M. Sutherland. *A catalogue of English newspapers and periodicals in the Bodleian Library, 1622–1800* (Oxford Bibliographical Society, Proceedings and Papers, IV, 163–344). Oxford, 1936.

138 [Muddiman, Joseph G.] *Tercentenary handlist of English and Welsh newspapers, magazines, and reviews.* 1920. Covers 1620–1920; published by *The Times.*

139 Mullins, Edward L. C. *A guide to the historical and archaeological publications of societies in England and Wales, 1901–1933.* 1968.

140 Mullins, Edward L. C. (ed.). *Texts and calendars: an analytical guide to serial publications* (Royal Historical Society Guides and Handbooks, no. 7). 1958. A first-rate list of source materials published by the national government, and by national and local historical societies.

141 Munby, Alan N. L. *Cambridge college libraries: aids for research students*. 2nd ed., Cambridge, 1962. A helpful introduction to the collections.

142 Myers, Denys P. (ed.). *Manual of collections of treaties and of collections relating to treaties* (Harvard Bibliographies, library ser.). Cambridge, Mass., 1922.

143 O'Donoghue, Freeman M. and H. M. Hake. *Catalogue of engraved British portraits in the British Museum*. 1908–25, 6 vols.

144 Ollard, Sidney L., Gordon Crosse and Maurice F. Bond (eds.). *A dictionary of English church history*. 3rd ed., rev., 1948.

145 Perrin, William G. (ed.). *Admiralty Library. Subject catalogue of printed books*. 1912. Part I, the historical section, provides an excellent general bibliography for naval history.

146 Piper, David (ed.). *Catalogue of the seventeenth-century portraits in the National Portrait Gallery, 1625–1714*. Cambridge, 1963.

147 Plomer, Henry R. *A dictionary of the booksellers and printers who were at work in England, Scotland, and Ireland from 1641 to 1667*. 1907. Cf. Esdaile (106).

148 Poole, Rachael E. (comp.). *Catalogue of portraits in the possession of the university, colleges, city, and county of Oxford*. Oxford, 1912–25, 3 vols.

149 Powicke, Frederick Maurice and E. B. Fryde (eds.). *Handbook of British chronology* (Royal Historical Society Guides and Handbooks, no. 2). 2nd ed., 1961. Lists rulers, high-ranking noblemen, various office-holders, parliaments and church councils.

150 *Public Record Office: lists and indexes*, 1892–1936, 55 vols.; *Supplementary series*, 1961–. Detailed lists and indexes of source materials in the Public Record Office.

151 Purvis, John S. *An introduction to ecclesiastical records*. 1954. Helpful for research in ecclesiastical administration.

152 *Reports and calendars issued by the Royal Commission on Historical Manuscripts*, 1874–. The indispensable guide to manuscript materials in private collections. Materials are listed, abstracted, calendared, or transcribed. For some of the principal collections relating to the period, see Grose (32), pp. 14–15; Mullins (140) describes the contents of the reports and calendars in considerable detail.

153 *Reports of the deputy keeper of the public records*. 1840–88. Lists, indexes, calendars, and inventories of materials in his custody.

154 *Reports of the Royal Commission on Public Records*. 3 vols., in *Parliamentary papers*, 1912–13, 1914 and 1919. Reports on national and local records.

155 Roberts, A. D. 'Searching for the texts of treaties', *Journal of Documentation*, 5 (Dec. 1949), 136–63.

156 Roberts, Richard A. *The reports of the Historical Manuscripts Commission* (Helps for Students of History, no. 22). 1920. A brief description of the Commission's work and the principal collections.

157 Rollins, Hyder E. *An analytical index to the ballad entries, 1557–1709, in the registers of the Stationers Company of London*. Chapel Hill, 1924.

158 Shaw, William A. *The knights of England: a complete record... of the knights of all the orders of chivalry in England, Scotland, and Ireland, and of knights bachelors*. 1906, 2 vols. A listing, with dates.

159 Somerville, Robert (ed.). *Handlist of record publications* (British Record Association, pamphlet no. 3). 1951.

160 Spokes, Peter S. (ed.). *Summary catalogue of manuscripts in the Bodleian Library relating to the city, county, and university of Oxford: accessions from 1916 to 1962* (Oxford Historical Society, new ser., XVII). 1964.

161 Steinberg, Sigfrid H. *A new dictionary of British history*. 1963.

162 Stephen, Leslie and Sidney Lee (eds.). *Dictionary of national biography*. 1885–1903, 63 vols. The most complete general work; still basic though obsolescent. An *Errata* volume appeared in 1904; for addenda and corrigenda see *BIHR*.

163 Stewart, James D. *et al.* (eds.). *British union catalogue of periodicals...in British libraries.* 1955–8, 4 vols.

164 *The subject index to periodicals.* 1915–. The best guide to periodicals containing articles on British history.

165 Sweet and Maxwell, Ltd, publ. *Sweet and Maxwell's Guide to law reports and statutes.* 4th ed., 1962.

166 Tanner, Joseph R. *et al.* (eds.). *Bibliotheca Pepysiana: a descriptive catalogue of the library of Samuel Pepys.* 1914–40, 4 vols. The library is at Magdalene College, Cambridge, and contains manuscripts as well as books.

167 Thirsk, Joan. *Sources of information on population, 1500–1760, and unexplored sources in local records.* Canterbury, 1965. A brief survey.

168 Thomas, Roger (ed.). *The Baxter treatises: a catalogue of the Richard Baxter papers (other than the letters) in Dr. Williams Library.* 1959.

169 Thomson, Theodore R. (ed.). *A catalogue of British family histories.* 2nd ed., 1935.

170 Tucker, Joseph E. 'Wing's *Short-title catalogue* and translations from the French, 1641–1700', *Papers of the Bibliographical Society of America,* **49** (1st quarter, 1955), 37–67. Sets forth additions and corrections.

171 Winfield, Percy H. *The chief sources of English legal history.* Cambridge, Mass., 1925.

172 Wing, Donald G. *A gallery of ghosts: books published between 1641–1700 not found in the Short-title catalogue.* New York, 1967. Refers to (173).

173 —— *Short-title catalogue of books printed in England, Scotland, Ireland, Wales, and British America, and of English books printed in other countries.* New York, 1945–51, 3 vols. Invaluable for books and their locations; for supplements see (172) and Tucker (170); also Sutherland (2161), p. 444, and Fry (112).

III GENERAL SURVEYS

174 Ashley, Maurice. *England in the seventeenth century* (Pelican History of England, VI). 1952. A brief readable account, with four chapters on the period.

175 Aylmer, Gerald E. *The struggle for the constitution: England in the seventeenth century.* 1963. A good survey, 1603–89, mainly political and constitutional.

176 Baker, Richard. *A chronicle of the kings of England* [continued to 1661 by Edward Phillips]. 4th ed., 1665. There is a further continuation to 1727 in the eds. of 1730 and 1733. A valuable work, much read for a century.

177 Bate [Bates], George and Thomas Skinner. *Elenchus motuum nuperorum in Anglia, or a short historical account of the rise and progress of the late troubles in England in two parts...Motus compositi, or the history of the composing the affairs of England.* 1685, 3 pts. The latter portion deals with the period to 1669. Bate was a court physician; Skinner physician to Monck, whose life he wrote.

178 Browning, Andrew (ed.). *English historical documents, 1660–1714* (*English historical documents,* VIII). 1953. The best collection of documents for the period, with useful bibliographies under various categories.

179 Burnet, Gilbert. *Bishop Burnet's History of his own time,* ed. Martin J. Routh. Oxford, 1823, 7 vols. The best complete edition, containing previously unpublished notes by the Earls of Dartmouth and Hardwicke and Speaker Onslow. For the period to 1685 the ed. by Osmund Airy (Oxford, 1897–1900, 2 vols.) is best. Although Burnet was at times inadequately informed and often careless, the work is indispensable for an understanding of the period, as well as a literary classic.

180 —— *Supplement to Burnet's History of my own time,* ed. Helen C. Foxcroft. Oxford, 1902. Includes his autobiography, letters, private meditations, and what survives of the original draft of the *History.*

181 Churchill, Winston L. S. *A history of the English-speaking peoples,* II, *The new world.* New York, 1956. See Book VI, 'The Restoration'. History in the grand manner, and worth reading, though essentially conventional in interpretation.

182 Clark, George N. *The later Stuarts, 1660–1714*. 2nd ed., Oxford, 1955. In the Oxford History of England. The standard survey, and a very good one. Contains fairly extensive bibliographical sections.

183 D'Orleans, Pierre J. *History of the Revolutions in England under the family of the Stuarts*, trans. by John Stevens. 1711. First published, Paris, 1693–4; a Catholic, royalist treatment, covering 1603–90.

184 Echard, Laurence. *The history of England from the first entrance of Julius Caesar and the Romans to the establishment of King William and Queen Mary upon the throne*. 1707–18, 3 vols. A Tory antidote to Kennet (189), but less valuable.

185 Feiling, Keith G. *England under the Tudors and Stuarts*. 1927. A brief survey.

186 Firth, Charles H. *A commentary on Macaulay's History of England*, ed. Godfrey Davies. 1938. Comprised of articles and lectures; provides needed corrections.

187 Hill, Christopher. *The century of revolution, 1603–1714*, in *A history of England*, ed. Christopher Brooke and Denis Mack Smith, vol. v. Edinburgh, 1961. Topical and analytical presentation. A very interesting and readable book, strongly reflecting the author's views; considerable attention to social, economic and intellectual factors.

188 Jones, Idris Deane. *The English revolution: an introduction to English history, 1603–1714*. 1931.

189 Kennet, White. *A complete history of England from the earliest time to the death of King William III*. 1706, 3 vols. A work of considerable stature, but with pronounced Whig views.

190 Lingard, John. *A history of England to 1688*. 1819–30, 8 vols. Dated, but still of some use as the work of a learned moderate Catholic.

191 Lockyer, Roger. *Tudor and Stuart Britain, 1471–1714*. 1964. An excellent survey, embodying recent scholarship.

192 Lodge, Richard. *The history of England from the Restoration to the death of William III (1660–1702)*. Vol. VIII of *The political history of England*, ed. William Hunt and Reginald L. Poole. 1905. Almost exclusively political in coverage; outmoded to some extent, but still useful for factual detail.

193 London County Council [Greater London Council]. *Survey of London*. 1900–. In progress; 35 vols. to date. A detailed topography, with many illustrations, plans and architectural drawings.

194 Macaulay, Thomas B. *The history of England from the accession of James II*. 1849–61, 5 vols. Covers in detail the years 1685–97, but has lengthy introduction. Indispensable, despite its age and the author's bias. The classic Whig interpretation, embodying redoubtable scholarship and a vivid prose style. The edition by Charles H. Firth (1913–15, 6 vols.) is profusely illustrated, with useful notes. For corrective comment see Firth (186).

195 Macpherson, James. *The history of Great Britain from the Restoration to the accession of the house of Hanover*. 1775, 2 vols.

196 —— (ed.). *Original papers containing the secret history of Great Britain from the Restoration to the accession of the house of Hanover*. 1775, 2 vols. Chiefly after 1688. Must be used with caution; for comment, see Davies (21), no. 97; Browning (178), p. 40.

197 Morpurgo, Jack E. (ed.). *Life under the Stuarts*. 1950. Popular; essays on various aspects of Stuart England.

198 Ogg, David. *England in the reign of Charles II*. 2nd ed., Oxford, 1955, 2 vols. The best general treatment of the reign.

199 —— *England in the reigns of James II and William III*. Corrected ed., Oxford, 1957. The best modern survey, solid and judicious.

200 Oldmixon, John. *The critical history of England*. 1724–6, 2 vols. Strong Whig point of view; Clarendon and Echard are attacked, Burnet defended.

201 —— *The history of England during the reigns of the royal house of Stuart*. 1730. Inaccurate and controversial, but represents considerable industry.

202 Parker, Samuel. *Bishop Parker's history of his own time*, translated from the Latin original by Thomas Newlin. 1727. Covers 1660–80.

203 Petrie, Charles. *The Stuarts*. 1937. Chap. 7 presents a picture of Restoration England; Tory and royalist sympathies.

204 Ranke, Leopold von. *A history of England principally in the seventeenth century.* Oxford, 1875, 6 vols. Originally published in German (Berlin, 1859–69). Primarily useful for foreign affairs. An appendix in vol. VI provides interesting historiographical comment on the writings of Clarendon, James II, and Burnet.

205 Rapin de Thoyras, Paul. *The history of England, written in French by Mr. Rapin de Thoyras.* 1726–47, 28 vols. The translation is by Nicholas Tindal, who continued the work from 1689 to 1727. The leading work of this kind before Hume; especially valuable for the Revolution, in which Rapin participated.

206 Trevelyan, George M. *England under the Stuarts* (vol. V of *A history of England*, ed. Charles W. C. Oman). 1904; later editions. A brilliant work which, though Whiggish and dated, is still useful.

207 Welwood, James. *Memoirs of the most material transactions in England for the last hundred years.* 1700; later edition by Francis Maseres, 1820. Goes to 1688. A Whig interpretation by the physician to William and Mary.

208 Williamson, James A. *A short history of British expansion: the old colonial empire.* 4th ed., 1953.

IV CONSTITUTIONAL AND ADMINISTRATIVE HISTORY

1 Printed Sources

209 *Acts of the privy council of England, colonial series*, ed. W. L. Grant and James Munro. 1908–12, 6 vols. The period is covered in vols. I and II.

210 Airy, Osmund (ed.). *The Lauderdale papers, 1639–1679* (Camden Society, new ser., XXXIV, XXXVI, XXXVIII). 1884–5. Important for the correspondence of those responsible for Scottish administration.

211 Akerman, John Y. (ed.). *Moneys received and paid for secret services of Charles II and James II, from 30th March 1679 to 25th December 1688* (Camden Society, old ser., LII). 1851.

212 Brady, Robert. *The great point of succession discussed, with a full and particular answer to the late pamphlet intituled A brief history of succession.* 1681. A reply to Somers (269), defending hereditary right.

213 Browning, Andrew and Doreen J. Milne. 'An exclusion bill division list', *BIHR*, **23** (Nov. 1950), 205–25.

214 Burnet, Gilbert. *The life and death of Sir Matthew Hale.* 1682.

215 *Calendar of state papers, colonial series*, ed. Noel Sainsbury *et al.* 1860–. Vols. I–XIII cover 1660–89.

216 *Calendar of state papers, domestic series*, ed. Mary A. E. Green *et al.* 1860–. Thirty vols. have been published covering the years 1660–87. Highly important for English concernments; a leading source for naval and military history, and of some use for Irish and foreign affairs.

217 *Calendar of state papers relating to Ireland, 1625–1670*, ed. Robert P. Mahaffy. 1900–10, 8 vols. Irish papers after 1670 are to be found in (216).

218 *Calendar of treasury books*, ed. William A. Shaw *et al.* 1904–. The leading source for financial history. Vols. I–IX cover 1660–92, and contain valuable introductions.

219 *Calendar of treasury papers*, ed. Joseph Redington. 1868–89, 6 vols. Deals only with papers of minor interest addressed to the treasury. Vol. I covers 1557–1696, but is almost entirely after 1660.

220 [Chandler, Richard]. *The history and proceedings of the House of Commons from the Restoration to the present time.* 1742–4, 14 vols. Sometimes called 'Chandler', who was the publisher.

221 Cobbett, William (ed.). *Parliamentary history of England.* 1806–20, 36 vols. Unsatisfactory, but still useful for want of something better. Based on scattered sources. Vols. IV and V relate to the period, and have reprints of some late seventeenth-century pamphlets.

222 Cobbett, William *et al. Collection of state trials and proceedings for high treason and other crimes and misdemeanors from the earliest period to the present time.* 1809–26, 33 vols. For the most part a reprint of materials already published. Vols. V–XII cover the years 1650–96.

223 Costin, William C. and J. Steven Watson. *The law and the working of the constitution: documents 1660–1914.* 1952, 2 vols. A useful compilation. Vol. I covers 1660–1783.

224 *Debate at large between the Lords and Commons...relating to the word 'abdicated' and the vacancy of the throne.* 1695. Debate in the convention, 1689.

225 De Beer, Esmond S. 'A list of the department of the lord chamberlain of the household, autumn, 1663', *BIHR*, **19** (no. 55, 1942–3), 13–24.

226 Dering, Edward. *The parliamentary diary of Sir Edward Dering, 1670–73*, ed. Basil D. Henning. New Haven, 1940.

227 Dugdale, William. *Origines juridiciales, or historical memorials of the English laws, courts of justice, forms of tryall.* 1666.

228 Elsynge, Henry. *The ancient method and manner of holding of parliaments in England.* 1660. Elsynge had been clerk of the House of Commons; he drew largely on Hakewell's *Modus tenendi parliamentum*, 1659.

229 *An exact collection of the debates of the House of Commons.* 1689. Deals with the proceedings of 1680–1, at Westminster and Oxford.

230 *The faithful register, or the debates of the House of Commons in four several parliaments.* 1689. Deals with 1680–5.

231 Grey, Anchitel. *Debates of the House of Commons from the year 1667 to the year 1694.* 1763, 10 vols. Valuable; Grey was M.P. for Derby.

232 Haley, Kenneth H. D. 'A list of the English peers, *c.* May, 1687', *EHR*, **69** (Apr. 1954), 302–6. 161 peers, divided into political and religious categories. Cf. Hosford (240).

233 Hamilton, Alexander H. A. *Quarter sessions from Queen Elizabeth to Queen Anne: illustrations of local government and history, drawn from original records.* 1878. Chiefly from Devonshire records.

234 Hardacre, Paul H. (ed.). 'Newgate, 1663—a letter of Sir Orlando Bridgeman, chief justice', *American Journal of Legal History*, **13** (Oct. 1969), 384–9. Illustrates legal problems of the time.

235 *Historical collections, or a brief account of the most remarkable transactions of the last two parliaments.* 1681.

236 Historical Manuscripts Commission. *Calendar of the manuscripts of the marquess of Ormonde.* Ormonde new ser., 1902–20, 8 vols. See vol. IV, 374–598, for the letters of Sir Richard Southwell to the duke of Ormonde, 1677–80, which provide a detailed account of the politics of the time and illustrate proceedings of the council.

237 —— *The manuscripts of the duke of Beaufort, K.G., the earl of Donoughmore, and others.* 12th report, app. IX, 1891. Includes a brief parliamentary diary, 1680–1.

238 —— *The manuscripts of the House of Lords.* A calendar. For the period, see reports 7–9 (1648–78) and 11–14 (1678–93); see Grose (32), no. 294. Of prime importance for the activities of the Lords.

239 —— *Supplementary report on the manuscripts of the late Montagu Bertie, 12th earl of Lindsey.* 1942. The collection includes various official papers, largely financial or economic in character.

240 Hosford, David H. 'The peerage and the Test Act: a list, *c.* November 1687', *BIHR*, **42** (May 1969), 116–20. A list of the French envoy, Bonrepaux, supposedly originating with the Prince of Orange's party.

241 Jones, James R. 'Court dependents in 1664', *BIHR*, **34** (May 1961), 81–91. A list of M.P.s, with introductory comment.

242 —— 'Shaftesbury's "worthy men": a Whig view of the parliament of 1679', *BIHR*, **30** (Nov. 1957), 232–41. An annotated list of Members of Parliament.

243 Jones, Philip E. *The fire court: calendar to the judgments and decrees of the court*, vol. I. 1966. The court dealt with matters arising from the Great Fire of London.

244 *Journals of the House of Commons*, VIII–X (1660–93). This and the *Lords' Journal* (245) are essentially minutes of proceedings, and do not contain debates.

245 *Journals of the House of Lords*, XI–XV (1660–96).
246 Kenyon, John P. (ed.). *The Stuart constitution, 1603–1688: documents and commentary*. Cambridge, 1966. Includes a bibliography.
247 'A letter from a person of quality to his friend in the country, giving an account of the debates and resolutions in the House of Lords in April and May, 1675', in Cobbett (221), IV, xxxviii–lxvii. Sometimes attributed to John Locke. The debates were on a test bill.
248 Macray, William D. (ed.). *Notes which passed at meetings of the privy council between Charles II and the earl of Clarendon* (Roxburghe Club). 1896. Covers 1660–7; has facsimiles.
249 *Memoirs relating to the impeachment of Thomas, earl of Danby...with an appendix containing the proceedings of parliament*. 1710.
250 Milward, John. *The diary of John Milward, esq., member of parliament for Derbyshire*, ed. Caroline Robbins. Cambridge, 1938. Covers 1666–8; a valuable diary. Appendix gives Arthur Capel's notes on debates, Oct.–Nov. 1667.
251 Muddiman, Joseph G. (ed.). *The Bloody Assizes* (Notable British Trials Series). Edinburgh, 1929. For attribution, see Grose (32), no. 2940.
252 Nottingham, Heneage Finch, earl of. *Lord Nottingham's 'Manual of chancery practice' and 'Prolegomena of chancery and equity'*, ed. David E. C. Yale (Selden Society, LXXIII, LXXIX). 1957, 1961.
253 Pickering, David (ed.). *Statutes at large from Magna Carta to 1806*. Cambridge, 1762–1807, 46 vols. Vol. I covers the period.
254 Pike, Clement E. (ed.). *Selections from the correspondence of Arthur Capel, earl of Essex, 1675–77* (Camden Society, 3rd ser., XXIV). 1913. Essex was lord lieutenant of Ireland at this time.
255 *The proceedings of the House of Commons touching the impeachment of Edward, late earl of Clarendon*. 1700. A valuable source.
256 *Proceedings of the House of Commons which met at Oxford*. 1681.
257 *A relation of the most material matters handled in parliament, relating to religion, property, and the liberty of the subject*. 1673. Covers Feb.–Nov. 1673. See (8).
258 *Return of the names of every member...in each parliament* [1213–1874]. 1878–91, 4 vols. The fullest list extant, though incomplete. For addenda and corrigenda, see indexes and also William W. Bean, *Notices of various errors and omissions* (1883).
259 Robbins, Caroline (ed.). 'Five speeches, 1661–1663, by Sir John Holland, M.P.', *BIHR*, **28** (Nov. 1955), 189–202. Includes debates on the ecclesiastical and military settlements.
260 —— 'Sir John Holland (1603–1701) in the convention of 1660', *BIHR*, **29** (Nov. 1956), 244–52. Four parliamentary speeches.
261 Roberts, Clayton. 'Sir Richard Temple's discourse on the parliament of 1667–1668', *HLQ*, **20** (Feb. 1957), 137–44.
262 Robertson, Charles G. (ed.). *Select statutes, cases, and documents to illustrate English constitutional history, 1660–1832*. 9th ed., 1949.
263 Rogers, James E. Thorold. *A complete collection of the protests of the Lords, including those which have been expunged*. Oxford, 1875, 3 vols. Valuable for dissenting opinion in the Lords: vol. I covers 1624–1741.
264 Rolle, Henry. *Un abridgment des plusieurs cases et resolutions del common ley*. 1668. Edited by Matthew Hale, Rolle having died in 1656. Among the first works to state legal principles as well as to summarize decisions.
265 Scobell, Henry. *Memorials of the method and manner of proceedings in parliament in passing bills*. 1656. Other editions in 1670, 1689.
266 Sheppard, William. *A grand abridgement of the common and statute law of England*. 1675, 3 vols. The first example of a combination of case law and statutes, but inferior to Rolle (264.)
267 Siebert, Frederick S. 'Regulation of the press in the seventeenth century: excerpts from the records of the court of the Stationers' Company', *Journalism Quarterly*, **13** (Dec. 1936), 381–93.
268 Simpson, Alan. 'Notes of a noble lord, 22 January to 12 February 1688/9', *EHR*, **52** (Jan. 1937), 87–98. Notes on proceedings in the Lords, presumably by the second earl of Clarendon, with whose diary they are compared.

269 Somers, John. *A brief history of the succession.* 1681 (?). Reprinted in *Harleian miscellany* (480), I, 461–77. Answered by Brady (212).

270 *The statutes of the realm*, ed. Alexander Luders *et al.* 1810–28, 11 vols. Of fundamental importance; preferable to other collections. For the period, see vols. V–VI.

271 Steele, Robert (ed.). *Bibliography of royal proclamations of the Tudor and Stuart sovereigns and of others published under authority, 1485–1714* (Bibliotheca Lindesiana). Oxford, 1910, 2 vols. Brief summaries.

272 Stephenson, Carl and Frederick G. Marcham (eds.). *Sources of English constitutional history*. New York, 1937. See sec. 10, 'The restored Stuarts'.

273 Stock, Leo F. (ed.). *Proceedings and debates of the British parliaments respecting North America.* Washington, 1924–7, 2 vols.

274 Temperley, Harold W. V. 'Documents illustrative of the powers of the privy council in the seventeenth century', *EHR*, **28** (Jan. 1913), 127–31. Designed as an appendix to (432); of limited value.

275 [Timberland, Ebenezer]. *The history and proceedings of the House of Lords from the Restoration to the present time.* 1742–3, 8 vols. Sometimes called 'Timberland', who was the publisher.

276 Tomlins, Thomas E. and John Raithby (eds.). *Statutes at large.* 1811, 10 vols. A work produced under private auspices; covers 1225–1800. Contains only selected, somewhat condensed statutes in force; hence inferior to *Statutes of the realm* (270). Cf. Pickering (253).

277 [Torbuck, John]. *A collection of the parliamentary debates in England.* 1739–41, 21 vols. Torbuck was the publisher. Covers 1668–1741; cf. Chandler (220) and Timberland (275).

278 *Votes and addresses of the hon. House of Commons...made this present year 1673.* 1673.

279 Yale, David E. C. (ed.). *Lord Nottingham's chancery cases* (Selden Society, LXXIII, LXXIX). 1957–61.

2 Surveys

280 Dodd, Arthur H. *The growth of responsible government: from James the First to Victoria.* 1956. A survey developed from lectures.

281 Egerton, Hugh E. *A short history of British colonial policy, 1606–1909*, rev. by Arthur P. Newton. 9th ed., 1932.

282 Hallam, Henry. *The constitutional history of England from the accession of Henry VII to the death of George II.* 1827, 2 vols.; 8th ed., 1855, 3 vols. A thoroughgoing Whig treatment, out of date but still of some value.

283 Harding, Alan. *Social history of English law.* Harmondsworth, 1966.

284 Holdsworth, William S. *A history of English law.* 7th ed. by Stanley B. Chrimes *et al.*, 1956–66, 16 vols. The fullest history; a monumental work. Vol. VI provides an admirable survey for the later Stuart era.

285 Jenks, Edward. *A short history of English law.* 4th ed., enlarged, 1928.

286 Keir, David L. *The constitutional history of modern Britain since 1485.* 8th ed., 1966. Solid and informative; one chapter on 1660–1714.

287 Keith, Arthur B. *Constitutional history of the first British empire.* Oxford, 1930.

288 Maitland, Frederic W. *The constitutional history of England.* Cambridge, 1908. Originally lectures; useful, but better on earlier phases of the subject.

289 Marcham, Frederick G. *A constitutional history of modern England, 1485 to the present.* New York, 1960. A useful textbook, organized topically.

290 Plucknett, Theodore F. T. *A concise history of the common law.* 5th ed., 1956. The best short history.

291 Taswell-Langmead, Thomas P. *English constitutional history.* 11th ed. by Theodore F. T. Plucknett, 1960. A fairly detailed treatment; older editions are out of date.

292 Thomson, Mark A. *A constitutional history of England, 1642 to 1801.* 1938. The fullest coverage of the later Stuart era.

3 Monographs

293 Amos, Andrew. *The English constitution in the reign of King Charles the Second.* 1857. Still of some use.

294 Andrews, Charles M. *British committees, commissions, and councils of trade and plantations, 1622–1675* (Johns Hopkins University Studies in Historical and Political Science, XXVI, nos. 1–3). Baltimore, 1908.

295 Baxter, Stephen B. *The development of the treasury, 1660–1702.* 1957. Cf. the introductions by William A. Shaw to the volumes of *Calendar of treasury books* (218).

296 Bieber, Ralph P. *The lords of trade and plantations, 1675–96.* Allentown, Pa., 1919. Cf. Root (428).

297 Cannan, Edwin. *The history of local rates in England.* 2nd ed., enlarged, 1912.

298 Collins, Edward D. 'Studies in the colonial policy of England, 1672–1680: the plantations, the Royal African Company, and the slave trade', *Annual Report*, American Historical Association, 1900, I, 139–92. Washington, 1901.

299 Craig, John H. M. *The mint: a history of the London mint from A.D. 287 to 1948.* Cambridge, 1953. Scattered references to the period; illustrations of Stuart coins.

300 Dowdell, Eric G. *A hundred years of quarter sessions: the government of Middlesex from 1660 to 1760.* Cambridge, 1932.

301 Dowell, Stephen. *A history of taxation and taxes in England from the earliest times to the present day.* 1884–5, 4 vols. A standard work, but inadequate for the period and out of date.

302 Elliott, T. H. *State papers domestic concerning the post office in the reign of Charles II* (Postal History Society). Bath, 1964.

303 Evans, Florence May Greir. *The principal secretary of state: a survey of the office from 1558 to 1680.* Manchester, 1923. A useful study, containing a valuable account of records of the office.

304 Fraser, Peter. *The intelligence of the secretaries of state and their monopoly of licensed news.* Cambridge, 1956. An excellent analysis of the news service of the period.

305 Gough, John W. *Fundamental law in English constitutional history.* Oxford, 1955. There are two chapters on the period.

306 Hall, Hubert. *A history of the custom-revenue in England from the earliest times to the year 1827.* 1885, 2 vols.

307 Hatsell, John. *Precedents of proceedings in the House of Commons.* 4th ed., 1818, 4 vols. As chief clerk of the Commons, Hatsell was in his day regarded as the best authority on its procedure.

308 Head, Ronald E. *Royal supremacy and the trials of bishops, 1558–1725* (Church Historical Society). 1962. Reveals the use of the royal supremacy in disciplining the bishops.

309 Hemmeon, Joseph C. *The history of the British post office.* Cambridge, Mass., 1912. An excellent account, but superseded by (330).

310 Henderson, Edith G. *Foundations of English administrative law: certiorari and mandamus in the seventeenth century.* Cambridge, Mass., 1963.

311 Henriques, Henry S. Q. *The return of the Jews to England, being a chapter in the history of English law.* 1905.

312 Holdsworth, William S. *An historical introduction to the land law.* Oxford, 1927.

313 —— *Sources and literature of English law.* Oxford, 1925. Some references to Hale.

314 Hughes, Edward E. *Studies in administration and finance, 1558–1825, with special reference to the history of salt taxation in England.* Manchester, 1934. An excellent specialized work; particularly useful for the development of the excise.

315 Hyde, James Wilson. *The early history of the post in grant and farm.* 1894. Goes to 1685.

316 Karraker, Cyrus H. *The seventeenth-century sheriff: a comparative study of the sheriff in England and the Chesapeake colonies, 1607–1689.* Philadelphia, 1930.

317 Kaye, Percy L. *English colonial administration under Lord Clarendon, 1660–1667* (Johns Hopkins University Studies in Historical and Political Science, XXIII, nos. 5–6). Baltimore, 1905.

318 Kemp, Betty. *King and Commons, 1660–1832*. 1957.

319 Laundy, Philip. *The office of speaker*. 1964. One chapter on the Restoration era.

320 Lee, Maurice, Jr. *The Cabal*. Urbana, Ill., 1965. The ablest treatment.

321 Maxwell-Lyte, Henry C. *Historical notes on the use of the great seal of England*. 1926. Largely quotations from documents in the Public Record Office.

322 Merewether, Henry A. and Archibald J. Stephens. *The history of the boroughs and municipal corporations of the United Kingdom, from the earliest to the present time*. 1835, 3 vols. An elaborate compilation of valuable data assembled for the purpose of influencing reform.

323 Oldfield, Thomas H. B. *The representative history of Great Britain and Ireland*. 1816, 6 vols.

324 Osborne, Bertram. *Justices of the peace, 1361–1848: a history of the justices of the peace for the counties of England*. Shaftesbury, 1960. Surveys the main events in the history of the office, with three chapters on the period.

325 Pape, Thomas. *The Restoration government and the corporation of Newcastle-under-Lyme* (Publications of the University of Manchester, Historical Series, no. 78). Manchester, 1940.

326 Pike, Luke O. *The constitutional history of the House of Lords*. 1894. Useful, particularly on legal aspects.

327 Porritt, Edward and Annie G. *The unreformed House of Commons: parliamentary representation before 1832*. Cambridge, 1909, 2 vols. The fullest work on the subject, but imperfectly organized.

328 Rex, Millicent B. *University representation in England, 1604–90*. 1954. A pioneer work of considerable value.

329 Roberts, Clayton. *The growth of responsible government in Stuart England*. Cambridge, 1966. A very substantial work; indispensable.

330 Robinson, Howard. *The British post office: a history*. Princeton, N.J., 1948. The standard work.

331 Roseveare, Henry. *The treasury: the evolution of a British institution*. 1969. Chap. 3 deals with 1667–1714.

332 Schoenfeld, Maxwell P. *The restored House of Lords*. The Hague, 1967. The focus is on the years 1660–2.

333 Senior, William. *Doctors' commons and the old court of admiralty: a short history of the civilians in England*. 1922.

334 Spence, George. *The equitable jurisdiction of the court of chancery*. 1846–9, 2 vols. Useful as a history of the court, but there is little directly on the period.

335 Squibb, George D. *The high court of chivalry: a study of the civil law in England*. Oxford, 1959.

336 Staff, Frank. *The penny post, 1680–1918*. 1964.

337 Stephen, James F. *A history of the criminal law of England*. 1883, 3 vols. Long a standard work.

338 Tanner, Joseph R. *English constitutional conflict in the seventeenth century, 1603–1689*. Cambridge, 1928.

339 Thomson, Mark A. *The secretaries of state, 1681–1782*. Oxford, 1932. Carries on from where Evans (303) leaves off; useful bibliography.

340 Thornton, Archibald P. *West India policy under the Restoration*. Oxford, 1956.

341 Todd, Thomas. *William Dockwra and the rest of the undertakers: the story of the London penny post, 1680–82*. Edinburgh, 1952. Includes extracts from newsbooks, broadsides, handbills, etc.

342 Trotter, Eleanor. *Seventeenth-century life in the country parish, with special reference to local government*. Cambridge, 1919. Based chiefly on quarter sessions records for the North Riding.

343 Turner, Edward R. *The cabinet council of England...1622–1784*. Baltimore, 1930, 2 vols. Contains masses of information; interpretations have been adversely criticized.

344 —— *The privy council of England...1603–1784*. Baltimore, 1927–8, 2 vols. Comment under (343) applies here as well.

345 Webb, Sidney and Beatrice. *English local government from the Revolution to the Municipal Corporations Act.* 1906–27, 7 vols. Deals with various matters before 1688, despite title. Important.

346 Weston, Corinne C. *English constitutional theory and the House of Lords, 1556–1832.* 1965.

347 Wilkinson, Bertie. *The coronation in history* (Historical Association Pamphlets, general series, no. 23). 1953.

348 Williams, Orlo C. *The clerical organization of the House of Commons, 1661–1850.* Oxford, 1954. A good survey.

349 Witcombe, Dennis T. *Charles II and the cavalier House of Commons, 1663–1674.* Manchester, 1966.

4 Biographies

350 Campbell, John, Baron. *The lives of the chief justices of England.* 3rd ed., 1874, 4 vols. Marred by inaccuracies.

351 —— *The lives of the lord chancellors and keepers of the great seal of England.* 4th ed., 1856–7, 10 vols. Strong Whig bias; inaccurate. Vols. IV and V cover the period.

352 Cherry, George L. *The convention parliament, 1689–1690.* New York, 1966. A useful biographical compilation, with some inaccuracies.

353 Foss, Edward. *The judges of England.* 1848–64, 9 vols. Valuable and generally reliable; abridged in one vol. as *Biographia juridica*, 1870.

354 Holdsworth, William S. *Some makers of English law.* Cambridge, 1938. Lectures. Includes Hale, Nottingham, and Jenkins.

355 Hyde, Harford Montgomery. *Judge Jeffreys.* 1940.

356 Irving, Henry B. *The life of Judge Jeffreys.* 1898. A not entirely successful attempt to defend Jeffreys.

357 Jacobsen, Gertrude Ann. *William Blathwayt: a late seventeenth-century English administrator* (Yale Historical Publications, Miscellany no. 21). New Haven, 1932. A study of the secretary-at-war, 1683–1704.

358 Keeton, George W. *Lord Chancellor Jeffreys and the Stuart cause.* 1965. The most ambitious attempt to rehabilitate Jeffreys.

359 Woodhead, John R. *The rulers of London, 1660–1689* (London and Middlesex Archaeological Society). 1966. A biographical roster of London aldermen and common councilmen.

5 Articles

360 Abbott, Wilbur C. 'The long Parliament of Charles II', *EHR*, **21** (Jan., Apr. 1906), 21–56, 254–85.

361 Aiken, William A. 'The admiralty in conflict and commission, 1679–1684', in William A. Aiken and Basil D. Henning (eds.)., *Conflict in Stuart England: essays in honour of Wallace Notestein*, New York, 1960, pp. 203–25.

362 Allan, D. G. G. 'Charles II's secretaries of state', *Hist. T.*, 8 (Dec. 1958), 856–63.

363 Aylmer, Gerald E. 'Place bills and the separation of powers: some seventeenth-century origins of the "non-political" civil service', *TRHS*, 5th ser., **15** (1965), 45–69.

364 Balfour, M. Melville. 'An incident in the life of a great lawyer', *LQR*, **41** (Jan. 1925), 71–8. A vindication of Judge Jeffreys.

365 Bell, Walter G. 'The birth of the London rate-payer', *Hist.*, **12** (July 1927), 117–29. Sees a 'modern municipal spirit' present in London only after the Great Fire.

366 Bieber, Ralph P. 'The British plantation councils of 1670–74', *EHR*, **40** (Jan. 1925), 93–106. Useful on administration and economic matters, as well as for the colonies.

367 Carlyle, Edward I. 'Clarendon and the privy council, 1660–67', *EHR*, **27** (Apr. 1912), 251–73.

368 Carroll, Roy. 'The by-election at Aldborough, 1673', *HLQ*, **28** (Feb. 1965), 157–78. Cross-currents of Restoration politics.

369 Cherry, George L. 'The role of the convention parliament (1688–89) in parliamentary supremacy', *JHI*, **17** (June 1956), 390–406.

370 Churchill, E. F. 'The dispensing power and the defence of the realm'. *LQR*, **37** (Oct. 1921), 412–41. Broad coverage chronologically, but there is something on the period.

371 —— 'The dispensing power of the crown in ecclesiastical affairs', *LQR*, **38** (July, Oct. 1922), 297–316, 420–34. Rather general, but useful because of the importance of the subject under James II.

372 Crawford, Clarence C. 'The suspension of the Habeas Corpus Act and the Revolution of 1689', *EHR*, **30** (Oct. 1915), 613–30.

373 —— 'The writ of habeas corpus', *American Law Review*, **42** (July–Aug. 1908), 481–99. There is considerable comment on the Habeas Corpus Act of 1679.

374 Crissey, Merrill H. and Godfrey Davies. 'Corruption in parliament, 1660–1677', *HLQ*, **6** (Nov. 1942), 106–14.

375 Cross, Arthur L. 'The English law courts at the close of the Revolution of 1688', *Michigan Law Review*, **15** (May 1917), 529–51. Interesting on court functionaries, fees, etc.

376 Davies, Godfrey. 'Council and cabinet, 1679–88', *EHR*, **37** (Jan. 1922), 47–66.

377 —— 'The general election of 1660', *HLQ*, **15** (May 1952), 211–35.

378 —— 'The treatment of constitutional history in Macaulay's History of England', *HLQ*, **2** (Jan. 1939), 179–204.

379 —— and Edith L. Klotz. 'The Habeas Corpus Act of 1679 in the House of Lords', *HLQ*, **3** (July 1940), 469–70. A note dealing with the vote on the bill.

380 De Beer, Esmond S. 'The great seal of James II: a reply to Sir Hilary Jenkinson', *Antiquaries Journal*, **42** (pt. 1, 1962), 81–90. See Jenkinson (400).

381 —— 'The House of Lords in the parliament of 1680', *BIHR*, **20** (1943–5), 22–37. Examines the composition and conduct of the House. Appendix has report of debate, attributed to Lord Huntingdon.

382 —— 'Members of the court party in the House of Commons, 1670–1678', *BIHR*, **11** (June 1933), 1–23.

383 Edie, Carolyn A. 'Succession and monarchy: the controversy of 1679–1681', *AHR*, **70** (Jan. 1965), 350–70.

384 Evans, Florence May Greir. 'Emoluments of the principal secretaries of state in the seventeenth century', *EHR*, **35** (Oct. 1920), 513–28.

385 Fryer, Charles E. 'The royal veto under Charles II', *EHR*, **32** (Jan. 1917), 103–11.

386 George, Mary Dorothy. 'Elections and electioneering, 1679–1681', *EHR*, **45** (Oct. 1930), 552–78.

387 George, Robert H. 'The charters granted to English parliamentary corporations in 1688', *EHR*, **55** (Jan. 1940), 47–56.

388 —— 'A note on the Bill of Rights: municipal liberties and freedom of parliamentary elections', *AHR*, **42** (July 1937), 670–9.

389 —— 'Parliamentary elections and electioneering in 1685', *TRHS*, 4th ser., **19** (1936), 167–95. A detailed and scholarly account.

390 Gill, Doris M. 'The relationship between the treasury and the excise and customs commissioners (1660–1714)', *Camb. Hist. J.*, **4** (no. 1, 1932), 94–9.

391 —— 'The treasury, 1660–1714', *EHR*, **46** (Oct. 1931), 600–22.

392 Greaves, Robert W. 'The earl of Huntingdon and the Leicester charter of 1684', *HLQ*, **15** (Aug. 1952), 371–91. Illustrates the regulation of a corporation.

393 Haffenden, Philip S. 'The crown and the colonial charters, 1675–1688', *William and Mary Quarterly*, 3rd ser., **15** (July, Oct. 1958), 297–311, 452–66. Focus is on the policies of James II.

394 Havighurst, Alfred F. 'James II and the twelve men in scarlet', *LQR*, **69** (Oct. 1953), 522–46. James's relations with his judges.

395 —— 'The judiciary and politics in the reign of Charles II', *LQR*, **66** (Jan., Apr. 1950), 62–78, 229–52.

396 Holdsworth, William S. 'Sir Matthew Hale', *LQR*, **39** (Oct. 1923), 402–26. A useful short analysis of the man and his accomplishments.

397 Holland, H. A. 'English legal authors before 1700', *Cambridge Law Journal*, **9** (no. 3, 1947), 292–329. A few pages are devoted to Restoration figures.

398 Hughes, Edward E. 'The English stamp duties, 1664–1764', *EHR*, **46** (Apr. 1941), 234–64.

399 Hurst, Gerald. 'Sir Matthew Hale', *LQR*, **70** (July 1954), 342–52.

400 Jenkinson, Hilary. 'What happened to the great seal of James II?', *Antiquaries Journal*, **21** (Jan.–Apr. 1943), 1–13. Disputes story that the seal was cast into the Thames. Cf. de Beer (380).

401 Jones, G. F. Trevallyn. 'The composition and leadership of the Presbyterian party in the Convention', *EHR*, **79** (Apr. 1964), 307–54. Deals with the parliament of 1660.

402 Jones, James R. 'Political groups and tactics in the convention of 1660', *Hist. J.*, **6** (no. 2, 1963), 159–77. Emphasizes the importance of the tactical skill of court managers.

403 —— 'Restoration election petitions', *Durham University Journal*, **53** (Mar. 1961), 49–57. Deals with disputed elections.

404 Karraker, Cyrus H. 'Spanish treasure, casual revenue of the crown', *JMH*, **5** (Sept. 1933), 301–18. Deals with the crown's interest in salvaging, 1683–8.

405 Keeton, George W. 'Judge Jeffreys as chief justice of Chester, 1680–83', *LQR*, **77** (Jan. 1961), 36–68. Provides background for Jeffreys's later career.

406 —— 'Judge Jeffreys: towards a reappraisal', *Welsh History Review*, **1** (no. 3, 1962), 265–78.

407 —— 'The judiciary and the constitutional struggle, 1660–88', *Journal of the Society of Public Teachers of Law*, **7** (Dec. 1962), 56–68.

408 Latham, Robert C. 'Payment of parliamentary wages: the last phase', *EHR*, **66** (Jan. 1951), 27–50. Focus is on the Cavalier Parliament.

409 Leftwich, Bertram R. 'The later history and administration of the customs revenue in England (1671–1814)', *TRHS*, 4th ser., **13** (1930), 187–203. Emphasizes the importance of customs officials after 1671.

410 Lipson, Ephraim. 'Elections to the exclusion parliaments, 1679–1681', *EHR*, **38** (Jan. 1913), 59–85.

411 Lovell, Colin R. 'The trial of peers in Great Britain', *AHR*, **55** (Oct. 1949), 69–81. Has a few references to the period.

412 Macdonald, Hugh. 'The law and defamatory biographies in the seventeenth century', *Review of English Studies*, **20** (July 1944), 177–98.

413 Mansfield, Harvey C., Jr. 'Party government and the settlement of 1688', *American Political Science Review*, **58** (Dec. 1964), 933–46.

414 Marshall, Lydia M. 'The levying of the hearth tax, 1662–1688', *EHR*, **51** (Oct. 1936), 628–46. Has a paraphrase of the Hearth Bill of 1676–77, and of Coventry's objections.

415 Mukerjee, H. N. 'Elections for the Convention and Cavalier Parliaments', *Notes and Queries*, **166** (9, 16 June 1934), 398–403, 417–21.

416 Mullett, Charles F. 'The Corporation Act and the election of English Protestant dissenters to corporation offices', *Virginia Law Review*, **21** (Apr. 1935), 641–64.

417 —— 'The legal position of English Protestant dissenters, 1660–1689', *Virginia Law Review*, **22** (Mar. 1936), 495–526.

418 Nutting, Helen A. 'The most wholesome law – the Habeas Corpus Act of 1679', *AHR*, **65** (Apr. 1960), 527–43. Important for examination of debates, 1668–79.

419 Plumb, John H. 'The elections to the Convention Parliament of 1688–9', *Camb. Hist. J.*, **5** (no. 3, 1937), 235–54.

420 Rich, Edwin E. 'The first earl of Shaftesbury's colonial policy', *TRHS*, 5th ser., **7** (1957), 47–70. Deals with the period 1667–76, when colonial affairs were dominated by Shaftesbury.

421 Robbins, Caroline. 'A note on general naturalization under the later Stuarts, and a speech in the House of Commons on the subject in 1664', *JMH*, **34** (June 1962), 168–77.

422 —— 'The Oxford session of the long parliament of Charles II, 9–31 October 1665', *BIHR*, **21** (no. 64, 1948), 214–24. Deals with contemporary reports, such as they are.

423 —— 'The repeal of the Triennial Act in 1664', *HLQ*, **12** (Feb. 1949), 121–40.

424 Roberts, Clayton. 'The growth of ministerial responsibility to parliament in later Stuart England', *JMH*, **28** (Sept. 1956), 215–33. Sees the uninterrupted winning of ministerial responsibility as beginning in 1660.

425 —— 'The impeachment of the earl of Clarendon', *Camb. Hist. J.*, **13** (no. 1, 1957), 1–18.

426 —— 'Privy council schemes and ministerial responsibility in later Stuart England', *AHR*, **64** (Apr. 1959), 564–82.

427 Root, Winfred T. 'The British plantation councils of 1670–74', *EHR*, **40** (Jan. 1925), 93–106. Based on journals of the councils, lost for two centuries.

428 —— 'The lords of trade and plantations, 1675–1696', *AHR*, **23** (Oct. 1917), 20–41. A contribution to a comparatively neglected era.

429 Sacret, Joseph H. 'The Restoration government and municipal corporations', *EHR*, **45** (Apr. 1930), 232–59.

430 Sainty, J. C. 'A reform in the tenure of offices during the reign of Charles II', *BIHR*, **41** (Nov. 1968), 150–65.

431 Sutherland, Lucy S. 'The law merchant in England in the seventeenth and eighteenth centuries', *TRHS*, 4th ser., **17** (1934), 149–76. Not much on the period, but useful in a general way.

432 Temperley, Harold W. V. 'Inner and outer cabinet and privy council between 1679 and 1783', *EHR*, **27** (Oct. 1912), 682–99.

433 Thomas, Roger. 'The seven bishops and their petition, 18 May 1688', *JEH*, **12** (Apr. 1961), 56–70.

434 Thomson, Gladys Scott. 'The bishops of Durham and the office of lord lieutenant in the seventeenth century', *EHR*, **40** (July 1925), 351–74.

435 Turberville, Arthur S. 'The house of lords in the reign of Charles II', *EHR*, **44** (July 1929), 400–17. For completion of this article, see (436).

436 —— 'The house of Lords under Charles II', *EHR*, **45** (Jan. 1930), 58–77. A continuation of (435).

437 Turner, Edward R. 'Charles II's part in governing England', *AHR*, **34** (Oct. 1928), 44–7. Contends that Charles took an active part in the routine of government.

438 —— 'Parliament and foreign affairs, 1603–1760', *EHR*, **34** (Apr. 1919), 172–97.

439 —— 'The privy council of 1679', *EHR*, **30** (Apr. 1915), 251–70.

440 Walker, James. 'The secret service under Charles II and James II', *TRHS*, 4th ser., **15** (1932), 211–42. Throws light on certain expenses related to the diplomatic service.

441 Williams, J. A. 'English Catholicism under Charles II: the legal position', *Recusant History*, **7** (Oct. 1963), 123–43.

442 Witcombe, Dennis T. 'The cavalier House of Commons: the session of 1663', *BIHR*, **32** (Nov. 1959), 181–91.

V POLITICAL HISTORY

1 Printed Sources

443 Ailesbury, Thomas Bruce, earl of. *The memoirs of Thomas Bruce, earl of Ailesbury* (Roxburghe Club). 1890, 2 vols. Unreliable but highly interesting; covers chiefly 1678–1715.

444 Anglesey, Arthur Annesley, earl of. *Memoirs of...Arthur, earl of Anglesey, late lord privy seal, intermixt with moral, political, and historical observations*, ed. Peter Pett. 1693. Picture of a puritanical type in profligate surroundings.

445 Bathurst, Allen B. (ed.). *Letters of two queens*. 1924. Chiefly those of the Princess of Orange, *c.* 1673–88, with some of Anne.

446 Beddard, Robert. 'The loyalist opposition in the interregnum: a letter of Dr. Francis Turner, bishop of Ely, on the Revolution of 1688', *BIHR*, **40** (May 1967), 101–9. The letter provides a detailed account of events, Dec. 1688–Feb. 1689.

POLITICS

447 Bentinck, Mechtild, Comtesse (ed.). *Lettres et mémoires de Marie reine d'Angleterre, épouse de Guillaume III*. The Hague, 1880. Correspondence of James II and Mary, 1687–8, and of Anne and Mary, 1688. Memoirs relate to 1688.

448 Bloxam, John R. (ed.). *Magdalen College and King James II, 1686–1689* (Oxford Historical Society, VI). Oxford, 1886. A comprehensive collection of documents.

449 Bohun, Edmund. *The diary and autobiography of Edmund Bohun*, ed. Samuel W. Rix. Beccles, 1853. Covers 1677–97.

450 —— *The history of the desertion, or an account of all the publick affairs in England*. 1689. Covers Sept. 1688–Feb. 1689; includes useful documents.

451 Bramston, John. *The autobiography of Sir John Bramston*, ed. Richard G. Neville, Lord Braybrooke (Camden Society, old ser., XXXII). 1845. Especially useful for 1685–90.

452 Bromley, George (ed.). *A collection of original royal letters written by King Charles the First and Second, King James the Second*. 1787.

453 Brown, Thomas. *Miscellanea aulica, or a collection of state treatises*. 1702. Useful for letters of Charles II and James, duke of York, and for documents dealing with foreign relations and Scottish affairs after 1660.

454 Buckingham, John Sheffield, duke of. *The works of John Sheffield...duke of Buckingham*, 2nd ed., corrected, 1729. Includes memoirs, mainly relating to naval affairs and Monmouth, and an account of the Revolution.

455 Bulstrode, Richard. *Memoirs and reflections upon the reign and government of King Charles the First and King Charles the Second*. 1721. Apologetic; written in his old age at St. Germain. Some genuine memoirs along with extracts from Clarendon and Warwick.

456 Burnet, Gilbert. *Some unpublished letters of Gilbert Burnet, the historian*, ed. Helen C. Foxcroft (Camden Miscellany, XI, 3rd ser., XIII, pp. 5–45). 1907. Newsletters to Halifax, written Jan.–Sept. 1680.

457 Campana de Cavelli, Emilia, Marquise. *Les derniers Stuarts à Saint-Germain en Laye: documents inédits et authentiques*. Paris, 1871, 2 vols. A valuable collection of documents from various archives on James II and Mary of Modena, 1673–89.

458 Chamberlayne, Edward. *Angliae notitia, or the present state of England*. 1669. A sort of almanac; useful for miscellaneous information. It went through 39 editions between 1669 and 1755.

459 Charles II. *The letters, speeches, and declarations of King Charles II*, ed. Arthur Bryant. 1935. A useful collection.

460 *A choice collection of papers relating to state affairs during the late Revolution*. 1703.

461 Clarendon, Edward Hyde, earl of. *The life of Edward, earl of Clarendon, being a continuation of the History of the Great Rebellion from the Restoration to his banishment in 1667*. Oxford, 1857, 2 vols. Includes portions of the life not included in the History; useful for Clarendon's ministry and final exile.

462 —— *Selections from The history of the Rebellion and Civil Wars and the Life, by himself*, ed. G. Huehns. 1955.

463 Clarke, James S. (ed.). *Life of James II...collected out of memoirs writ of his own hand*. 1816, 2 vols. Originally compiled by William Dicconson, who had access to James's letters, papers, etc. It is now impossible to tell how much is directly from James's writings and how much from Dicconson.

464 Coad, John. *A memorandum of the wonderful providences of God to a poor unworthy creature, during the time of the duke of Monmouth's rebellion and to the revolution in 1688*. 1849. A contemporary account, by one transported to Jamaica.

465 Coate, Mary. 'William Morrice and the restoration of Charles II', *EHR*, **33** (July 1918), 367–77. Letters from the spring of 1660, for the most part.

466 *Collection of papers relating to the present juncture of affairs in England*. 12 pts., 1688–9. Pamphlets.

467 *A collection of scarce and valuable tracts...selected from...public as well as private libraries, particularly that of the late Lord Somers*. 1748–52, 16 vols. An important collection. A later edition, 'revised, augmented, and arranged' by Sir Walter Scott, in 13 vols., appeared in 1809–15.

468 *A collection of state tracts publish'd on occasion of the late revolution in 1688 and during the reign of King William III.* 1705–7, 3 vols.

469 Collins, Arthur (ed.). *Letters and memorials of state in the reigns of Queen Mary, Queen Elizabeth, King James, King Charles I, part of the reign of King Charles II, and Oliver's usurpation.* 1746, 2 vols. A valuable collection of letters of the Sidney family.

470 Davies, Godfrey. 'Three letters on Monmouth's rebellion, 1685', *EHR*, **35** (Jan. 1920), 113–16.

471 Doble, Charles E. (ed.). *Correspondence of Henry, earl of Clarendon, and James, earl of Abingdon, chiefly relating to the Monmouth insurrection (1683–1685)* (Oxford Historical Society, Collectanea, III, 3rd ser., XXXII, 245–78). Oxford, 1896.

472 Dunham, William H., Jr., and Stanley M. Pargellis. *Complaint and reform in England, 1436–1714.* New York, 1937. Contemporary writings on politics, society, economics, etc.; includes nine tracts published 1660–82.

473 Ellis, George J. W. Agar (Baron Dover) (ed.). *Letters written during the years 1686, 1687, and 1688, and addressed to John Ellis, esq.* 1829, 2 vols. Useful for events leading to and connected with the Revolution.

474 Ellis, Henry (ed.). *Original letters illustrative of English history, including numerous royal letters.* 1824–46, 11 vols. in three series.

475 Feiling, Keith G. 'Two speeches of Charles II', *EHR*, **45** (Apr. 1930), 291–3. Comment on parliament and on foreign affairs.

476 Grey, Forde, Lord. *Secret history of the Rye House plot and of Monmouth's rebellion, written by Ford, Lord Grey, in 1685.* 1754. Cf. (676).

477 Guizot, François F. P. (ed.). *Collection des mémoires relatifs à la Révolution d'Angleterre.* Paris, 25 pts., 1823–5. Includes Clarendon, Burnet, Reresby, James II. Prefaces by Guizot were published separately as *Portraits politiques* (Paris, 1851), and trans. by Andrew R. Scoble as *Monk's contemporaries* (1851).

478 Gumble, Thomas. *The life of General Monck, duke of Albemarle.* 1671. Gumble was Monck's chaplain; useful for 1659–60.

479 Hardwicke, Philip Yorke, earl of (ed.). *Miscellaneous state papers from 1501 to 1726.* 1778, 2 vols. Known as Hardwicke state papers; includes material on Monmouth's rebellion.

480 *The Harleian miscellany: a collection of scarce, curious, and entertaining pamphlets and tracts...found in the late earl of Oxford's library.* 1744–6, 8 vols. There are also two early nineteenth-century editions. See *Contents of the Harleian miscellany, with an index.* Sydney, 1885.

481 Heath, James. *A brief chronicle of the late intestine wars in the three kingdoms of England, Scotland, and Ireland...from...1637 to 1663.* Oxford, 1663. The 2nd ed., 1676, provides a continuation by J. Phillips to 1675. Royalist bias; relies on newspapers.

482 —— *The glories and magnificent triumphs of the blessed restitution of King Charles II, from his arrival in Holland, 1659/60, till this present.* 1662.

483 Henrietta Maria, Queen. *Lettres de Henriette-Marie de France, reine d'Angleterre, à sa sœur Christine, duchesse de Savoie*, ed. Hermann Ferrero. Turin, 1881. Covers 1628–66.

484 Historical Manuscripts Commission. *Calendar of the manuscripts of the marquess of Bath, preserved at Longleat, Wiltshire.* 1904–7, 2 vols. Harley papers, letters from Burnet, and other Restoration material.

485 —— *The Le Fleming manuscripts.* 12th rept., app. VII. 1890. Valuable series of newsletters, *c.* 1660–1700; extracts from Sir Daniel Fleming's account book, 1656–88.

486 —— *The Lindsey manuscripts.* 14th rept., app. IX. 1895. Chiefly papers of the earl of Danby, 1667–88.

487 —— *The manuscripts of Sir William Fitzherbert, bart., and others.* 13th rept., app. VI. 1893. Papers relating to the Popish Plot; also letters of Monck and Edward Coleman.

488 —— *The manuscripts of the right honourable F. J. Savile Foljambe, of Osberton.* 15th rept., app. V. 1897. Contains letters from James, duke of York, to William of Orange, 1678–9.

POLITICS

489 Historical Manuscripts Commission. *Pine-Coffin manuscripts*. 5th rept., pp. 370–86. 1876. Selections from newsletters, *c*. 1685–1700.

490 —— *Report on the manuscripts of the earl of Denbigh*. 1911. Dyckvelt's letters, 1672–1702, newsletters, and other papers.

491 —— *Sutherland manuscripts*. 5th rept., pp. 135–214. 1876. Includes some useful newsletters.

492 Japikse, Nicolaas. *Correspondentie van Willem III en Hans Willem Bentinck*. The Hague, 1927–35, 4 vols. Much is from Welbeck Abbey manuscripts; introduction in Dutch and English, text largely in French.

493 Jones, William. *A just and modest vindication of the proceedings of the two last parliaments*. 1681. Also attributed to Algernon Sidney and Lord Somers. Reprinted in Cobbett (221).

494 Le Neve, Peter. *Le Neve's pedigrees of the knights made by King Charles II, King James II, King William III, and...Queen Anne*, ed. George W. Marshall (Harleian Society Publications, VIII). 1873.

495 Lonsdale, John Lowther, Viscount. *Memoir of the reign of James II*. York, 1808. Valuable as a record of opinions rather than facts. For a continuation, ed. Charles H. Firth, see *EHR*, **30** (Jan. 1915), 90–7.

496 Ludlow, Edmund. *The memoirs of Edmund Ludlow*, ed. Charles H. Firth. Oxford, 1894, 2 vols. About half of vol. II deals with the years 1660–72.

497 Luttrell, Narcissus. *A brief historical relation of state affairs from September 1678 to April 1714*. Oxford, 1857, 6 vols. Valuable as a record of newsworthy items, largely from newspapers, etc.

498 Macdonald, Hugh (ed.). *Observations upon a late libel, called A letter from a person of quality to his friend concerning the King's declaration, etc*. Cambridge, 1940. A moderate Tory political tract, written upon the dissolution of the Oxford parliament, attributed to Halifax.

499 Macray, William D. *et al*. (eds.). *Calendar of the Clarendon state papers preserved in the Bodleian Library*. Oxford, 1869–. 4 vols. to date. Vol. IV goes to Apr. 1660.

500 Marlborough, Sarah Churchill, duchess of. *Memoirs of Sarah, duchess of Marlborough, together with her characters of contemporaries and her opinions*, ed. William King. 1930. Only the memoirs are useful for the period.

501 Monmouth, James Scott, duke of. *Original letters of the duke of Monmouth in the Bodleian Library*, ed. George Duckett (Camden Miscellany, VIII, new ser., XXXI). 1883. Several letters from 1685.

502 Muller, Pieter L. (ed.). *Wilhelm III von Oranien und Georg Friedrich von Waldeck*. The Hague, 1873–80, 2 vols. Correspondence in French, 1675–92; particularly useful for English affairs, 1688–90.

503 North, Roger. *Examen, or an enquiry into the credit and veracity of a pretended complete history...together with some memoirs occasionally inserted*. 1740. A Tory criticism of Kennet's *Complete history*, to be used with caution; valuable documents.

504 —— *The lives of the right hon. Francis North, Baron Guilford, the hon. Sir Dudley North, and the hon. and rev. Dr. John North*, ed. Augustus Jessopp. 1890, 3 vols. Also contains autobiography of the author. This and Guilford's life are valuable for the legal and political history of the latter years of Charles II.

505 Nottingham, Heneage Finch, earl of. *An exact and most impartial accompt of the indictment, arraignment, trial, and judgment...of nine and twenty regicides*. 1660.

506 Plumb, John H. and Alan Simpson. 'A letter of William, Prince of Orange, to Danby on the flight of James II', *Camb. Hist. J.*, **5** (no. 1, 1935), 107–8.

507 Price, John. *The mystery and method of his majesty's happy restauration*. 1680. Valuable; Price accompanied Monck.

508 Robbins, Caroline. 'Six letters by Andrew Marvell', *Études anglaises*, **17** (Jan.–Mar. 1964), 47–55.

509 Rugg, Thomas. *The diurnal of Thomas Rugg, 1659–1661*, ed. William L. Sachse (Camden Society, 3rd ser., XCI). 1961. An annalistic journal, comparable to Luttrell (497), kept by a London barber-surgeon.

510 Ruland, Virginia L. 'A royalist account of Hugh Peters' arrest', *HLQ*, **18** (Feb. 1955), 178–82. A reprint from *Parliamentary intelligencer*; defamatory and scurrilous.

511 S., W. *A compleat collection of the lives...of those persons lately executed.* 1661. Short lives of regicides.

512 Shaftesbury, Anthony Ashley Cooper, earl of. *Memoirs, letters, and speeches of Anthony Ashley Cooper, first earl of Shaftesbury,...with other papers illustrating his life*, ed. William D. Christie. 1859. Mostly incorporated in Christie's *Life* (616).

513 Sidney, Algernon. *Letters...to the honourable Henry Savile, ambassador in France in the year 1679.* 1742.

514 Sidney, Henry. *Diary of the times of Charles II by Henry Sidney, including his correspondence with the countess of Sutherland and other distinguished persons*, ed. Robert W. Blencowe. 1843, 2 vols. The diary covers 1679–82; the correspondence 1679–81 and 1684–9.

515 Singer, Samuel W. (ed.). *The correspondence of Henry Hyde, earl of Clarendon, and of his brother Laurence Hyde, earl of Rochester, with the diary of Lord Clarendon from 1687 to 1690.* 1828, 2 vols.

516 Sitwell, George. *Letters of the Sitwells and Sacheverells.* Scarborough, 1900–1, 2 vols. Contains much material to be found in (594). Public events and country life in the seventeenth and eighteenth centuries.

517 Skinner, Thomas. *The life of General Monck, late duke of Albemarle*, ed. William Webster. 2nd ed., corrected, 1724. Skinner d. 1679; a mere compilation.

518 Speke, Hugh. *Some memoirs of the most remarkable passages and transactions on the late happy revolution in 1688.* Dublin, 1709.

519 Sprat, Thomas. *A true account and declaration of the horrid conspiracy to assassinate the late King...ordered to be published by his late majesty.* 1685. The official account of the Rye House plot.

520 *State tracts, in two parts: the first being a collection of several treatises relating to the government, privately printed in the reign of King Charles II; the second part consisting of a further collection...1660 to 1689.* 1692–3. Part I was published separately in 1689.

521 Stone, Thora G. (ed.). *England under the Restoration (1660–1688).* 1923. A useful collection of extracts from primary sources; deals with social and economic, as well as political, aspects of the period.

522 Straka, Gerald M. (ed.). *The Revolution of 1688: Whig triumph or palace revolution?* Boston, 1963. Extracts from contemporary and later writers.

523 Tanner, Joseph R. 'The flight of Princess Anne', *EHR*, **8** (Oct. 1893), 740–1. Letter from Pepys to Lord Dartmouth, 26 November 1688.

524 Thibaudeau, Alphonse W. (ed.). *Catalogue of the collection of autograph letters and historical documents formed...by Alfred Morrison:* second series, *The Bulstrode papers*, I. 1897. Newsletters to Sir Richard Bulstrode while a resident at Brussels; covers 1667–75.

525 Thompson, Edward M. (ed.). *Correspondence of the family of Hatton, being chiefly letters addressed to Christopher, first viscount Hatton, A.D. 1601–1704* (Camden Society, new ser., XXII–XXIII). 1878. Valuable for the period.

526 Toynbee, Margaret R. 'An early correspondence of Queen Mary of Modena', *Notes and Queries*, **188** (1945), 90–4, 112–18, 135–40. Correspondence with Baroness Bellasyse, 1675–82.

527 Warcup, Edmund. 'The journals of Edmund Warcup, 1676–84', ed. Keith G. Feiling and F. R. D. Needham, *EHR*, **40** (Apr. 1925), 235–60. Warcup was involved in the Popish Plot.

528 Wilkins, William (ed.). *Political ballads of the seventeenth and eighteenth centuries.* 1860, 2 vols.

2 Surveys

529 Dalrymple, John. *Memoirs of Great Britain and Ireland.* 1771–3, 2 vols. Later ed. 1790, 3 vols., but first ed. is preferable. Vol. II consists of valuable documents.

530 Kennet, White. *A register and chronicle ecclesiastical and civil, containing matters of fact...with...notes and references towards discovering and connecting the true history of England from the restoration of Charles II.* 1728. Whig partisanship, but valuable, especially for 1660–2.

531 Mackinnon, James. *A history of modern liberty*, IV, *The struggle with the Stuarts, 1647–1689*. 1941. Essentially a general treatment of England and Scotland.

532 Mackintosh, James. *History of the revolution in England in 1688, comprising a view of the reign of James II, from his accession to the enterprise of the Prince of Orange.* 1834. Whig partisanship, but a careful work providing useful documents.

533 Marriott, John A. R. *The crisis of English liberty: a history of the Stuart monarchy and the puritan revolution.* Oxford, 1930. Over a hundred pages are devoted to the period.

534 Mazure, François A. J. *Histoire de la révolution de 1688 en Angleterre.* Paris, 1825, 3 vols. Covers 1660–88; has extracts from diplomatic despatches.

535 Ralph, James. *The history of England during the reigns of King William, Queen Anne, and King George I, with an introductory review of the reigns of the royal brothers, Charles and James.* 1744–6, 2 vols. Vol. I covers 1660–88. A careful work, making use of pamphlet literature.

536 Somerville, Thomas. *The history of political transactions and of parties from the restoration of King Charles the Second to the death of King William.* 1792. Chiefly after 1688.

537 Turberville, Arthur S. *Commonwealth and restoration.* Rev. ed., 1936. A rather brief treatment.

3 Monographs

538 Abbott, Wilbur C. *Colonel Thomas Blood, crown-stealer, 1618–1680.* New Haven, 1911. Reprinted in his *Conflicts with oblivion*, New Haven, 1924, pp. 103–60.

539 Acton, John E. E. D., Lord. *Lectures on modern history*, ed. John N. Figgis and Reginald V. Laurence. 1906. Includes lectures on the rise of the Whigs and on the English revolution.

540 Ashley, Maurice. *The Glorious Revolution of 1688.* 1966. An interesting descriptive account.

541 Bickley, Francis L. *The Cavendish family.* 1911. Chap. 6 deals with William, first duke of Devonshire.

542 Brett, Arthur C. A. *Charles II and his court.* 1910.

543 Buranelli, Vincent. *The king and the Quaker: a study of William Penn and James II.* Philadelphia, 1962. Maintains that James acted in good faith regarding religious toleration and had no intention of subverting the rights of Englishmen. No new evidence, or critical reinterpretation of the old.

544 Carr, John Dickson. *The murder of Sir Edmund Godfrey.* 1936. An investigation by a writer of detective fiction.

545 Carswell, John. *The descent on England: a study of the English revolution of 1688 and its European background.* 1969. Emphasis on European and Atlantic aspects.

546 Cooke, George W. *The history of party.* 1836–7, 3 vols. Vol. I covers 1666–1714. Superseded by Feiling (555).

547 Crawfurd, Raymond H. P. *The last days of Charles II.* Oxford, 1909. An investigation of the causes of Charles's death.

548 Davies, Godfrey. *Essays on the later Stuarts.* San Marino, Calif., 1958. Includes 'Charles II in 1660' and 'Tory churchmen and James II'.

549 —— *The restoration of Charles II, 1658–1660.* San Marino, Calif., 1955. A detailed narrative, designed to 'complete' Gardiner and Firth.

550 Dodd, Arthur H. *Studies in Stuart Wales.* Cardiff, 1952. Has chapters on 'The dawn of party politics' and 'The Glorious Revolution'.

551 Dunn, Mary M. *William Penn: politics and conscience.* Princeton, 1967. A good analysis of Penn as a politician, based primarily on his political pamphlets.

552 Echard, Laurence. *The history of the revolution and the establishment of England in...1688.* 1725. Provides background treatment of the reigns of Charles II and James II.

553 Edie, Carolyn A. The Irish cattle bills: a study in Restoration politics (*American Philosophical Society, Transactions*, new ser., LX, pt. 2). Philadelphia, 1970.

554 Emerson, William R. *Monmouth's rebellion*. New Haven, 1951. Undergraduate prize essay. The most original part is concerned with William of Orange's responsibility for the rebellion.

555 Feiling, Keith G. *History of the Tory party, 1640–1714*. Oxford, 1924. The best account; sympathetic toward moderate Toryism.

556 Fitzgerald, Brian. *The Anglo-Irish, three representative types: Cork, Ormonde, Swift, 1602–1745*. 1952.

557 Folger Shakespeare Library. *The restoration of the Stuarts: blessing or disaster?* (Report of the Folger Library Conference). Washington, 1960. A collection of papers on aspects of the Restoration.

558 Fox, Charles James. *A history of the early part of the reign of James II*, ed. Vassall Fox, Lord Holland. 1808. Appendix has correspondence of Barillon, French ambassador to London, with Louis XIV, 1684–5.

559 George, Mary Dorothy. *English political caricature: a study of opinion and propaganda*, vol. I. Oxford, 1959. Three chapters on the period.

560 Guizot, François P. G. *History of Richard Cromwell and the restoration of Charles II*, trans. Andrew R. Scoble. 1856, 2 vols. Contains despatches of the French ambassador.

561 —— *Monk, or the fall of the republic and the restoration of the monarchy in England in 1660*, trans. Andrew R. Scoble. 1851. Has copious diplomatic despatches, 1659–60.

562 Handover, Phyllis M. *A history of the London Gazette, 1665–1965*. 1965.

563 Hardacre, Paul H. *The royalists during the puritan revolution*. The Hague, 1956. The last chapter deals with the treatment of the royalists by Charles II and his government.

564 Hay, Malcolm V. *The enigma of James II*. 1938. Criticizes Churchill (1586).

565 —— *Winston Churchill and James II of England*. 1934. Defends authenticity of Clarke (463), and James II himself. Unconvincing.

566 Hertz, Gerald B. *English public opinion after the Restoration*. 1902. Seeks to present 'the people's idea of politics', 1660–1702.

567 Illick, Joseph E. *William Penn the politician: his relations with the English government*. Ithaca, N.Y., 1966. A solid work with extensive documentation.

568 Inderwick, Frederick A. *Side-lights on the Stuarts*. 1888. Has chapters on touching for scrofula and Monmouth's rebellion.

569 Jones, James R. *The first Whigs: the politics of the exclusion crisis, 1678–1683*. 1961. A valuable work, setting the crisis in its historical perspective as part of the struggle between representative government and absolutism.

570 Kent, Clement B. R. *The early history of the Tories, from the accession of Charles the Second to the death of William the Third*. 1908. Superseded by Feiling (555).

571 Kenyon, John P. *The nobility in the Revolution of 1688*. Hull, 1963. An inaugural lecture.

572 —— *The Stuarts: a study in English kingship*. 1958. Chapters on individual reigns.

573 Kitchin, George. *Sir Roger L'Estrange: a contribution to the history of the press in the seventeenth century*. 1913. Contains list of his political works and the chief sources for his life.

574 Lacey, Douglas R. *Dissent and parliamentary politics in England, 1661–1689*. New Brunswick, N. J., 1969. An illuminating study based on thorough research.

575 Landon, Michael. *The triumph of the lawyers: their role in English politics, 1678–1689*. University, Ala., 1970.

576 Levin, Jennifer. *The charter controversy in the city of London, 1660–88, and its consequences*. 1969.

577 Little, Bryan D. *The Monmouth episode*. 1956.

578 Macky, John. *Memoirs of the secret services of John Macky*. 1733. Includes characters of late seventeenth-century figures.

579 Marks, Alfred. *Who killed Sir Edmund Berry Godfrey?* 1905. Argues that Godfrey committed suicide; Catholic presentation.

580 Moore, George. *The history of the British revolution of 1688–89*. 1817.

581 Morley, Iris. *A thousand lives: an account of the English revolutionary movement, 1660–1685*. 1954. Concerned with the background and bases of Monmouth's support.

582 Morrah, Patrick. *1660: the year of the Restoration*. 1960. Popular in tone, but makes extensive use of primary sources.

583 Nobbs, Douglas. *England and Scotland, 1560–1707*. 1952. Surveys political and religious developments in the two countries.

584 Parry, Edward A. *The Bloody Assize*. 1929.

585 Pinkham, Lucile. *William III and the respectable revolution*. Cambridge, Mass., 1954. Sees William as actively engaged in fulfilling a lifelong aim to secure the English throne; controversial.

586 Plumb, John H. *The growth of political stability in England, 1675–1725*. 1967. Important for the growth of the electorate and the executive.

587 —— *Men and centuries*. Boston, 1963. Essays. Mostly eighteenth-century, but there are interesting pieces on the first earl of Shaftesbury and Evelyn.

588 *Revolution politics, being a complete collection of all the reports, lies, and stories which were forerunners of the great revolution in 1688*. 1733. Sometimes attributed to Gilbert Burnet.

589 Ronalds, Francis S. *The attempted Whig revolution of 1678–1681*. Urbana, Ill., 1937. Should be read with Jones (569). Emphasis on prominent figures; detailed bibliography.

590 Rowse, Alfred L. *The early Churchills*. 1956. An interesting account, going to 1722.

591 Salmon, Thomas. *An impartial examination of Bishop Burnet's History of his own times*. 1724. One of the numerous replies to Burnet.

592 Sharpe, Reginald R. *London and the kingdom: a history derived mainly from the archives at Guildhall*. 1894–5, 3 vols. Vol. II deals with 1603–1714, and there are important documents in vol. III.

593 Siebert, Frederick S. *Freedom of the press in England, 1476–1776: the rise and decline of government controls*. Urbana, Ill., 1952.

594 Sitwell, George. *The first Whig: an account of the parliamentary career of William Sacheverell*. Scarborough, 1894. Deals with the origins of political parties; cf. Sitwell, *Letters* (516).

595 Trevelyan, George M. *The English revolution, 1688–1689*. 1938. The best-known exposition apart from Macaulay; Whiggish in character.

596 Ward, Robert Plumer. *An historical essay on the real character and amount of the precedent of the Revolution of 1688*. 1838. A Tory interpretation.

597 Western, John R. *The English militia in the eighteenth century: the story of a political issue, 1660–1802*. 1965. A valuable work, based on much unpublished source material. Essentially a study of English politics and local government, rather than of military affairs.

598 Woods, Maurice. *A history of the Tory party in the seventeenth and eighteenth centuries*. 1924. Superseded, for the period, by Feiling (555).

4 Biographies

599 Airy, Osmund. *Charles II*. 1901.

600 Ashley, Maurice. *John Wildman, plotter and postmaster: a study of the English republican movement in the seventeenth century*. 1947. Biography of William III's postmaster-general.

601 Baxter, Stephen B. *William III and the defense of European liberty, 1650–1702*. 1966. The best biography; makes use of Dutch as well as English materials.

602 Beaven, Alfred B. *The aldermen of the city of London temp. Henry III–1908*. 1908, 2 vols. Provides much biographical data, and numerous corrections of the *Dictionary of National Biography*.

603 Beaven, Murray L. R. *Sir William Temple*. Oxford, 1908. A prize essay; inadequate.

604 Beresford, John. *The godfather of Downing Street: Sir George Downing, 1623–84*. 1925. Describes the varied activities of an opportunist politician; chiefly important for his negotiations with the Netherlands.

605 Bowen, Marjorie (pseud.). *The third Mary Stuart*. 1929. Contains Mary's memoirs, letters, and meditations.

606 Boyer, Abel. *The history of King William III*. 1702–3, 3 vols. Treatment by a contemporary Huguenot journalist.

607 Brown, Louise Fargo. *The first earl of Shaftesbury*. New York, 1933. Concentrates on Shaftesbury's earlier years, but goes beyond Christie (616), especially regarding commerce and colonization. Superseded by Haley (639).

608 Browning, Andrew. *Thomas Osborne, earl of Danby and duke of Leeds, 1632–1712*. Glasgow, 1944–51, 3 vols. An elaborate, scholarly work. Vol. II contains letters, vol. III various papers.

609 Bryant, Arthur. *King Charles II*. Rev. ed., 1955. The most satisfactory biography.

610 Cardigan, Chandos S. C. Brudenell-Bruce, earl of. *The life and loyalties of Thomas Bruce*. 1951. Treats the life of the second earl of Ailesbury, closely associated with Charles II and James II; over-sympathetic and under-documented.

611 Carswell, John. *The old cause: three biographical studies in Whiggism*. 1954. Includes Thomas, first marquess of Wharton (1648–1715).

612 Carte, Thomas. *An history of the life of James, duke of Ormonde, 1610–1688*. Oxford, 1851, 6 vols. The most elaborate account, to be read with Gardiner (636).

613 Chapman, Hester W. *The great Villiers: a study of George Villiers, second duke of Buckingham, 1628–1687*. 1949. A barely adequate treatment.

614 —— *Mary II, Queen of England*. 1953. The most satisfactory treatment.

615 —— *Privileged persons: four seventeenth-century studies*. 1966. Includes the second earl of Ailesbury (1656–1741).

616 Christie, William D. *A life of Anthony Ashley Cooper, first earl of Shaftesbury, 1621–1683*. 1871, 2 vols. Incorporates *Memoirs* (512); superseded by Haley (639).

617 Clarkson, Thomas. *Memoirs of the public and private life of William Penn*. 1813, 2 vols. A later ed., 1849, has a preface by W. E. Forster replying to charges made against Penn by Macaulay in his *History*.

618 Cleugh, James. *Prince Rupert*. 1934. Popular.

619 Corbett, Julian S. *Monk*. 1889.

620 Craik, Henry. *The life of Edward, earl of Clarendon*. 1911, 2 vols. A sympathetic work, less important than Lister (659), but making use of new materials.

621 Davies, John D. G. *Honest George Monck*. 1936. Laudatory.

622 Dixon, William H. *William Penn, an historical biography founded on family and state papers*. 1851. Penn as statesman; a reply to Macaulay.

623 D'Oyley, Elizabeth. *James, duke of Monmouth*. 1938. Popular.

624 Edinger, George A. *Rupert of the Rhine, the pirate prince*. 1936. Popular.

625 Elliot, Hugh F. H. *The life of Sidney, earl Godolphin, lord high treasurer of England*. 1888. For a more modern treatment, see Lever (658).

626 Ewald, Alexander C. *The life and times of the hon. Algernon Sydney*. 1873, 2 vols.

627 Fea, Allan. *King Monmouth, being a history of the career of James Scott, 'the Protestant duke'*. 1902. A popular life.

628 Feilding, Cecilia Mary, countess of Denbigh. *Royalist father and roundhead son, being the memoirs of the first and second earls of Denbigh, 1600–1675*. 1915.

629 Ferguson, James. *Robert Ferguson the plotter, or the secret of the Rye House conspiracy*. Edinburgh, 1887. Based largely on his letters.

630 Firebrace, Cordell W. *Honest Harry, being a biography of Sir Henry Firebrace, 1619–1691*. 1932. Life of a staunch royalist, chiefly important for pre-Restoration years.

631 Fletcher, Joseph S. *Yorkshiremen of the Restoration*. 1921. Twelve biographical essays, including Reresby and Halifax.

632 Forneron, Henri (ed.). *Louise de Kéroualle, duchesse de Portsmouth, 1649–1734*. Paris, 1886. Based on French archives, but rather slight. An English translation (1887) is untrustworthy.

633 Foxcroft, Helen C. *A character of the Trimmer, being a short life of the first marquis of Halifax*. Cambridge, 1947. A recast, updated version of (634), without the writings.

634 Foxcroft, Helen C. *The life and letters of Sir George Savile, bart., first marquis of Halifax, with a new edition of his works*. 1898, 2 vols. Authoritative; vol. II contains a reprint of his works and a bibliography.

635 Gardner, Winifred A. H. C. (Lady Burghclere). *George Villiers, second duke of Buckingham, 1628–1687*. 1903.

636 —— *The life of James, first duke of Ormonde, 1610–1688*. 1912, 2 vols. Cf. Carte (612).

637 Haile, Martin. *Queen Mary of Modena: her life and letters*. 1905. Based on unpublished materials in foreign archives.

638 Haley, Kenneth H. D. *Charles II* (Historical Association, General Series, no. 63). 1966. A brief evaluation.

639 —— *The first earl of Shaftesbury*. Oxford, 1968. A massive work of admirable scholarship, superseding Christie (616) and Brown (607).

640 Hamilton, Elizabeth, Lady. *The backstairs dragon: a life of Robert Harley, earl of Oxford*. 1969.

641 Harris, William. *An historical and critical account of the life of Charles the Second, after the manner of Mr. Bayle*. 1766, 2 vols. Nonconformist point of view; chiefly valuable for notes.

642 Hartmann, Cyril H. *Clifford of the Cabal: a life of Thomas, first Lord Clifford of Chudleigh*. 1937. Makes use of Clifford's papers.

643 —— *The King's friend: a life of Charles Berkeley, viscount Fitzhardinge, earl of Falmouth, 1630–1665*. 1951. Completes a trilogy, with (642) and (804), on circumstances leading up to the Treaty of Dover.

644 Henslowe, J. R. *Anne Hyde, duchess of York*. 1915. Popular.

645 Higham, Florence M. G. *King James the Second*. 1934. Reasonably adequate, but inferior to Turner (691).

646 Hopkirk, Mary. *Queen over the water: Mary Beatrice of Modena, queen of James II*. 1953.

647 Horwitz, Henry. *Revolution politicks: the career of Daniel Finch, second earl of Nottingham, 1647–1730*. 1968. Not a full biography; an outline of his career through chapters illuminating its more important aspects.

648 Japikse, Nicolaas. *Prins Willem III, de Stadhouder-Koning* (Nederlandsche Historische Bibliotheck, XVII, XIX). Amsterdam, 1930–3, 2 vols. A valuable work, making extensive use of source materials.

649 Jones, G. F. Trevallyn. *Saw-pit Wharton: the political career from 1640 to 1691 of Philip, fourth Lord Wharton*. 1967.

650 Jones, George H. *Charles Middleton: the life and times of a Restoration politician*. Chicago, 1968. A scholarly work, making extensive use of manuscript materials.

651 Kaufman, Helen A. *Conscientious cavalier: Colonel Bullen Reymes, M.P., F.R.S., the man and his times*. 1962.

652 Kenyon, John P. *Robert Spencer, earl of Sunderland, 1641–1702*. 1958. A first-rate biography.

653 Kirby, Ethyn W. *William Prynne: a study in puritanism*. Cambridge, Mass., 1931. Chiefly valuable as a guide to Prynne's pamphlets; has extensive bibliography. Some inaccuracies in citations.

654 Klose, Curt. *George Savile, Marquis von Halifax, als Politiker und Staatsdenker, 1633–1695*. Breslau, 1936. A brief life.

655 Lamont, William M. *Marginal Prynne, 1600–1669*. 1963. A valuable study of Prynne's ideas in relation to those of his contemporaries, but there is only one chapter on the period.

656 Lane, Jane (pseud. for Elaine Dakers). *Titus Oates*. 1949. Popular.

657 Lediard, Thomas. *Life of John, duke of Marlborough*. 1736, 3 vols. Detailed treatment by a close observer; includes documents favourable to Marlborough.

658 Lever, Tresham. *Godolphin: his life and times*. 1952.

659 Lister, Thomas H. *Life and administration of Edward, first earl of Clarendon*. 1837–8, 3 vols. Still the best life, despite its age. Vol. III contains correspondence, 1660–7. Should be used with Craik (620).

660 Lodge, Edmund. *Portraits of illustrious personages of Great Britain...with biographical and historical memoirs of their lives and actions*. 1821–4, 4 vols.

661 Longueville, Thomas. *The adventures of King James II of England.* 1904. Based mainly on Ailesbury (443).
662 Mackay, Janet. *Catherine of Braganza.* 1937. Popular.
663 Mackenzie, William C. *The life and times of John Maitland, duke of Lauderdale, 1616–1692.* 1923. Not entirely satisfactory for English affairs.
664 Madgett, Nicholas and J. F. H. Dutems. *Histoire de Jean Churchill, duc de Marlborough.* Paris, 1806, 3 vols. Based on Lediard (657); written by order of Napoleon.
665 Meadley, George W. *Memoirs of Algernon Sydney.* 1813.
666 *Memoirs of the life of Sir Stephen Fox.* 1717. Life of an active politician and philanthropist.
667 Middleton, Dorothy. *The life of Charles, second earl of Middleton.* 1957. Inadequate; cf. Jones (650).
668 Muddiman, Joseph G. *The King's journalist, 1659–1689.* 1923. Virtually a life of Henry Muddiman.
669 Nicholas, Donald. *Mr. Secretary Nicholas, 1593–1669: his life and letters.* 1955.
670 Nicholson, Thomas C. and Arthur S. Turberville. *Charles Talbot, duke of Shrewsbury.* Cambridge, 1930.
671 Ogg, David. *William III.* 1956. A good short treatment.
672 Oliver, Harold J. *Sir Robert Howard, 1626–1698: a critical biography.* Durham, N.C., 1963. Howard was a Whig M.P. and privy councillor, as well as a dramatist.
673 Oman, Carola. *Mary of Modena.* 1962. A sound and readable biography, though somewhat superficial.
674 Pearson, Hesketh. *Charles II: his life and likeness.* 1960. Popular.
675 Porritt, Derrick J. *The duke of Monmouth.* Ilfracombe, 1953.
676 Price, Cecil. *Cold Caleb: the scandalous life of Ford Grey, first earl of Tankerville, 1655–1701.* 1956. Study of a Whig politician and zealous exclusionist. Cf. Grey (476).
677 Rait, Robert S. (ed.). *Five Stuart princesses.* 1902. Includes Mary of Orange and Henrietta of Orleans.
678 Reid, Stuart J. *John and Sarah, duke and duchess of Marlborough, 1660–1744.* 1914. By the archivist at Blenheim. Highly sympathetic, particularly toward the duchess; not entirely superseded.
679 Robb, Nesca A. *William of Orange: a personal portrait.* 1966. 2 vols. Inferior to Baxter (601).
680 Roberts, George. *The life, progresses, and rebellion of James, duke of Monmouth.* 1844, 2 vols. Includes account of the Bloody Assize. Sound but out of date; should be supplemented by Fea (627).
681 Russell, Lord John. *The life of William Lord Russell, with some account of the times in which he lived.* 1819. Rather a history of the times than a biography.
682 Scott, Eva. *Rupert, Prince Palatine.* 1899.
683 —— *Six Stuart sovereigns, 1512–1701.* 1935. Includes Charles II and James II; popular in tone.
684 Seccombe, Thomas (ed.). *Lives of twelve bad men: original studies of eminent scoundrels by various hands.* 1894. Includes Oates and Jeffreys.
685 Somerville, Dorothy H. *The king of hearts: Charles Talbot, duke of Shrewsbury.* 1962. Adds little to Nicholson and Turberville (670).
686 Strickland, Agnes. *Lives of the queens of England*, ed. John F. Kirk. Philadelphia, 1907, 16 vols. Originally published 1840–8. Antiquated and uncritical.
687 Tibbutt, Harry G. *Colonel John Okey, 1606–1662* (Bedfordshire Historical Record Society, XXXV). 1955. A narrative interspersed with numerous documents.
688 Townshend, Dorothea. *George Digby, second earl of Bristol.* 1924.
689 Traill, Henry D. *William the Third.* 1888. Slight and out of date; cf. Baxter (601).
690 Trevor, Arthur H., Viscount Dungannon. *The life and times of William III.* 1835–6, 2 vols. Emphasis on William's relations with Charles II and James II. Includes documents. Cf. Baxter (601).
691 Turner, Francis C. *James II.* New York, 1948. The best biography.
692 Warburton, Eliot. *Memoirs of Prince Rupert and the cavaliers, including their private correspondence from the original manuscripts.* 1849, 3 vols. Antiquated, but the letters are of some interest.

693 Warner, Oliver M. W. *Hero of the Restoration: a life of General George Monck, first duke of Albemarle, K.G.* 1936. One of several laudatory accounts; cf. Davies (621).

694 Waterson, Nellie M. *Mary II.* Durham, N.C., 1928.

5 Articles

695 Abbott, Wilbur C. 'English conspiracy and dissent, 1660–1674', *AHR*, **14** (Apr., July 1909), 503–28, 696–722.

696 —— 'Origin of English political parties', *AHR*, **24** (July 1919), 578–602.

697 —— 'The origin of Titus Oates' story', *EHR*, **25** (Jan. 1910), 126–9.

698 —— 'What was a Whig?', in Stanley M. Pargellis (ed.), *The quest for political unity in world history* (American Historical Association, Annual Report, 1942), III, 253–67. Washington, 1944.

699 Ashley, Maurice. 'Is there a case for James II?', *Hist. T.*, **13** (May 1963), 347–52. Sees James as a masochist rather than a bigot.

700 —— 'King James II and the Revolution of 1688: some reflections on the historiography', in Henry E. Bell and R. L. Ollard (eds.), *Historical essays, 1600–1750, presented to David Ogg*, 1963, pp. 185–202.

701 Beddard, Robert. 'The commission for ecclesiastical promotions, 1681–1684: an instrument of Tory reaction', *Hist. J.*, **10** (no. 1, 1967), 11–40. Claims that the commission provided for a 'Yorkist' invasion of the hierarchy.

702 —— 'The Guildhall declaration of 11 December 1688 and the counter-revolution of the loyalists', *Hist. J.*, **11** (no. 3, 1968), 403–20.

703 Benson, Donald R. 'Halifax and the trimmers', *HLQ*, **27** (Feb. 1964), 115–34. Deals with the identity of the trimmers.

704 Birrell, T. A. 'Roger North and political morality in the later Stuart period', *Scrutiny*, **17** (Mar. 1951), 282–98.

705 Browning, Andrew. 'Parties and party organization in the reign of Charles II', *TRHS*, 4th ser., **30** (1948), 21–36.

706 Buranelli, Vincent. 'William Penn and James II', *Proceedings of the American Philosophical Society*, **104** (1960), 35–53. Seeks to account for the friendship between the two. See also (543).

707 Burrage, Champlin. 'Fifth monarchy insurrections', *EHR*, **25** (Oct. 1910), 722–52.

708 Catterall, Ralph C. H. 'Sir George Downing and the regicides', *AHR*, **17** (Jan. 1912), 268–89. Discusses successful attempt of the government to apprehend regicides who had fled to the Netherlands. Cf. Beresford (604).

709 Cole, Alan. 'The Quakers and the English Revolution', *PP*, no. 10 (Nov. 1956), 39–54.

710 Davies, Godfrey. 'Charles II in 1660', *HLQ*, **19** (May 1956), 245–75. Analyses contemporary biographical treatment of Charles in the light of those who knew him well.

711 —— 'The political career of Sir Richard Temple (1634–1697) and Buckingham politics', *HLQ*, **4** (Oct. 1940), 47–83.

712 De Beer, Esmond S. 'Executions following the "Bloody Assize"', *BIHR*, **4** (no. 10, 1926), 36–9.

713 Evans, A. M. 'The imprisonment of the earl of Danby in the Tower (1679–1684)', *TRHS*, 4th ser. **12** (1929), 105–36.

714 —— 'Yorkshire and the Revolution of 1688', *Yorkshire Archaeological Journal*, **29** (1929), 258–85. Based on Hornby Castle papers and other original sources.

715 Firth, Charles H. 'Edward Hyde, earl of Clarendon, as statesman, historian, and chancellor of the University', in his *Essays historical and literary*, Oxford, 1939, pp. 103–28. Also separately published, Oxford, 1909; a commemorative lecture.

716 —— 'The Stewart restoration', in *CMH*, v, 92–115.

717 Foxcroft, Helen C. 'New light on George Savile, first marquis of Halifax, "the trimmer"', *Hist*, **26** (Dec. 1941), 176–87.

718 Furley, O. W. 'The Whig exclusionists: pamphlet literature in the exclusion campaign, 1678–81', *Camb. Hist. J.*, **13** (no. 1, 1957), 19–36.

719 Gardner, William B. 'The later years of John Maitland, second earl and first duke of Lauderdale', *JMH*, **20** (June 1948), 113–22. Sympathetic.

720 Grose, Clyde L. 'Charles the Second of England', *AHR*, **43** (Apr. 1938), 533–41. A brief and not very penetrating evaluation of Charles, sparked by recent publications.

721 Humphreys, Arthur L. 'Some sources of history for the Monmouth rebellion and the Bloody Assizes', *Proceedings of the Somersetshire Archaeological and Natural History Society*, **38** (1892), 312–26. Criticizes older sources.

722 Jones, James R. 'The first Whig party in Norfolk', *Durham University Journal*, **46** (Dec. 1953), 13–21.

723 —— 'The Green Ribbon Club', *Durham University Journal*, **49** (Dec. 1956), 17–20. Deals with the Whig club of exclusionist days.

724 —— 'James II's Whig collaborators', *Hist. J.*, **3** (no. 1, 1960), 65–73. Concerned with those who collaborated with James in 1687–8 in a project for packing parliament.

725 Kenyon, John P. 'The birth of the Old Pretender', *Hist. T.*, **13** (June 1963), 418–26.

726 —— 'The earl of Sunderland and the Revolution of 1688', *Camb. Hist. J.*, **11** (no. 3, 1955), 272–96.

727 —— 'The exclusion crisis', *Hist. T.*, **14** (Apr., May 1964), 252–9, 344–9.

728 —— 'William III, part I', *Hist. T.*, **9** (Sept. 1959), 581–8. Evaluates William as a successful but not a popular monarch.

729 Lemoine, Jean M. P. J. and André Lichtenberger. 'Louise de Kéroualle, duchesse de Portsmouth', *Revue des deux mondes*, 5th ser., **14** (1903), 114–46, 358–96. A good account, based on newly discovered manuscripts.

730 McCutcheon, Roger P. 'Pepys in the newspapers of 1679–1680', *AHR*, **32** (Oct. 1926), 61–4. Deals with charges against Pepys.

731 Milne, Doreen J. 'The results of the Rye House plot and their influence upon the Revolution of 1688', *TRHS*, 5th ser., **1** (1951), 91–108.

732 Mitchell, A. A. 'The Revolution of 1688 and the flight of James II', *Hist. T.* **15** (July 1965), 496–504. A reappraisal of James's reasons for leaving England.

733 Morgan, William T. 'What was a Tory?', in Stanley M. Pargellis (ed.), *The quest for political unity in world history* (American Historical Association, Annual Report, 1942), III, 269–86. Washington, 1944.

734 Muddiman, Joseph G. 'The mystery of Sir Edmund Berry Godfrey', *National Review*, **84** (Sept. 1924), 138–45.

735 Mullett, Charles F. 'A case of allegiance: William Sherlock and the Revolution of 1688', *HLQ*, **10** (Nov. 1946), 83–104.

736 —— 'Religion, politics, and oaths in the Glorious Revolution', *Review of Politics*, **10** (Oct. 1948), 462–74. Concerned with fugitive pieces of political literature.

737 Petrie, Charles. 'James the Second: a revaluation', *Nineteenth Century*, **114** (Oct. 1933), 475–84. Defends James against treatment at the hands of Winston Churchill.

738 Pollock, John. 'The policy of Charles II and James II', *CMH*, IX, 198–235. A general treatment of the two reigns.

739 Priestley, Margaret. 'London merchants and opposition politics in Charles II's reign', *BIHR*, **29** (Nov. 1956), 205–19.

740 Ranft, B. M. 'The significance of the political career of Samuel Pepys', *JMH*, **24** (Dec. 1952), 368–75. Pepys's career in the Commons.

741 Sachse, William L. 'The mob and the Revolution of 1688', *JBS*, **4** (Nov. 1964), 23–40.

742 Salmon, J. H. M. 'Algernon Sidney and the Rye House plot', *Hist. T.*, **4** (Oct. 1954), 698–705.

743 Schafer, Robert G. 'The making of a Tory', *HLQ*, **23** (Feb. 1960), 123–44. Deals with Sir James Brydges, eighth baron Chandos of Sudeley.

744 Temperley, Harold W. V. 'The Revolution and the Revolution settlement in Great Britain', *CMH*, V, 236–77.

745 Vellacott, Paul C. 'The struggle of James II with the University of Cambridge', in *In memoriam: A. W. Ward*, Cambridge, 1924, pp. 81–101.

746 Walcott, Robert. 'The idea of party in the writing of later Stuart history', *JBS*, **2** (May 1962), 54–61.

747 Walker, James. 'The censorship of the press during the reign of Charles II', *Hist.*, new ser., **33** (Oct. 1950), 219–38.

748 —— 'Dissent and republicanism after the Restoration', *Baptist Quarterly*, **8** (Jan. 1937), 263–80.

749 —— 'The English exiles in Holland during the reigns of Charles II and James II', *TRHS*, 4th ser., **30** (1948), 111–25.

750 Whiting, George W. 'The condition of the London theaters, 1679–83: a reflection of the political situation', *Mod. Phil.*, **25** (Nov. 1927), 195–206.

751 —— 'Political satire in London stage plays, 1680–83', *Mod. Phil.*, **28** (Aug. 1930), 29–43.

752 Wood, Alfred C. 'The Revolution of 1688 in the north of England', *Transactions of the Thoroton Society*, **44** (1941), 72–104. A survey, somewhat superseded by Browning (608).

VI FOREIGN RELATIONS

1 Printed Sources

753 Arlington, Henry Bennet, earl of. *The right honourable the earl of Arlington's letters to Sir William Temple, bart.*, ed. Thomas Bebington. 1701, 2 vols. From 1665 to 1670. Also letters to Sir Richard Fanshawe and others during their embassies in Spain (1664–74) and to Sir Robert Southwell in Portugal.

754 Avaux, Jean Antoine de Mesmes, comte d'. *Negociations du comte d'Avaux en Hollande*. Paris, 1752–3, 6 vols. English trans., 1754. Useful for activities of William of Orange prior to his invasion of England.

755 *Calendar of state papers, Venetian*, ed. Allen B. Hinds, vols. XXXII–XXXVIII. 1931–47. These vols. cover 1659–75, the present limit of the publication.

756 Chalmers, George (ed.). *A collection of treaties between Great Britain and other powers*. 1790, 2 vols.

757 Christie, William D. (ed.). *Letters addressed from London to Sir Joseph Williamson while plenipotentiary at the congress of Cologne in the years 1673 and 1674* (Camden Society, new ser., VIII–IX). 1874. Chiefly on domestic and parliamentary affairs.

758 Cooper, William D. (ed.). *Savile correspondence; letters to and from Henry Savile, esq., envoy at Paris and vice-chamberlain to Charles II and James II, including letters from his brother George, marquess of Halifax* (Camden Society, old ser., LXXI). 1858. Savile's letters cover 1679–82; Halifax's, 1679–86.

759 'Copies of several letters received from and writ to the right honourable the lord Arlington and Mr. Trevor, secretaries of state in the reign of Charles the Second, by the honourable Charles Bertie, esq.,...as envoy extraordinary to the King of Denmark, to adjust the difference of the flag', *Retrospective Review*, 2nd ser., **2** (1827), 177–205.

760 Davenport, Francis G. (ed.). *European treaties bearing on the history of the United States and its dependencies*, vol. II (1650–97). Washington, 1929. Translations.

761 Dumont, Jean (Baron de Carlscroon). *Corps universel diplomatique du droit des gens*. Amsterdam, 1726–31, 8 vols. An important collection of treaties.

762 Ellis, Henry (ed.). 'Relation of the Lord Fauconberg's embassy to the states of Italy in the year 1669', *Archaeologia*, **37** (1857), 158–88. A report to Charles II.

763 Estrades, Godefroi, comte d'. *Lettres, mémoires, et négociations de Monsieur le comte d'Estrades, pendant les années 1663 jusques 1668*, ed. J. Aymon. Brussels, 1709. An English translation appeared in 1711.

764 Etherege, George. *The letterbook of Sir George Etherege*, ed. Sybil Rosenfeld. Oxford, 1928. Etherege was minister at Ratisbon, 1685–8, but the letter-book has more to offer on the social and literary side than on the diplomatic. On Etherege see Dobrée (820).

765 Fanshawe, Ann. *The memoirs of Ann Lady Fanshawe*, ed. Herbert C. Fanshawe. 1907. Useful for Charles II's marriage, and for relations with Iberian countries.

766 Feiling, Keith G. 'Henrietta Stuart, duchess of Orleans, and the origins of the Treaty of Dover', *EHR*, **47** (Oct. 1932), 642–5. A letter, in French, from the duchess to Charles II.

767 Firth, Charles H. 'Secretary Thurloe on the relations of England and Holland', *EHR*, **21** (Apr. 1906), 319–27. Drawn up by Thurloe in 1661 for Clarendon's benefit.

768 Grose, Clyde L. 'French ambassadors' reports on financial relations with members of parliament, 1677–1681', *EHR*, **44** (Oct. 1929), 625–8. See also (835).

769 Harris, William. *A complete collection of all the marine treaties subsisting between Great Britain and France, Spain, Portugal, Austria, Russia, Denmark, Sweden*, etc. 1779.

770 Historical Manuscripts Commission. *The manuscripts of J. M. Heathcote, esq., Conington Castle*. Norwich, 1899. Chiefly the correspondence of Richard Fanshawe, ambassador to Portugal and Spain, 1661–6.

771 —— *Report on the manuscripts of Allan George Finch, esq., of Burley-on-the-Hill, Rutland*, vol. I. 1913. Correspondence of Heneage Finch, earl of Winchilsea, during his Turkish embassy, 1660–8.

772 Jenkinson, Charles, earl of Liverpool. *A collection of all the treaties of peace, alliance, and commerce between Great Britain and other powers*. 1785, 3 vols. Covers 1648–1783; translations only.

773 Jusserand, Jean A. A. J. (ed.). *Recueil des instructions données aux ambassadeurs et ministres de France*, vols. XXIV–XXV: *Angleterre*. Paris, 1929. The vols. cover 1648–90; valuable for continental negotiations in which England participated.

774 Kenyon, John P. 'Charles II and William of Orange in 1680', *BIHR*, **30** (May 1957), 95–101. Three letters of the Earl of Sunderland.

775 *Letters from the secretaries of state and other persons, in the reign of King Charles the Second, to Francis Parry, esq., English envoy in Portugal*. 1817. Letters of Henry Bennet, earl of Arlington, Henry Coventry, and others.

776 Lindenow, Christopher. *The first triple alliance: the letters of Christopher Lindenow, Danish envoy to London, 1668–1672*, ed. Waldemar Westergaard. New Haven, 1947. Useful for the diplomacy of Charles II's middle years, as viewed from London.

777 *List of despatches of ambassadors from France to England, 1509–1714*, ed. Armand Baschet, in *Reports of the deputy keeper of the public records*, **39**, 1878, app. 1, pp. 573–826.

778 Middlebush, Frederick A. 'Charles II and Louis XIV in 1683', *EHR*, **38** (Apr. 1923), 258–60. Prints anonymous letter from The Hague, describing supposed Anglo-French alliance, Cf. de Beer (828).

779 —— (ed.). *The despatches of Thomas Plott (1681–1682) and Thomas Chudleigh (1682–1685), English envoys at The Hague*. The Hague, 1926. A full-dress edition, throwing light on the complexities of contemporary English policy.

780 Miège, Guy. *A relation of three embassies from his sacred majesty Charles II to the great duke of Muscovie*. 1669. Written by a diplomatic aide.

781 *Original letters and negotiations of Sir Richard Fanshaw, the earl of Sandwich, the earl of Sunderland, and Sir William Godolphin,...wherein divers matters between the three crowns of England, Spain, and Portugal from 1663 to 1678 are set in a clearer light than is anywhere else extant*. 1724, 2 vols. Amplifies materials found in Arlington's and Coventry's letters to Parry (775).

782 Orlich, Leopold von (ed.). 'Briefe aus England über die Zeit von 1674 bis 1678', in *Gesandtschafts Berichten des Ministers Otto von Schwerin des Jüngen an den Grossen Kurfürsten Friedrich Wilhelm*. Berlin, 1837. Reports of the Prussian envoy.

783 Perwich, William. *The despatches of William Perwich, English agent in Paris, 1669–77*, ed. M. Beryl Curran (Camden Society, 3rd ser., v). 1903.

784 Prinsterer, Gulielmus G. van (ed.). *Archives ou correspondance inédite de la maison d'Orange-Nassau*, 2nd ser., 1584–1688. Leyden, 1857–62, 5 vols. Important for Anglo-Dutch relations; vol. v has correspondence of William III.

785 Temple, William. *Letters to the King, the Prince of Orange,...and other persons*. 1703.

786 —— *Letters written by Sir William Temple, bart., and other ministers of state, containing an account of the most important transactions...in Christendom from 1665 to 1672*, ed. Jonathan Swift. 1700, 2 vols.

787 —— *The works of Sir William Temple, bart.*, ed. Jonathan Swift. 1814, 4 vols. Includes observations on the United Provinces, letters from European capitals, and other correspondence and essays.

788 Vast, Henri. *Les grands traités du règne de Louis XIV*. Paris, 3 pts., 1893–9. Introduction is informative on preliminary negotiations; valuable bibliographical notes for each treaty.

789 Wicquefort, Abraham van. *The ambassador and his functions*, trans. John Digby. 1716. First published in French in 1681; useful for protocol, as well as for general questions of personnel and extraterritoriality.

790 William III. *Original letters from King William III, then Prince of Orange, to King Charles II, Lord Arlington, etc.*, ed. Robert Sanderson. 1704. From 1668 to 1677.

2 Surveys

791 Jones, James R. *Britain and Europe in the seventeenth century*. 1966. A brief but useful survey.

792 Klopp, Onno. *Der Fall des Hauses Stuart und die Succession des Hauses Hannover*. Vienna, 1875–88, 14 vols. Covers 1660–1715, more particularly from about 1678. Based largely on Austrian despatches from London. A detailed and valuable work, very important for foreign relations despite a pro-Austrian, anti-French bias.

793 Petrie, Charles. *Earlier diplomatic history, 1492–1713*. 1949. A general survey of European diplomacy.

794 Seeley, John R. *The growth of British policy*. Cambridge, 1895, 2 vols. Covers 1558–1714. Dated, but still of some value.

795 Zeller, Gaston, *Les temps modernes*, in Pierre Renouvin, *Histoire des relations internationales*, vol. III. Paris, 1955. Covers 1660–1789.

3 Monographs

796 Abbott, George F. *Under the Turk in Constantinople: a record of Sir John Finch's embassy, 1674–1681*. 1920. Investigates Levantine relations.

797 Anderson, Matthew S. *Britain's discovery of Russia, 1553–1815*. 1958. A study of Anglo-Russian relations, emphasizing English reactions.

798 Clark, Ruth. *Sir William Trumbull in Paris, 1685–86*. Cambridge, 1938. Deals with English diplomacy in connection with the revocation of the Edict of Nantes.

799 Feiling, Keith G. *British foreign policy, 1660–1672*. 1930. Mainly concerned with the secret Treaty of Dover.

800 Firth, Charles H. and Sophia C. Lomas (eds.). *Notes on the diplomatic relations of England and France, 1603–1688; lists of ambassadors from England to France and from France to England*. Oxford, 1906.

801 Geyl, Pieter C. A. *Oranje en Stuart, 1641–1672*. Utrecht, 1939. For English translation, see *Orange and Stuart, 1641–1672*, New York, 1969.

802 Grovestins, Charles F. Sirtema de, Baron. *Histoire des luttes et rivalités politiques entre les puissances maritimes et la France, durant la seconde moitié du XVIIe siècle*. Paris, 1851–4, 8 vols.

803 Haley, Kenneth H. D. *William of Orange and the English opposition, 1672–1674*.

Oxford, 1953. Deals with attempts to detach England from the French alliance.

804 Hartmann, Cyril H. *Charles II and Madame*. 1934. Contains correspondence of Charles and his sister Henrietta; valuable for light thrown on the secret Treaty of Dover. A revision, *The King my brother*, was published in 1954.

805 Head, Frederick W. *The fallen Stuarts*. Cambridge, 1901. Deals with the influence of European politics upon Stuart fortunes, 1660–1748.

806 Horn, David B. (ed.). *British diplomatic representatives, 1689–1789*. 1932. Has some information on Restoration diplomats still in service under William III.

807 Japikse, Nicolaas. *De verwikkelingen tusschen de republiek en Engeland van 1660–1665*. Leyden, 1900. A study of Anglo-Dutch relations.

808 Jusserand, Jean A. A. J. *A French ambassador at the court of Charles II: le comte de Cominges*. 1892. Chiefly concerned with the year 1665, and based on the count's unpublished correspondence. An appendix contains the original text of French despatches. A lively and instructive work.

809 King, Harold L. *Brandenburg and the English Revolution of 1688*. Oberlin, 1914.

810 Lachs, Phyllis S. *The diplomatic corps under Charles II and James II*. New Brunswick, 1965. An excellent study, with useful bibliographical comment.

811 Lubimenko, Inna I. *Les relations commerciales et politiques de l'Angleterre avec la Russie avant Pierre le Grand*. Paris, 1933.

812 Muilenburg, James. *The embassy of Everaard van Weede, lord of Dykvelt, to England in 1687* (University Studies, University of Nebraska, vol. xx, nos. 3, 4). Lincoln, 1920. A detailed account of negotiations with James II.

813 Picavet, Camille G. *La diplomatie française au temps de Louis XIV (1661–1715)*. Paris, 1930. Deals with foreign policy as well as the diplomatic corps.

814 Prestage, Edgar. *The diplomatic relations of Portugal with France, England, and Holland from 1640 to 1668*. Watford, 1925.

815 Trevelyan, Mary C. *William the Third and the defence of Holland, 1672–4*. 1930.

4 Biographies

816 Barbour, Violet, *Henry Bennet, earl of Arlington, secretary of state to Charles II*. Washington, 1914. A scholarly work, but somewhat slight.

817 Boyer, Abel. *Memoirs of the life and negotiations of Sir William Temple*. 1714. Covers the years 1665–81.

818 Cartwright, Julia. *Madame: a life of Henrietta, daughter of Charles I and duchess of Orleans*. 1894. A competent study; includes letters from Charles II from Archives des Affaires Étrangères.

819 Courtenay, Thomas P. *Memoirs of the life, works, and correspondence of Sir William Temple*. 1836, 2 vols.

820 Dobrée, Bonamy. *Essays in biography, 1680–1720*. Oxford, 1924. Includes essay on George Etherege, dramatist, employed by Charles II on diplomatic missions. See also Etherege (764).

821 Lefèvre-Pontalis, G. Antonin. *John de Witt*. 1885, 2 vols. Of some value for Anglo-Dutch relations under Charles II.

822 Pribram, Alfred F. *Franz Paul, Freiherr von Lisola, 1613–1674, und die Politik seiner Zeit*. Leipzig, 1894.

823 Wynne, William. *The life of Sir Leoline Jenkins*. 1724, 2 vols. Largely correspondence, 1673–9. Jenkins was English representative at the congress at Cologne and at Nimeguen.

5 Articles

824 Anderson, Matthew S. 'English views of Russia in the seventeenth century', *Slavonic and East European Review*, **33** (Dec. 1954), 140–60.

825 Barbour, Violet. 'Consular service in the reign of Charles II', *AHR*, **33** (Apr. 1928), 533–78.

826 Brinkmann, Carl. 'Charles II and the bishop of Munster int he Anglo-Dutch war of 1665–66', *EHR*, **21** (Oct. 1906), 686–98.
827 —— 'Relations between England and Germany, 1660–88', *EHR*, **24** (Apr., July 1909), 247–77, 448–69.
828 De Beer, Esmond S. 'Charles II and Louis XIV in 1683', *EHR*, **39** (Jan. 1924), 86–9. Comments on Middlebush (778).
829 —— 'The marquis of Albeville and his brothers', *EHR*, **45** (July 1930), 397–408. Albeville was James II's envoy to the United Provinces.
830 George, Robert H. 'The financial relations of Louis XIV and James II', *JMH*, **3** (Sept. 1931), 392–413.
831 Grose, Clyde L. 'The Anglo-Dutch alliance of 1678', *EHR*, **39** (July, Oct. 1924), 349–72, 526–51.
832 —— 'The Anglo-Portuguese marriage of 1662', *Hispanic American Historical Review*, **10** (Aug. 1930), 313–52. An extensively documented article.
833 —— 'The Dunkirk money, 1662', *JMH*, **5** (March 1933), 1–18.
834 —— 'England and Dunkirk', *AHR*, **39** (Oct. 1933), 1–27. Primarily concerned with 1658–62.
835 —— 'Louis XIV's financial relations with Charles II and the English parliament', *JMH*, **1** (June 1929), 177–204. See also related documents (768).
836 Haley, Kenneth H. D. 'The Anglo-Dutch rapprochement of 1677', *EHR*, **73** (Oct. 1958), 614–48.
837 Japikse, Nicolaas. 'Louis XIV et la guerre anglo-hollandaise de 1665–1667', *Revue historique*, **98** (May 1908), 22–60.
838 Lee, Maurice D., Jr. 'The earl of Arlington and the Treaty of Dover', *JBS*, no. 1 (Nov. 1961), 58–70.
839 Robbins, Caroline. 'Carlisle and Marvell in Russia, Sweden, and Denmark, 1663–1664', *History of Ideas Newsletter*, **3** (no. 1, 1957), 8–17. Carlisle, ambassador to northern powers, employed Marvell as secretary.
840 Rowen, Herbert H. 'John de Witt and the Triple Alliance', *JMH*, **26** (March 1954), 1–14.
841 Saint-Léger, Alexandre de. 'L'acquisition de Dunkerque et de Mardyck par Louis XIV [1662]', *Revue d'histoire moderne et contemporaine*, **2** (1901), 233–45.
842 Schoolcraft, Henry L. 'England and Denmark, 1660–1667', *EHR*, **25** (July 1910), 457–79.
843 Swaine, Stephen A. 'The English acquisition and loss of Dunkirk', *TRHS*, new ser., **1** (1883), 93–118.
844 Ternois, René. 'Saint-Évremond et la politique anglaise, 1665–1674', *XVIIe siècle*, no. 57 (1962), 3–23. Saint-Évremond, exiled in England, served on a mission to Holland in 1672.
845 Wood, Alfred C. 'The English embassy at Constantinople, 1660–1762', *EHR*, **40** (Oct. 1925), 533–61. A few pages deal with the period.

VII SOCIAL HISTORY

1 Printed Sources

846 Aubrey, John. '*Brief lives', chiefly of contemporaries, set down by John Aubrey between the years 1669 and 1696*, ed. Andrew Clark. Oxford, 1898, 2 vols. Miscellaneous comment on various persons. See also the unbowdlerised ed. (1959) by Oliver L. Dick. Cf. Powell (1058) and Collier (954).
847 Aulnoy, Marie C. J. de Berneville, comtesse d'. *Memoirs of the court of England in 1675*, ed. George D. Gilbert. 1927. Originally published in Paris in 1695.
848 Blome, Richard. *The gentleman's recreation*. 1686. The most important contemporary work on English manners, etc.
849 Blundell, William. *Cavalier: letters of William Blundell to his friends, 1620–98*, ed. Margaret Blundell. 1933. Interesting letters of a Catholic gentleman, most of them after 1660.

850 Blundell, William. *Crosby records: a cavalier's note book, being notes, anecdotes, and observations of William Blundell*, ed. Thomas E. Gibson. 1880. A valuable picture of the fortunes of a Lancashire Catholic family.

851 Bryant, Arthur. *Postman's horn: an anthology of the letters of latter seventeenth century England*. 1936. An artificial selection, but a highly interesting and illuminating one.

852 Burrell, Timothy. *Extracts from the journal and account book of Timothy Burrell, 1683–1714*, ed. Robert W. Blencowe (Sussex Archaeological Collections, III, 117–72). 1850.

853 Cardigan, Chandos S. C. Brudenell-Bruce, earl of. *Domestic expenses of a nobleman's household, 1687, being an extract from the analysis book kept by Simon Urlin for Robert, first earl of Ailesbury* (Bedfordshire Historical Record Society, XXXII, 108–42). Bedford, 1952.

854 Chesterfield, Philip Stanhope, earl of. *Letters...to several...individuals of the time of Charles II, James II, William III, and Queen Anne, with some of their replies*. 1829. Interesting private letters, mainly from 1656 to 1689.

855 —— *Philip Stanhope...his correspondence with various ladies...and letters exchanged with Sir Charles Sedley, John Dryden, Charles Cotton, Mr. Bates*. 1930.

856 Collier, Jeremy. *A short view of the immorality and profaneness of the English stage*. 1698.

857 Cooper, William D. *Lists of foreign Protestants and aliens resident in England, 1618–1688* (Camden Society, old ser., LXXXII). 1862.

858 Cotton, Charles. *The compleat gamester*. 1674. Reprinted in Hartmann (877).

859 Courtin, Antoine de. *The rules of civility, or certain ways of deportment observed in France amongst all persons of quality*. 1671. Translated from the French; a widely used etiquette book, setting a new standard.

860 Coxere, Edward. *Adventure by sea of Edward Coxere: a relation of the several adventures by sea, with the dangers, difficulties, and hardships met for several years*, ed. E. H. W. Meyerstein. 1946. Life of a merchant seaman.

861 Dillon, Harold A., Viscount (ed.). 'Some familiar letters of Charles II and James, duke of York, addressed to their daughter and niece, the countess of Litchfield', *Archaeologia*, 58 (1902), 153–88.

862 Ebsworth, Joseph W. (ed.). *The Bagford ballads, illustrating the last years of the Stuarts* (Ballad Society). Hertford, 1878, 2 vols. Collected by John Bagford, antiquary, for Robert Harley, earl of Oxford.

863 —— *The Roxburghe ballads, illustrating the last years of the Stuarts* (Ballad Society). Hertford, 1871–99, 9 vols.

864 Evelyn, John. *The diary of John Evelyn*, ed. Esmond S. de Beer. Oxford, 1955, 6 vols. The definitive text, elaborately edited.

865 —— *The life of Mrs. Godolphin*, ed. Harriet Sampson. 1939. The subject was a maid of honour at Charles II's court; religious interest.

866 —— *London revived: considerations for its rebuilding in 1666*, ed. Esmond S. de Beer. Oxford, 1938. A plan for rebuilding London after the Great Fire.

867 Fawcett, Frank Burlington (ed.). *Broadside ballads of the Restoration period, from the Jersey collection known as the Osterley Park ballads*. 1930.

868 Fell, Sarah. *The household account book of Sarah Fell, of Swarthmoor Hall, 1673–78*, ed. Norman Penney. Cambridge, 1920. Useful for both Quaker and social history.

869 Fiennes, Celia. *The journeys of Celia Fiennes*, ed. Christopher Morris. 1947. Observations made on journeys between 1685 and 1703.

870 Gailhard, Jean. *The compleat gentleman, or directions for the education of youth as to their breeding at home and travelling abroad*. 1678, 2 pts.

871 Gardiner, Dorothy (ed.). *The Oxinden and Peyton letters, 1642–1670*. 1937. Letters of Kentish families.

872 Giffard, Martha, Lady. *Martha, Lady Giffard, her life and correspondence, 1664–1722: a sequel to the letters of Dorothy Osborne*, ed. Julia G. Longe. 1911. Life of Sir William Temple's sister.

873 Grammont, Anthony Hamilton, comte de. *Memoirs of the comte de Gramont*, trans. Peter Quennell; introduction by Cyril H. Hartmann. 1930. First published in French, 1713. A vivid picture of court life, without any

pretence to factual accuracy. An annotated ed. of the French text, by Claire-Élaine Engel, was published at Monaco in 1958.

874 Graunt, John. *Natural and political observations made upon the bills of mortality*, ed. Walter F. Willcox. Baltimore, 1939. First published in 1662.

875 Hale, Matthew. *A discourse touching provision for the poor*. 1683. A modern ed. appeared in 1927.

876 —— *A tryal of witches...at the assizes held at Bury St. Edmunds...before Sir Matthew Hale*. 1683. The trial occurred in 1664. Reprinted in Cobbett (222), vol. VI.

877 Hartmann, Cyril H. (ed.). *Games and gamesters of the Restoration*. 1930. Includes Cotton (858) and Lucas (999).

878 Heath, Helen T. (ed.). *The letters of Samuel Pepys and his family circle*. Oxford, 1955.

879 Hotten, John C. *The original lists of persons of quality, emigrants, etc., who went from Great Britain to the American plantations, 1600–1700*. 1874.

880 Jouvin [Jorevin] de Rochefort, Albert. *Le voyageur d'Europe où sont les voyages de France...d'Angleterre*. Paris, 1672, 6 vols. The section dealing with England and Ireland was reprinted in *The Antiquarian Repertory* (1809), IV, 549–622.

881 Kerr, Russell J. and Ida C. Duncan (eds.). *The Portledge papers*. 1928. Covers 1687–97. Newsy letters written from London to a Devonshire squire.

882 Lang, Andrew (ed.). *Social England illustrated: a collection of seventeenth-century tracts*. 1903. Vol. VI of *An English garner*, ed. Edward Arber. Contains three tracts from the period.

883 Lennep, William van *et al.* (eds.). *The London stage, 1660–1800: a calendar of plays, entertainments, and afterpieces, together with casts, box-receipts, and contemporary comment compiled from the playbills, newspapers, and theatrical diaries of the period*. Part I: 1660–1700. Carbondale, Ill., 1965. Invaluable for theatre history.

884 Locke, John. *Locke's travels in France, 1675–1679, as related in his journals, correspondence, and other papers*, ed. John Lough. Cambridge, 1953.

885 Lodge, Eleanor C. (ed.). *The account book of a Kentish estate (Godinton), 1616–1704*. Oxford, 1927.

886 Lowe, Roger. *The diary of Roger Lowe of Ashton-in-Makerfield, Lancashire, 1663–74*, ed. William L. Sachse. 1938. Diary of a mercer's apprentice, portraying rural life and a nonconformist environment.

887 Macgrath, John R. (ed.). *The Flemings in Oxford, being documents selected from the Rydal papers in illustration of the lives and ways of Oxford men, 1650–1700* (Oxford Historical Society, XLIV, LXII, LXXIX). Oxford, 1904–24.

888 Magalotti, Count Lorenzo. *Travels of Cosmo III, grand duke of Tuscany, through England, 1669*. 1821. Informative, but deals with only a small part of the country.

889 Mills, Peter and John Oliver. *The survey of building sites in the city of London after the great fire of 1666*. London Topographical Society, 1946–65, 5 vols.

890 Mundy, Peter. *The travels of Peter Mundy...V: Travels in south-west England and western India, with a diary of events in London, 1658–1663, and in Penryn, 1664–1667*, ed. Richard C. Temple and Lavinia M. Anstey (Hakluyt Society, 2nd ser., LXXVIII). 1936.

891 Myddelton, W. M. (ed.). *Chirk Castle accounts, 1666–1753*. Horncastle, 1931.

892 Newcastle, Margaret Cavendish, duchess of. *The life of...William Cavendish, duke of...Newcastle*, ed. Charles H. Firth. 1906. First printed in 1667.

893 Newton, Evelyn C. Legh, Lady (ed.). *Lyme letters, 1660–1760*. 1925. Letters are not printed in their entirety.

894 Newton, Samuel. *The diary of Samuel Newton, alderman of Cambridge (1662–1717)*, ed. John E. Foster (Cambridge Antiquarian Society, octavo ser. publications, no. 23). 1890.

895 Ogilby, John. *Britannia, or an illustration of the kingdom of England and the dominion of Wales by a geographical and historical description of the principal roads*. 1675. A hundred double-page plates and 200 pages of text.

896 —— *The relation of his Majesties entertainment passing through the city of London to his coronation*. 1661.

897 Pepys, Samuel. *The diary of Samuel Pepys*, ed. Henry B. Wheatley. 1893–9, 10 vols. Covers 1659–69; a classic. Three vols. of new and complete edition by Robert Latham and William Matthews now in print (Berkeley, 1970).

898 Prideaux, Humphrey. *Letters of Humphrey Prideaux, sometime dean of Norwich, to John Ellis, sometime under-secretary of state, 1674–1722*, ed. Edward M. Thompson (Camden Society, new ser., XV). 1875. Much amusing gossip, especially about Oxford, 1674–85.

899 Reresby, John. *Memoirs of Sir John Reresby: the complete text and a selection of his letters*, ed. Andrew Browning. Glasgow, 1936. The best edition; useful for parliament and for Yorkshire society.

900 Rollins, Hyder E. (ed.). *The Pepys ballads*. Cambridge, Mass., 1929–32, 8 vols. Vols. III–IV cover the period; the ballads (with one exception) are after 1675.

901 Russell, Rachel Wriothesley, Lady. *Letters* of *Rachel, Lady Russell*, ed. Lord John Russell. 1853. 2 vols. 96 letters previously unpublished, covering 1670–1723. The best ed.; cf. (902).

902 —— *Some account of the life of Rachael Wriothesley, Lady Russell*, ed. Mary Berry. 1819. Includes letters to her husband, Lord William Russell, 1672–82. But see (901), which is preferable.

903 Shaw, William A. (ed.). *Letters of denization and acts of naturalization for aliens in England and Ireland, 1603–1700*. Lymington, 1911. Introduction gives history of the law and documentary sources.

904 Sitwell, George R. *Letters of the Sitwells and Sacheverells...illustrating country life and public events in the seventeenth and eighteenth centuries*. Scarborough, 1900–1, 2 vols.

905 Smith, David Nichol (ed.). *Characters from the histories and memoirs of the seventeenth century, with an essay on the character*. Oxford, 1918. An excellent survey, but deals mainly with the first half of the century.

906 Sorbière, Samuel de. *Relation d'un voyage en Angleterre, où sont touchées plusieurs choses qui regardent l'état des sciences et de la religion et autres matières curieuses*. Paris, 1664. An English translation was published in 1709. Sorbière was a man of scientific ability; his criticism of English government and religion provoked comment. See Sprat (907).

907 Sprat, Thomas. *Observations on M. de Sorbier's voyage into England*. 1665. Cf. Sorbière (906).

908 Taswell, William. *Autobiography and anecdotes by William Taswell...1651–1682*, ed. George P. Elliott (Camden Miscellany, II, old ser., LV). 1853. Covers 1651–82; vivid description of the Fire of London.

909 Thoresby, Ralph. *Diary of Ralph Thoresby (1677–1724) [and] letters of eminent men addressed to Ralph Thoresby*, ed. Joseph Hunter. 1830–2, 4 vols. Pertains to a north-country antiquarian and topographer.

910 Thornton, Alice. *The autobiography of Mrs. Alice Thornton, of East Newton, co. York*, ed. Charles Jackson (Surtees Society, LXII). Durham, 1875. Covers 1629–69, with an appendix of letters, 1651–92.

911 Verney, Frances Parthenope, Lady, and Margaret Maria, Lady Verney. *Memoirs of the Verney family...compiled from the letters...at Claydon House*. 1892–9, 4 vols. Valuable history of a county family; vol. IV deals with the period.

912 Warwick, Mary Rich, countess of. *Autobiography of Mary, countess of Warwick*, ed. Thomas C. Croker (Percy Society). 1848. Illustrates social and religious aspects of puritanism.

913 Wilding, James. *The account book of James Wilding, 1682–88*, ed. E. Gordon Duff (Oxford Historical Society, V). *Collectanea*, 1st ser., I, pp. 249–68. Oxford, 1885. Accounts of an Oxford undergraduate.

914 Wilson, John H. (ed.). *The Rochester–Savile letters* (Ohio State University Contributions in Language and Literature, no. 8). Columbus, 1941. The second earl of Rochester's correspondence with Henry Savile.

915 Wood, Anthony à. *The life and times of Anthony Wood, antiquary, at Oxford, 1632–95, as described by himself*, ed. Andrew Clark (Oxford Historical Society, XIX, XXI, XXVI, XXX, XL). Oxford, 1891–1900. Valuable for social life at Oxford University, as well as for other matters of wider interest.

2 Surveys

916 Ashley, Maurice. *Life in Stuart England*. 1964.
917 Boehn, Max von. *Modes and manners*. 1932–5, 4 vols. Translated from the German; vol. III covers the seventeenth century.
918 Bryant, Arthur. *The England of Charles II*. 1934. An admirable brief survey.
919 Carritt, Edgar F. *A calendar of British taste, from 1600 to 1800*. 1949.
920 Coate, Mary. *Social life in Stuart England*. 1924. Essays on various aspects of society.
921 Cole, Rufus I. *Human history: the seventeenth century and the Stuart family*. Freeport, Maine, *c.* 1959, 2 vols. The work of an amateur historian, with emphasis on environment.
922 Hill, Christopher. *Reformation to industrial revolution: the making of modern English society*, vol. I, 1530–1780. New York, 1967. Erudite, provocative and readable.
923 Leys, Mary D. R. *Catholics in England, 1559–1829: a social history*. 1961.
924 Mitchell, Rosamund J. and Mary D. R. Leys. *A history of London life*. 1958. A survey, with one chapter entitled 'John Evelyn's London'.
925 Quennell, Marjorie and Charles H. B. *A history of everyday things in England*, vol. II, 1500–1799. 4th ed., rev., 1950. A popular work, containing a considerable amount of miscellaneous information.
926 Sydney, William C. *Social life in England from the Restoration to the Revolution, 1660–1690*. 1892. Old fashioned and somewhat diffuse, but useful for miscellaneous information.
927 Traill, Henry D. and James S. Mann (eds.). *Social England*. Illustrated ed., vols. III–IV, 1903. Articles by various authors covering many aspects of the period; excellent illustrations.
928 Trevelyan, George M. *English social history: a survey of six centuries, Chaucer to Queen Victoria*. 1942. An admirable survey, though somewhat dated, containing a chapter on 'Restoration England'.

3 Monographs

929 Adams, William H. D. *The merry monarch, or England under Charles II: its art, literature, and society*. 1885, 2 vols.
930 Andrews, Alexander. *History of British journalism from the foundation of the newspaper press in England to the repeal of the Stamp Act in 1855*. 1859. 2 vols.
931 Ascoli, Georges. *La Grande-Bretagne devant l'opinion française au XVIIe siècle*. Paris, 1930, 2 vols. An exhaustive study, drawn chiefly from the accounts of French travellers.
932 Ashley, Maurice. *The Stuarts in love, with some reflections on love and marriage in the sixteenth and seventeenth centuries*. 1963. Four chapters on the period, as well as interesting general comment.
933 Ashton, John. *A history of English lotteries*. 1893.
934 —— *The history of gambling in England*. 1898.
935 Bastide, Charles. *The Anglo-French entente in the seventeenth century*. 1914. An instructive study of French influence upon England.
936 Bebb, Evelyn D. *Nonconformity and social and economic life, 1660–1800: some problems of the present as they appeared in the past*. 1935.
937 Bell, Walter G. *The great fire of London in 1666*. Rev. ed., 1951. A valuable work, largely derived from unexploited sources.
938 —— *The great plague in London in 1665*. Rev. ed., 1951. Based on extensive research; shows Defoe's *Journal* (961) to be essentially a work of fiction.
939 Beloff, Max. *Public order and popular disturbances, 1660–1714*. 1938.
940 Beresford, John. *Gossip of the seventeenth and eighteenth centuries*. New York, 1924. Has two chapters on Anne Hyde.
941 Bonar, James. *Theories of population from Raleigh to Arthur Young*. 1931. Harrington, Graunt, Petty, and Halley are among those treated.

942 Boswell [Murrie], Eleanore. *The Restoration court stage.* Cambridge, Mass., 1932. Interesting theatre history, 1660–1702.

943 Bouch, Charles M. L. and Gwilym P. Jones. *A short economic and social history of the lake counties, 1500–1830.* Manchester, 1961. A broad-based study, involving other factors as well.

944 Bourne, Henry Richard Fox. *English newspapers: chapters in the history of journalism.* 1887, 2 vols. See vol. I, chap. 2, 'Under the licensing acts, 1660–1695'.

945 Bradley, Rose M. *The English housewife in the seventeenth and eighteenth centuries.* 1912.

946 Brears, Charles. *Lincolnshire in the seventeenth and eighteenth centuries, compiled from national, county, and parish records.* Hull, 1940.

947 Brett-James, Norman G. *The growth of Stuart London.* 1935. A substantial and informative work.

948 Brooke, Iris. *Dress and undress: the Restoration and eighteenth centuries.* 1958. Interesting discussion of formal and informal costume.

949 Castells, Francis de P. *English freemasonry in its period of transition, A.D. 1600–1700.* 1931.

950 Chalklin, C. W. *Seventeenth-century Kent: a social and economic history.* 1965.

951 Charlanne, Louis. *L'influence française en Angleterre au XVIIe siècle.* Paris, 1906. Social and literary coverage, mainly after 1660.

952 Clark, Alice. *The working life of women in the seventeenth century.* 1919. A full investigation; appendix has list of wage assessments.

953 Clark, George N. *Three aspects of Stuart England.* New York, 1960. Three lectures, dealing with insularity, social structure, and freedom.

954 Collier, John. *The scandal and credulities of John Aubrey.* 1931. Prints some previously suppressed portions of the 'Brief Lives'.

955 Cooper, Charles H. *Annals of Cambridge.* Cambridge, 1842–1908, 5 vols.

956 Crofts, John E. *Packhorse, waggon, and post: land carriage and communications under the Tudors and Stuarts.* 1967. A detailed descriptive work, drawn from a wide range of sources.

957 Cunningham, William. *Alien immigrants to England.* 1897.

958 Cunnington, Cecil W. and Phillis. *Handbook of English costume in the seventeenth century.* 1955. A convenient reference work, amply illustrated.

959 Davis, Dorothy. *A history of shopping.* 1966. Especially chap. 7, 'Some items for a Restoration gentleman'.

960 Dean, Charles G. T. *The Royal Hospital, Chelsea.* 1950.

961 Defoe, Daniel. *A journal of the plague year*, ed. Louis A. Landa. Oxford, 1969. First published in 1722; fictional, but based on fact. See Bell (938).

962 Downes, John. *Roscius anglicanus, or an historical review of the stage*, ed. Montague Summers. 1928. First published in 1708. First-hand information on actors and the theatre, 1641–1706.

963 Drummond, Jack C. and Anne Wilbraham. *The Englishman's food: a history of five centuries of English diet.* 2nd ed., enlarged, 1958. Includes discussion of the relationship of diet and health.

964 Dutton, Ralph. *English court life from Henry VII to George II.* 1963. Seeks to show the influence of the reigning monarch on court life.

965 Ellis, Aytoun. *The penny universities: a history of the coffee-houses.* 1956.

966 Emden, Cecil. *Pepys himself.* 1963. Pepys's character; mostly from the diary.

967 Evelyn, Helen. *The history of the Evelyn family.* 1915.

968 Ewen, Cecil H. L'Estrange. *Witchcraft and demonianism: a concise account derived from sworn depositions and confessions obtained in the courts of England and Wales.* 1933. The period is well represented in the documents.

969 —— *Witch hunting and witch trials: the indictments for witchcraft from the records of 1373 assizes held for the home circuit, 1559–1736.* 1929.

970 Fairholt, Frederick W. *Costumes in England*, ed. Harold A. Dillon. 1896, 2 vols. Still a standard reference work.

971 —— *Tobacco: its history and associations.* 1859.

972 Fitzgerald, Percy H. *The new history of the English stage, from the Restoration to the liberty of the theatres in connection with the patent houses.* 1882, 2 vols. Based on contemporary material.

973 Fussell, George E. *The English rural labourer: his house, furniture, clothing, and food, from Tudor to Victorian times.* 1949.

974 —— and K. R. *The English countryman: his life and work, A.D. 1500–1900.* 1955. Makes wide use of source materials, as does (975).

975 —— *The English countrywoman: a farmhouse social history, A.D. 1500–1900.* 1953.

976 Gillespie, James E. *The influence of oversea expansion on England to 1700.* New York, 1920. Organization is topical.

977 Glass, David V. and D. E. C. Eversley (eds.). *Population in history: essays in historical demography.* 1965. Some references to the period, but treatment of Great Britain bears mainly on the eighteenth century.

978 Gray, Benjamin K. *A history of English philanthropy from the dissolution of the monasteries to the taking of the first census.* 1905. Cf. Owen (1012).

979 Hampson, Ethel M. *The treatment of poverty in Cambridgeshire, 1597–1834* (Cambridge Studies in Economic History). Cambridge, 1934. Scattered references to the period.

980 Hartmann, Cyril H. *La belle Stuart: memoirs of court and society in the times of Frances Theresa, duchess of Richmond and Lennox.* 1924.

981 Hearsey, John E. N. *London and the Great Fire.* 1965.

982 Hill, James W. F. *Tudor and Stuart Lincoln.* Cambridge, 1956. Scholarly; two chapters on the later Stuart era.

983 Hiscock, Walter G. *John Evelyn and Mrs. Godolphin.* 1951. A different view of court life from that presented by Gilmour (1049) and Wilson (1064). See also Evelyn (865).

984 Hole, Christina. *English home-life, 1500 to 1800.* 1947. Scattered information on the period.

985 —— *The English housewife in the seventeenth century.* 1953.

986 —— *English sports and pastimes.* 1949. Considerable miscellaneous information, arranged topically.

987 Hore, John P. *History of Newmarket and the annals of the turf.* 1886, 3 vols. A detailed work containing many extracts from original sources.

988 Hotson, J. Leslie. *The Commonwealth and Restoration stage.* Cambridge, Mass., 1928.

989 Howard, Clare M. *English travellers of the renaissance.* 1914. Goes from the sixteenth to the early eighteenth century.

990 Jackman, William T. *The development of transportation in modern England.* 1916, 2 vols.

991 Kay, Frederick G. *Royal mail: the story of the posts in England from the time of Edward IV to the present day.* 1951.

992 Kittredge, George L. *Witchcraft in old and New England.* New York, 1929. Interesting, but there is relatively little on the period.

993 Laslett, Peter. *The world we have lost.* 1965. Examines the social structure of seventeenth- and eighteenth-century England.

994 Leasor, James. *The Plague and the Fire.* New York, 1961. Popular.

995 Lennard, Reginald (ed.). *Englishmen at rest and play: some phases of English leisure, 1558–1714.* Oxford, 1931.

996 Lillywhite, Bryant. *London coffee houses: a reference book of coffee houses of the seventeenth, eighteenth, and nineteenth centuries.* 1964. Detailed and useful.

997 Lloyd, Arnold. *Quaker social history, 1669–1738.* 1950.

998 Longueville, Thomas. *Rochester and other literary rakes of the court of Charles II, with some account of their surroundings.* 1902.

999 Lucas, Theophilus. *Memoirs of the lives, intrigues, and comical adventures of the most famous gamesters and celebrated sharpers in the reigns of Charles II, James II, William III, and Queen Anne.* 1714. Also to be found in Hartmann (877).

1000 McAfee, Helen. *Pepys on the Restoration stage.* New Haven, 1916. Comment from the diary.

1001 Maitland, William *et al. The history of London from its foundation by the Romans to the present time.* 1756, 2 vols. First pub. 1739; the 1756 ed. contains additional material.

1002 Malcolm, James P. *Miscellaneous anecdotes illustrative of the manners and history of Europe during the reigns of Charles II, James II, William III, and Queen Anne.* 1811. Largely quotations from English newspapers of the time.

1003 Marburg, Clara. *Mr. Pepys and Mr. Evelyn.* Philadelphia, 1935. Includes correspondence.

1004 Marshall, Dorothy. *The English poor in the eighteenth century: a study in social and administrative history.* 1926. Restoration material is scattered through the book.

1005 Mason, John E. *Gentlefolk in the making: the history of English courtesy literature from 1531 to 1774.* Philadelphia, 1935. A doctoral dissertation.

1006 Mendelsohn, Oscar A. *Drinking with Pepys.* 1963. Quotations from Pepys, with incidental comment.

1007 Moir, Esther. *The discovery of Britain: the English tourists, 1540–1840.* 1964. Chap. 4 deals with Celia Fiennes: see (869).

1008 Newdigate-Newdegate, Anne E., Lady. *Cavalier and puritan in the days of the Stuarts.* 1901. From private papers and diary of Sir Richard Newdigate, as well as newsletters to him (1675–89).

1009 Newton, Evelyn C. Legh, Lady. *The house of Lyme from its foundation to the end of the eighteenth century.* 1917. Of considerable interest; deals with Cheshire family.

1010 Nicoll, Allardyce. *A history of English drama, 1660–1900.* Cambridge, 1952–9, 6 vols. Vol. I covers 1660–1700. Useful for theatre history.

1011 Notestein, Wallace. *A history of witchcraft in England from 1558 to 1718.* Washington, 1911. Based on careful research.

1012 Owen, David E. *English philanthropy, 1660–1960.* Cambridge, Mass., 1964. The best survey; cf. Gray (978).

1013 Parkes, Joan. *Travel in England in the seventeenth century.* 1925. The best survey; gives extracts from contemporary printed sources.

1014 Perks, Sydney. *The history of the Mansion House.* Cambridge, 1922. Has appendix on the rebuilding of London after the Great Fire.

1015 Pinchbeck, Ivy. *Children in English society, I, From Tudor times to the eighteenth century.* 1969.

1016 Pitt, Moses. *The cry of the oppressed, being a true and tragical account of the unparalleled sufferings of the multitudes of poor imprisoned debtors.* 1691. One of the earliest pleas for prison reform.

1017 Priestley, Harold E. *London: the years of change.* 1966. Describes the growth of London in the seventeenth century.

1018 Reddaway, Thomas F. *The rebuilding of London after the Great Fire.* 1940. Based on exacting research; should be read with Evelyn (866).

1019 Ribton-Turner, Charles J. *A history of vagrants and vagrancy and beggars and begging.* 1887.

1020 Richardson, Albert E. and H. Donaldson Eberlein. *The English inn past and present: a review of its history and social life.* 1925. A little scattered material on the period.

1021 Roberts, George. *The social history of the people of the southern counties of England in past centuries.* 1856.

1022 Robinson, Edward F. *The early history of coffee houses in England, with some account of the first use of coffee and a bibliography of the subject.* 1893.

1023 Robson-Scott, William D. *German travellers in England, 1400–1800.* Oxford, 1953. Describes several visits during the period.

1024 Roth, Cecil. *A history of the Jews in England.* 3rd ed., Oxford, 1964.

1025 Sachse, William L. *The colonial American in Britain.* Madison, Wis., 1956. Some references to the period, but chiefly later.

1026 Samuel, Wilfred S. *Some notes on seventeenth-century London Jews* (Jewish Historical Society). 1937. Based on careful research in scattered sources.

1027 Scott, Walter S. *Green retreats: the story of Vauxhall Gardens, 1661–1859.* 1955.

1028 Sells, Arthur Lytton. *The paradise of travellers: the Italian influence on Englishmen in the seventeenth century.* Bloomington, Ind., 1964. Scholarly and interesting, but little on the period.

1029 Smith, Edward. *Foreign visitors in England and what they have thought of us.* 1889. Includes four from the period.

1030 Southworth, James G. *Vauxhall Gardens: a chapter in the social history of England.* New York, 1941. Informative.

1031 Stenton, Doris M. *The English woman in history.* 1957.

1032 Stoye, John W. *English travellers abroad, 1604–67: their influence in English society and politics.* 1952.

1033 Strutt, Joseph. *The sports and pastimes of the people of England,* ed. J. Charles Cox. 1903. First published 1801.

1034 Summers, Montague. *The Restoration theatre.* 1934.

1035 Tanner, Joseph R. *Mr. Pepys: an introduction to the diary together with a sketch of his later life.* 1925. Useful for the general reader.

1036 Thomas, Gertrude Z. *Richer than spices: how a royal bride's dowry introduced cane, lacquer, cottons, tea, and porcelain to England, and so revolutionized taste, manners, craftsmanship, and history in both England and America.* New York, 1965.

1037 Thomson, Gladys Scott. *Life in a noble household, 1641–1700.* 1937. A detailed picture of life at Woburn, based upon household papers.

1038 —— *The Russells in Bloomsbury, 1669–1771.* 1940. A mine of information for the student of social history.

1039 Wheatley, Henry B. *London past and present.* 1891, 3 vols. Encyclopaedic work; valuable for miscellaneous information.

1040 Whitaker, Wilfred B. *Sunday in Tudor and Stuart times.* 1933.

1041 Wildeblood, Joan and Peter Brinson. *The polite world: a guide to English manners and deportment from the thirteenth to the nineteenth century.* 1965. Contains considerable miscellaneous information.

1042 Williams, J. B. [pseud. for Joseph G. Muddiman]. *History of English journalism to the foundation of the Gazette.* 1908. A useful survey to 1665.

1043 Wilson, John H. *All the king's ladies: actresses of the Restoration.* Chicago, 1958.

1044 —— *The court wits of the Restoration: an introduction.* Princeton, N.J., 1948. An interesting account of various free-living writers.

1045 Wingfield-Stratford, Esmé C. *The squire and his relations.* 1956. Contains little on the period, but is of some general interest.

4 Biographies

1046 Barnard, Etwell A. B. *A seventeenth-century country gentleman: Sir Francis Throckmorton, 1640–80.* Cambridge, 1944. Based on a ledger kept by Throckmorton's steward.

1047 Cartwright, Julia (Mrs Henry Ady). *Sacharissa: some account of Dorothy Sidney, countess of Sutherland, her family and friends, 1617–1684.* 4th ed., 1926.

1048 Clark, Ruth. *Anthony Hamilton: his life and works and his family.* 1921. Deals with the author of the well-known *Memoirs* (873).

1049 Gilmour, Margaret. *The great lady: a biography of Barbara Villiers, mistress of Charles II.* 1944.

1050 Grant, Douglas. *Margaret the first: a biography of Margaret Cavendish, duchess of Newcastle, 1623–73.* 1957.

1051 Harris, Brice. *Charles Sackville, sixth earl of Dorset: patron and poet of the Restoration.* Urbana, Ill., 1940.

1052 Hawkes, Arthur J. *Sir Roger Bradshaigh of Haigh, knight and baronet, 1628–1684* (Lancashire and Cheshire Antiquarian Society, Chetham Miscellanies, new ser., VIII). Manchester, 1945. Bradshaigh was active in Lancashire affairs.

1053 Notestein, Wallace. *English folk: a book of characters.* New York, 1938. Sketches of several Restoration figures, including Lowe (886) and Alice Thornton (910).

1054 —— *Four worthies.* 1956. Includes Anne Clifford and Oliver Heywood (1672).

1055 Petherick, Maurice. *Restoration rogues.* 1951. Includes Col. Blood, Barbara Palmer, duchess of Cleveland, Popish Plot figures, etc.

1056 Pinto, Vivian de Sola. *Enthusiast in wit: a portrait of John Wilmot, earl of Rochester.* 1962. A reworking of his *Rochester: portrait of a Restoration poet*, 1935.

1057 —— *Sir Charles Sedley, 1639–1701: a study in the life and literature of the Restoration.* 1927. Part 1 deals with the life of this court wit.

1058 Powell, Anthony D. *John Aubrey and his friends.* Rev. ed., 1963. An excellent biographical study. See Aubrey (846).

1059 Prinz, Johannes. *John Wilmot, earl of Rochester: his life and writings.* Leipzig, 1927.

1060 Steinman, George S. *Althorp memoirs, or biographical notices of Lady Denham, the countess of Shrewsbury, the countess of Falmouth, Mrs. Jenyns, the duchess of Tyrconnel, and Lucy Walter.* Oxford, 1869.

1061 —— *A memoir of Barbara, duchess of Cleveland.* Oxford, 1871. Additions and corrections were published in 1874 and 1878.

1062 Ward, Estelle F. *Christopher Monck, duke of Albemarle.* 1915. Life of George Monck's son.

1063 Wheatley, Henry B. *Samuel Pepys and the world he lived in.* 1880.

1064 Wilson, John H. *Nell Gwynn, royal mistress.* New York, 1952.

1065 —— *A rake and his times: George Villiers, second duke of Buckingham.* New York, 1954.

5 Articles

1066 Abbott, Wilbur C. 'The Restoration press', *Proceedings of the Massachusetts Historical Society*, **67** (1945), 22–54. A good survey article.

1067 —— 'The serious Pepys', in his *Conflicts with oblivion*, New Haven, 1924, pp. 3–33.

1068 Ashley, Maurice. 'Love and marriage in seventeenth-century England', *Hist. T.*, **8** (Oct. 1958), 667–75. Cf. (932).

1069 Baker, John N. L. 'England in the seventeenth century', in Henry C. Darby (ed.), *An historical geography of England before A.D. 1800*, Cambridge, 1936, pp. 387–443.

1070 Bell, Robert. 'Social amusements under the Restoration', *Fortnightly Review*, **2** (1865), 193–205, 299–309, 460–75.

1071 Braithwaite, Alfred W. 'The mystery of Swarthmoor Hall', *JFHS*, **51** (no. 1, 1965), 22–9. Deals with a quarrel over possession.

1072 Campbell, Mildred. '"Of people either too few or too many": the conflict of opinion on population and its relation to emigration', in William A. Aiken and Basil D. Henning (eds.), *Conflict in Stuart England: essays in honour of Wallace Notestein*, New York, 1960, pp. 171–201.

1073 Dawson, Warren R. 'The London coffee-houses and the beginnings of Lloyd's', *Essays by Divers Hands, Being the Transactions of the Royal Society of Literature of the United Kingdom*, new ser., **11** (1932), 69–111.

1074 Ditchfield, Peter H. 'The errors of Lord Macaulay in his estimation of the squires and parsons of the seventeenth century', *TRHS*, 3rd ser., **9** (1915), 77–93.

1075 Edie, Carolyn A. 'New buildings, new taxes, and old interests: an urban problem of the 1670s', *JBS*, **6** (May 1967), 35–63.

1076 Engel, Claire-Élaine. 'English visitors at Louis XIV's court', *Hist. T.*, **9** (June 1959), 424–31.

1077 Firth, Charles H. 'Macaulay's third chapter', *Hist.*, **17** (Oct. 1932), 201–19. Commentary on 'The state of England in 1685'. See also (186).

1078 Fordham, Herbert G. 'John Ogilby (1600–1676): his *Britannia*, and the British itineraries of the eighteenth century', *Lib.*, 4th ser., **6** (Sept. 1925), 157–78. Deals with Ogilby's extraordinary road survey; see Ogilby (895).

1079 Gay, Edwin F. 'Sir Richard Temple: the debt settlement and estate litigation, 1653–1675', *HLQ*, **6** (May 1943), 255–91. Temple's successful efforts to maintain the family fortunes.

1080 Glass, David V. 'Gregory King's estimate of the population of England and Wales, 1695', *Population Studies*, **3** (Mar. 1950), 338–74. A careful investigation; see King (1118).

1081 Gourgey, Brenda. 'Cosmetics and perfumes in Stuart times', *Hist. T.*, **16** (Sept. 1966), 633–9.

1082 Gwynn, Robin D. 'The arrival of Huguenot refugees in England, 1680–1705', *Hug. Soc. Proc.*, **21** (no. 4, 1969), 366–73. Informative tables on numbers, place of origin, etc.

1083 Hampson, Ethel M. 'Settlement and removal in Cambridgeshire, 1662–1834', *Camb. Hist. J.*, **2** (no. 3, 1928), 273–89. While for the most part too late, there is some significant material for the period.

1084 Hartmann, Cyril H. 'Rochester's marriage', *Hist. T.*, **5** (Dec. 1955), 840–9. Deals with the second earl.

1085 Hill, Christopher. 'The diary of John Evelyn', *Hist.*, **42** (Feb. 1957), 12–18. A review of the de Beer ed. (864).

1086 Hoffman, Daniel G. 'Tylden's almanac: the chapbook of a royalist in the Restoration', *Journal of Rutgers University Library*, **16** (June 1953), 49–55. A description of the chapbook.

1087 Kirby, Chester H. 'The English game law system', *AHR*, **38** (Jan. 1933), 240–62. Includes discussion of the basic game law of 1671.

1088 Laslett, Peter and John Harrison. 'Clayworth and Cogenhoe', in Henry E. Bell and R. L. Ollard (eds.), *Historical essays, 1600–1750, presented to David Ogg*, 1963, pp. 157–84. Interesting study of the populations of two villages.

1089 Latham, Robert C. 'Roger Lowe, shopkeeper and nonconformist', *Hist.*, **26** (June 1941), 19–35. Concerned with the relevance of Lowe's diary (886) to the controversy over the relations between puritanism and capitalism.

1090 McCulloch, Samuel C. 'Some conflicting views of the clergy in England in the second half of the seventeenth century', *Historical Magazine of the Protestant Episcopal Church*, **16** (Sept. 1947), 267–77. Discusses the state of the clergy in the period.

1091 McWilliam, N. 'French impressions of English character, 1663–95', *French Quarterly*, **2** (Dec. 1920), 176–84. Based on the reactions of seven travellers.

1092 Mayo, Charles H. 'The social status of the clergy in the seventeenth and eighteenth centuries', *EHR*, **37** (Apr. 1922), 258–66. A modification of Macaulay's picture of the clergy.

1093 Parks, George B. 'John Evelyn and the art of travel', *HLQ*, **10** (May 1947), 251–76. Interesting, but largely before 1660.

1094 Routh, Enid M. G. 'The English at Tangier', *EHR*, **26** (July 1911), 469–81. Life at the outpost *temp.* Charles II.

1095 Sachse, William L. 'Harvard men in England, 1642–1714', Colonial Society of Massachusetts, xxxv, *Transactions, 1942–46*, pp. 119–44. Boston, 1951. Activities of alumni who returned, or visited England.

1096 Shaw, William A. 'The English government and the relief of Protestant refugees', *EHR*, **9** (Oct. 1894), 662–83. Mostly after 1689.

1097 Smith, Abbot E. 'The transportation of convicts to the American colonies in the seventeenth century', *AHR*, **39** (Jan. 1934), 232–49.

1098 Spate, Oscar H. K. 'The growth of London, A.D. 1660–1800', in Henry C. Darby (ed.), *An historical geography of England before A.D. 1800*, Cambridge, 1936, pp. 529–48.

1099 Speck, William A. 'Social status in late Stuart England', *PP*, no. 34 (July 1966), 127–9. An answer to Stone (1102), emphasizing the hostility of the landed classes toward men engaged in business and the professions.

1100 Srigley, Michael. 'The great frost fair of 1683–84', *Hist. T.*, **10** (Dec. 1960), 848–55.

1101 Stone, Lawrence. 'Marriage among the English nobility in the sixteenth and seventeenth centuries', *Comparative Studies in Society and History*, **3** (Jan. 1961), 182–206. Some references to the period, but coverage is primarily 1540–1640.

1102 —— 'Social mobility in England, 1500–1700', *PP*, no. 33 (Apr. 1966), 16–55. For an answer, see Speck (1099).

1103 Ternois, René. 'Les français en Angleterre au temps de Charles II, 1660–1676', *Revue de littérature comparée*, **34** (1960), 196–211. Adds something to Ascoli (931).

1104 Ustick, W. Lee. 'Changing ideals of aristocratic character and conduct in seventeenth-century England', *Mod. Phil.*, **30** (Nov. 1932), 147–66. Largely before 1660.

1105 Vellacott, Paul C. 'The diary of a country gentleman in 1688', *Camb. Hist. J.*, **2** (no. 1, 1926), 48–62. Includes excerpts.

1106 Waller, R. D. 'Lorenzo Magalotti in England, 1668–9', *Italian Studies*, **1** (no. 2, 1937), 49–66. See Magalotti (888).

1107 Williams, J. B. [pseud. for Joseph G. Muddiman]. 'Newsbooks and letters of news of the Restoration', *EHR*, **23** (Apr. 1908), 252–76.

VIII ECONOMIC HISTORY

1 Printed Sources

1108 Balderston, Marion. 'William Penn's twenty-three ships, with notes on some of their passengers', *Pennsylvania Genealogical Magazine*, **23** (no. 2, 1963), 27–67. Covers 1681–2; gives entries from port books on cargo.

1109 Barlow, R. Fred and Henry Yule (eds.). *The diary of William Hedges, esq., afterwards Sir William Hedges, during his agency in Bengal, as well as on his voyage out and return overland, 1681–87* (Hakluyt Society, 1st ser., LXXIV–LXXV, LXXVIII). 1887–9. Includes memoirs of Job Charnock (founder of Calcutta), biographical information on Thomas Pitt, etc.

1110 Brent, J. Theodore (ed.). *Early voyages and travels in the Levant* (Hakluyt Society, 1st ser., LXXXVII). 1893. Includes extracts from diaries of Dr John Covel, chaplain at Constantinople, 1670–9.

1111 Carr, Cecil T. (ed.). *Select charters of trading companies, A.D. 1530–1707* (Selden Society, XXVIII). 1913. Restoration charters include those of the African Company, Royal Fishing Company, Fire Office, and White Paper Makers; valuable introduction.

1112 Child, Josiah. *A new discourse of trade*. 1693.

1113 Claypoole, James. *James Claypoole's letter book: London and Philadelphia, 1681–1684*, ed. Marion Balderston. San Marino, Calif., 1967. Letters of a Quaker merchant.

1114 *A collection of the names of the merchants living in and about the city of London*. 1677. Later ed. by John C. Hotten, entitled *The little London directory of 1677*, 1863. Gives addresses as well as names.

1115 Dalby, Thomas. *An historical account of the rise and growth of the West India colonies, and of the great advantage they are to England in respect of trade*. 1690. Also in *Harleian miscellany* (480), IX, 403–45.

1116 Donnan, Elizabeth. *Documents illustrative of the history of the slave trade to America*. Washington, 1930–2, 3 vols. Vol. I contains nearly 200 pages devoted to 1660–89, many pertaining to England.

1117 Evelyn, John. *Sylva, or a discourse of forest-trees and the propagation of timber*, ed. John Nisbet. 1908, 2 vols. An influential work and long a standard authority; first published in 1664.

1118 King, Gregory. *Two tracts*, ed. George E. Barnett. Baltimore, 1936. Important late-seventeenth-century treatises, one on the 'state and condition' of England (1696), the other on the maritime trade of England in 1688.

1119 Lansdowne, Henry W. E. Petty-Fitzmaurice, marquess of (ed.). *The Petty–Southwell correspondence, 1676–1687*. 1928. Repr. New York, 1967. A highly interesting correspondence, illuminating various aspects of the contemporary scene. Supplements (1127).

1120 McCulloch, John R. (ed.). *Early English tracts on commerce*. Cambridge, 1952. A valuable collection, first published in 1859, including four tracts from the period.

1121 McGrath, Patrick (ed.). *Merchants and merchandise in seventeenth-century Bristol* (Bristol Record Society, XIX). Bristol, 1955. Documents selected from local and national records to illustrate various aspects of the subject.

1122 McLachlan, Jean. 'Documents illustrating Anglo-Spanish trade between the commercial treaty of 1667 and the commercial treaty and the asiento contract of 1713', *Camb. Hist. J.*, 4 (no. 3, 1934), 299–311. Should be used in connection with Nettels (1266).

1123 Morse, Hosea Ballou. *The chronicles of the East India Company trading to China, 1635–1834.* Oxford, 1926–9, 5 vols. There is a little material for the period, pertaining to Taiwan and Amoy, in vol. I.

1124 Mun, Thomas. *England's treasure by foreign trade.* 1664. Written about 1630 by one of the first opponents of mercantilism; many reprints.

1125 Parsloe, Guy (ed.). *Wardens' accounts of the Worshipful Company of Founders of the city of London, 1497–1681.* 1964. Accounts of a lesser livery company, illustrating various aspects of London life.

1126 Petty, William. *The economic writings of Sir William Petty*, ed. Charles H. Hull. Cambridge, 1899, 2 vols. Reprints various works; important.

1127 —— *The Petty papers: some unpublished writings of Sir William Petty*, ed. Henry W. E. Petty-Fitzmaurice, marquess of Lansdowne. 1927, 2 vols. Valuable; contains comment on religion and politics as well as economic subjects. Supplemented by (1119).

1128 Rich, Edwin E. (ed.). *Minutes of the Hudson's Bay Company.* The years 1671–4 and 1679–84 have been covered in the Publications of the Champlain Society, vols. V, VIII–IX, Toronto, 1942 and 1945–6. A very useful contribution to business history.

1129 Sainsbury, Ethel B. *A calendar of the court minutes, etc., of the East India Company.* Oxford, 1907–. Eleven vols. to date. Vols. VI–XI cover the years 1660–79.

1130 Sellers, Maud (ed.). *The acts and ordinances of the Eastland Company* (Camden Society, 3rd ser., XI). 1906. Documents of merchant adventurers of York, trading in the Baltic region.

1131 Yarranton, Andrew. *England's improvement by sea and land to outdo the Dutch without fighting.* 1677–81, 2 pts. Discusses a variety of subjects: national granaries, canals, land banks, etc.

2 Surveys

1132 Clapham, John. *A concise economic history of Britain: from the earliest times to 1750.* Cambridge, 1949. Excellent introductory survey.

1133 Clark, George N. *The wealth of England from 1496 to 1760.* Oxford, 1946. A good survey of economic developments.

1134 Cunningham, William. *The growth of English industry and commerce in modern times.* 6th ed., Cambridge, 1919, 2 vols. Still valuable, but largely superseded by Lipson (1137).

1135 Dietz, Frederick C. *Economic history of England.* New York, 1942.

1136 Innes, Arthur D. *The maritime and colonial expansion of England under the Stuarts, 1603–1714*, 1932.

1137 Lipson, Ephraim. *The economic history of England*, vols. II and III, *The age of mercantilism.* 6th ed., repr. 1964. The fullest general account, largely superseding Cunningham (1134).

1138 Wilson, Charles. *England's apprenticeship, 1603–1763.* 1965. Excellent; about a third of the work is devoted to the years 1660–1700. Useful bibliography.

3 Monographs

1139 Åström, Sven-Erik. *From cloth to iron: the Anglo-Baltic trade in the late seventeenth century.* Helsingfors, 1963.

1140 Bal Krishna. *Commercial relations between India and England, 1601 to 1757.* 1924. Has two chapters on the period.

1141 Barnes, Donald G. *A history of the English corn laws, from 1660–1846.* 1930.

1142 Beer, George L. *The old colonial system, 1660–1754*, pt. 1, *The establishment of the system, 1660–1688.* New York, 1912, 2 vols.

1143 Bevan, Wilson L. *Sir William Petty: a study in English economic literature* (Publications of the American Economic Association, IX, no. 4). Baltimore, 1894.

1144 Beveridge, William H., Lord. *Prices and wages in England from the twelfth to the nineteenth century*, I, *Price tables: the mercantile era.* 1939. Covers 1550–1830, superseding Rogers (1200).

1145 Blagden, Cyprian. *The Stationers' Company: a history, 1403–1959.* 1960. One chapter on the period.

1146 Bowden, Peter J. *The wool trade in Tudor and Stuart England.* 1962.

1147 Brooke, George C. *English coins.* 3rd ed., 1950.

1148 Bruce, John. *Annals of the honorable East India Company from...1660 to... 1707–8.* 1810, 3 vols. By the Company's historiographer.

1149 Coleman, Donald C. *The British paper industry, 1495–1860: a study in industrial growth.* Oxford, 1958.

1150 —— *Sir John Banks, baronet and businessman: a study of business, politics, and society in later Stuart England.* Oxford, 1963.

1151 Cornewall-Jones, R. J. *The British merchant service, being a history of the British mercantile marine from the earliest times to the present day.* 1898. Deals mostly with the nineteenth century.

1152 Court, William H. B. *The rise of the Midland industries, 1600–1838.* 1938.

1153 Cullen, Louis M. *Anglo-Irish trade, 1660–1800.* Manchester, 1968.

1154 Davies, Kenneth G. *The Royal African Company.* 1957. Important for both English economic and African history.

1155 Davis, Ralph. *The rise of the English shipping industry in the seventeenth and eighteenth centuries.* 1962.

1156 Dunlap, Olive J. and Richard D. Denman. *English apprenticeship and child labour: a history.* 1912.

1157 Eames, James B. *The English in China, being an account of the intercourse and relations between England and China.* 1909. A scholarly work, covering 1600–1843, on trade relations only.

1158 Feavearyear, Albert E. *The pound sterling: a history of English money*, 2nd ed., rev. by E. Victor Morgan. Oxford, 1963. The best summary; useful for the development of credit during the period.

1159 Flinn, Michael W. *Men of iron: the Crowleys in the early iron industry.* Edinburgh, 1962. Of limited value for the period.

1160 Girtin, Thomas. *The triple crowns: a narrative history of the Drapers' Company, 1364–1964.* 1958.

1161 Grubb, Isabel. *Quakerism and industry before 1800.* 1930.

1162 Handover, Phyllis M. *Printing in London from 1476 to modern times.* 1960. Originally lectures. Good for economic and technological aspects.

1163 Harper, Lawrence A. *The English navigation laws: a seventeenth-century experiment in social engineering.* New York, 1939. Deals mostly with the latter part of the century.

1164 Heal, Ambrose. *London goldsmiths, 1200–1800: a record of the names and addresses of the craftsmen, their shop-signs and trade-cards.* Cambridge, 1935. Pp. 11–20 treat of Pepys's relations with the goldsmiths. See also Richards (1199).

1165 Heaton, Herbert. *The Yorkshire woollen and worsted industries from the earliest times up to the industrial revolution.* Oxford, 1920.

1166 Heawood, Edward. *A history of geographical discovery in the seventeenth and eighteenth centuries.* Cambridge, 1912.

1167 Heckscher, Eli F. *Mercantilism*, rev. by E. F. Söderlund, 1955, 2 vols. The standard work.

1168 Herbert, William. *The history of the twelve great livery companies of London.* 1833–6, 2 vols. The standard work; useful for documents.

1169 Hewins, William A. S. *English trade and finance chiefly in the seventeenth century.* 1892. Of limited value.

1170 Hinton, Raymond W. K. *The Eastland trade and the common weal in the seventeenth century*. Cambridge, 1959. A useful work; appendix has much rich material.

1171 Horsefield, John Keith. *British monetary experiments, 1650–1710*. 1960.

1172 Houblon, Alice F. A. *The Houblon family: its story and times*. 1907, 2 vols. Account of a family of merchants and bankers.

1173 Johnson, Arthur H. *The history of the Worshipful Company of the Drapers of London*. Oxford, 1914–22, 5 vols. Vol. III contains the history from 1603; vol. IV has many documents of the seventeenth century.

1174 Johnson, Edgar A. J. *Predecessors of Adam Smith: the growth of British economic thought*. 1937. Includes six previously published articles.

1175 Johnson, John de M. and Strickland Gibson. *Print and privilege at Oxford to the year 1700*. 1946. Deals with the development of printing and publishing by the University.

1176 Judah, Charles B., Jr. *The North American fisheries and British policy to 1713* (University of Illinois Studies in the Social Sciences, XVIII). Urbana, 1933.

1177 Kelsall, Roger Keith. *Wage regulation under the Statute of Artificers*. 1938. Appendix gives chronological list of wage assessments, 1563–1778.

1178 Kennedy, William. *English taxation, 1640–1799: an essay on policy and opinion*. 1913. Deals with the effects rather than the details of taxation.

1179 Khan, Shafaat Ahmad. *The East India trade in the seventeenth century, in its political and economic aspects*. 1923. Deals only with Anglo-Indian trade; notes refer to many contemporary pamphlets.

1180 Knoop, Douglas and Gwilym P. Jones. *The London mason in the seventeenth century*. 1935.

1181 Kramer, Stella. *The English craft gilds: studies in their progress and decline*. New York, 1927. Based on her *English craft gilds and the government* (Columbia University Studies in History, Economics, and Public Law, XXIII, no. 4). New York, 1905.

1182 Lawler, John. *Book auctions in England in the seventeenth century, 1676–1700*. 1898. Has a chronological list of the book auctions of the period; some prices are given.

1183 Letwin, William L. *The origins of scientific economics: English economic thought, 1660–1776*. 1963.

1184 Lewis, George R. *The stannaries: a study of the English tin miner* (Harvard Economic Studies, III). Boston, 1908. Little on the period; some statistics.

1185 Lipson, Ephraim. *The history of the woollen and worsted industries*. Rev. ed., 1953. Scattered material on the period.

1186 Lounsbury, Ralph G. *The British fishery at Newfoundland* (Yale Historical Publications, Miscellany no. 27). New Haven, 1934.

1187 McLachlan, Jean O. *Trade and peace with old Spain, 1667–1750*. Cambridge, 1940. Stresses importance of England's trade with Spain, apart from the Spanish colonies; deals mainly with the eighteenth century. See also Nettels (1266).

1188 Martin, John B. '*The Grasshopper' in Lombard Street*. 1892. Contains useful information about early bankers and banking; reprints in facsimile *The mystery of the new fashioned goldsmiths or bankers* (1676).

1189 Mumby, Frank A. *Publishing and bookselling: a history from the earliest times to the present day*. Rev. ed., 1956. Pertains to Britain.

1190 Nef, John U. *The rise of the British coal industry*. 1932, 2 vols. Covers the period 1550–1700.

1191 Oman, Charles W. C. *The coinage of England*. 1931. An established work, with one chapter on the period.

1192 Parkinson, Cyril Northcote. *The rise of the port of Liverpool*. Liverpool, 1952. Of limited relevance, but interesting.

1193 Pasquier, Maurice. *Sir William Petty: ses idées économiques*. Paris, 1903.

1194 Plant, Marjorie. *The English book trade: an economic history of the making and sale of books*. 2nd ed. rev., 1965.

1195 Price, Jacob M. *The tobacco adventure to Russia: enterprise, politics, and diplomacy in the quest for a northern market for English colonial tobacco*,

1676–1722 (American Philosophical Society, Transactions, new ser., LI, pt. 1). Philadelphia, 1961.

1196 Pritchard, Earl H. *Anglo-Chinese relations during the seventeenth and eighteenth centuries* (University of Illinois Studies in the Social Sciences, XVII, nos. 1, 2). Urbana, 1930. Has chapter on the origin of the China trade.

1197 Ramsay, George D. *English overseas trade during the centuries of emergence.* 1957. The best general survey of English foreign trade, but there is little on the period.

1198 Rich, Edwin E. *The history of the Hudson's Bay Company*, vol. I. 1958. Covers 1670–1763. See also (1128).

1199 Richards, Richard D. *The early history of banking in England.* 1929. Useful on the goldsmith bankers; shows that the Stop of the Exchequer was less serious than has been supposed. See Browning (178), p. 277, for works with which this should be read.

1200 Rogers, James E. Thorold. *A history of agriculture and prices in England, 1259–1793.* Oxford, 1866–1902, 7 vols. A monumental work, but somewhat inaccurate; superseded and amplified by Beveridge (1144) and Gras (1297).

1201 —— *Six centuries of work and wages: the history of English labour.* 11th ed., 1912. The conclusions have been subject to criticism.

1202 Scott, William R. *The constitution and finance of English, Scottish, and Irish joint-stock companies to 1720.* Cambridge, 1910–12, 3 vols. A detailed examination of great importance.

1203 Shillington, Violet M. and Annie B. W. Chapman. *The commercial relations of England and Portugal.* 1907. A brief study based on diplomatic correspondence.

1204 Simon, André L. *The history of the wine trade in England.* 1906–9, 3 vols. Vol. III deals with the seventeenth century; valuable.

1205 Smout, T. Christopher. *Scottish trade on the eve of union, 1660–1707.* Edinburgh, 1963. There is considerable information on trade with England.

1206 Stephens, W. B. *Seventeenth-century Exeter: a study of industrial and commercial development, 1625–88.* Exeter, 1958.

1207 Suviranta, Bruno K. *Theory of the balance of trade in England: a study in mercantilism.* Repr., New York, 1967. Examines the theory as it appeared in seventeenth-century writings.

1208 Tucker, Graham S. L. *Progress and profits in British economic thought, 1650–1850.* Cambridge, 1960. Chapter 2, 'The problem of interest in the seventeenth century' focuses on the Restoration period.

1209 Tveite, Svein. *Engelsk–Norsk trelasthandel, 1640–1710.* Bergen-Oslo, 1961. Deals with timber trade.

1210 Unwin, George. *The guilds and companies of London.* 1908. A valuable study, but chiefly before 1660, except chap. 8, 'Antecedents of the trade union'. Useful bibliographical information.

1211 Wadsworth, Alfred P. and Julia de Lacy Mann. *The cotton trade and industrial Lancashire, 1600–1780.* Manchester, 1931. Some statistical as well as other information on the period.

1212 Watson, John Steven. *A history of the Salters' Company.* 1963.

1213 Westerfield, Ray B. 'Middlemen in English business, particularly between 1660 and 1760', *Transactions of the Connecticut Academy of Arts and Sciences*, **19** (May 1915), 111–445.

1214 Willan, Thomas S. *The English coasting trade, 1600–1750.* Manchester, 1938.

1215 —— *River navigation in England, 1660–1750.* 1936.

1216 Willson, Beckles. *The Great Company, being a history of the honourable Company of Merchants-Adventurers trading into Hudson's Bay.* 1900, 2 vols.

1217 —— *Ledger and sword, or the honourable Company of Merchants of England trading to the East Indies (1599–1874).* 1903, 2 vols.

1218 Wilson, Charles H. *Profit and power: a study of England and the Dutch Wars.* 1957. Deals almost entirely with the first two wars; stresses dominating effects of economic needs.

1219 Wood, Alfred C. *A history of the Levant Company.* 1935.

1220 Zook, George F. *The Company of Royal Adventurers trading into Africa.* 1919. Covers 1660–72; repr. from *Journal of Negro history*, **4** (Apr. 1919), 134–231.

4 Biographies

1221 Fitzmaurice, Edmund G., Baron. *The life of Sir William Petty, 1623–1687.* 1895. Lists Petty's works in appendix.

1222 Letwin, William L. *Sir Josiah Child, merchant economist.* Boston, Mass., 1959.

1223 Papillon, Alexander F. W. *Memoirs of Thomas Papillon of London, merchant (1623–1702).* Reading, 1887. Useful for trade and politics; of Huguenot interest.

1224 Pearson, John B. *A biographical sketch of the chaplains to the Levant Company maintained at Constantinople, Aleppo, and Smyrna, 1611–1706.* Cambridge, 1883.

1225 Strauss, Erich. *Sir William Petty: portrait of a genius.* 1954.

5 Articles

1226 Ambrose, Gwilym. 'English traders at Aleppo (1658–1756)', *EcHR*, **3** (Oct. 1931), 246–67.

1227 Aylmer, Gerald E. 'The last years of purveyance, 1610–1660', *EcHR*, 2nd ser., **10** (no. 1, 1957), 81–93. Shows the landed classes insisting upon its abolition in 1660.

1228 Bailyn, Bernard. 'Communication and trade: the Atlantic in the seventeenth century', *Journal of Economic History*, **13** (no. 4, 1953), 378–87. Regards second third of the century as formative period of north Atlantic trade.

1229 Barbour, Violet. 'Dutch and English merchant shipping in the seventeenth century', *EcHR*, **2** (Jan. 1930), 261–90.

1230 Boxer, Charles R. 'English shipping in the Brazil trade, 1640–1665', *MM*, **37** (July 1951), 197–230.

1231 Brinkmann, Carl. 'England and the Hanse under Charles II', *EHR*, **23** (Oct. 1908), 683–708.

1232 Brown, E. H. Phelps and Sheila V. Hopkins. 'Seven centuries of building wages', *Economica*, new ser., **22** (Aug. 1955), 195–206. Has data for 1655–87 and 1687–1701.

1233 Browning, Andrew. 'The stop of the Exchequer', *Hist.*, **14** (Jan. 1930), 333–7. A 'revision' of Richards (1273).

1234 Chaudhuri, K. N. 'Treasure and trade balances: the East India Company's export trade, 1660–1720', *EcHR*, 2nd ser., **21** (Dec. 1968), 480–502.

1235 Clark, Dorothy K. 'Edward Backwell as a royal agent', *EcHR*, **9** (Nov. 1938), 45–55. Financial activities of a London goldsmith.

1236 —— 'A Restoration goldsmith-banking house: the Vine on Lombard Street', in *Essays in modern English history in honor of Wilbur Cortez Abbott*, Cambridge, Mass., 1941, pp. 3–47.

1237 Clarkson, L. A. 'The leather crafts in Tudor and Stuart England', *AgHR*, **14** (pt. 1, 1966), 25–39. Has statistics for the period.

1238 Coleman, Donald C. 'The early British paper industry and the Huguenots', *Hug. Soc. Proc.*, **19** (1957), 210–25.

1239 —— 'Labour in the British economy of the seventeenth century', *EcHR*, 2nd ser., **8** (no. 3, 1956), 280–95.

1240 —— 'London scriveners and the estate market in the later seventeenth century', *EcHR*, 2nd ser., **4** (no. 2, 1951), 221–30.

1241 Darby, Henry C. 'The draining of the fens, A.D. 1600–1800', in his *Historical geography of England before A.D. 1800*, Cambridge, 1936, pp. 444–64.

1242 Davies, Kenneth G. 'Joint-stock investment in the later seventeenth century', *EcHR*, 2nd ser., **4** (no. 3, 1952), 283–301.

1243 Davis, Ralph. 'Earnings of capital in the English shipping industry, 1670–1730', *Journal of Economic History*, **17** (Sept. 1957), 409–25.

1244 Davis, Ralph. 'English foreign trade, 1660–1700', *EcHR*, 2nd ser., **7** (no. 1, 1954), 150–66. Includes table analysing foreign trade, 1663–9.

1245 —— 'Merchant shipping in the economy of the late seventeenth century', *EcHR*, 2nd ser., **9** (no. 1, 1956), 59–73.

1246 Flinn, Michael W. 'The growth of the English iron industry, 1660–1760', *EcHR*, 2nd ser., **11** (no. 1, 1958), 144–53. Of some use, though for the most part beyond the period.

1247 Grampp, William. 'The liberal elements in English mercantilism', *Quarterly Journal of Economics*, **66** (Nov. 1952), 465–501. Includes discussion of Petty and Temple.

1248 Gravil, R. 'Trading to Spain and Portugal, 1670–1700', *Business History*, **10** (July 1968), 69–88. Based mainly on the papers of John Oldbury.

1249 Gregory, Theodor E. 'The economics of employment in England, 1660–1713', *Economica*, **1** (no. 1, 1921), 37–51.

1250 Habakkuk, H. John. 'Long-term rate of interest and the price of land in the seventeenth century', *EcHR*, 2nd ser., **5** (no. 1, 1952), 26–45.

1251 Haig, Robert L. 'New light on the King's printing office, 1680–1730', *Studies in Bibliography*, **8** (1956), 157–67.

1252 Hall, Daniel G. E. 'Anglo-French trade relations under Charles II', *Hist.*, **7** (Apr. 1922), 17–30.

1253 Hobsbawm, Eric J. 'The seventeenth century in the development of capitalism', *Science and Society*, **24** (Spring 1960), 97–112. Sees the seventeenth century as crucial in the victory of the capitalist economy; deals with Europe generally, with special reference to England.

1254 Hudson, Winthrop S. 'Puritanism and the spirit of capitalism', *Church Hist.*, **18** (Mar. 1949), 3–17. A critique of Tawney's treatment of Baxter.

1255 Hughes, Edward. 'The negotiations for a commercial treaty between England and Scotland in 1668', *Scottish Historical Review*, **24** (Oct. 1926), 30–47.

1256 Iddesleigh, Stafford H. Northcote, earl of. 'The closing of the exchequer by Charles II in 1672', in his *Lectures and essays*, Edinburgh, 1887, pp. 244–85.

1257 Johnson, Alfred F. 'The King's printers, 1660–1742', *Lib.*, 5th ser., **3** (June 1948), 33–8.

1258 Judges, Arthur V. 'The origins of English banking', *Hist.*, new ser., **16** (July 1931), 138–45.

1259 Kelsall, R. Keith. 'Two East Yorkshire wage assessments, 1669, 1679', *EHR*, **52** (Apr. 1937), 283–9.

1260 Koenigsberger, Helmut. 'English merchants in Naples and Sicily in the seventeenth century', *EHR*, **62** (July 1947), 304–26. Includes discussion of difficulties with local authorities.

1261 Lloyd, Christopher. 'Bartholomew Sharp, buccaneer', *MM*, **42** (1956), 291–301. Deals with voyages of the 1670s and 1680s.

1262 Lodge, Richard. 'The English factory at Lisbon: some chapters on its history', *TRHS*, 4th ser., **16** (1933), 211–47.

1263 McGovney, Dudley O. 'The navigation acts as applied to European trade', *AHR*, **9** (July 1904), 725–34.

1264 Miller, C. William. 'Henry Herringman, Restoration bookseller-publisher', *Papers of the Bibliographical Society of America*, **42** (1948), 292–306. Deals with a prominent publisher of 'polite literature'.

1265 Moller, Asta. 'Coal mining in the seventeenth century', *TRHS*, 4th ser., **8** (1925), 79–97. Concerned with financial and commercial aspects of the subject.

1266 Nettels, Curtis P. 'England and the Spanish-American trade, 1680–1715', *JMH*, **3** (Mar. 1931), 1–32. Important; should be read with McLachlan (1187) and Hall (1252).

1267 Packard, Laurence B. 'International rivalry and free trade origins, 1660–78'. *Quarterly Journal of Economics*, **37** (May 1923), 412–35.

1268 Price, Jacob M. 'Notes on some London price-currents, 1667–1715', *EcHR*, 2nd ser., **7** (no. 2, 1954), 240–50. A bibliographical essay dealing with contemporary price lists.

1269 Priestley, Margaret. 'Anglo-French trade and the "unfavorable balance" controversy, 1660–1685', *EcHR*, 2nd ser., **4** (no. 1, 1951), 37–52. Concerned primarily with the cloth trade.

1270 Richards, Richard D. 'The evolution of paper money in England', *Quarterly Journal of Economics*, **41** (May 1927), 361–404. Shows that by the end of the seventeenth century paper money was established in England.

1271 —— 'Mr. Pepys and the goldsmith bankers', *Ec. Hist.*, **2** (Jan. 1933), 500–20.

1272 —— 'A pre-Bank of England English banker – Edward Backwell', *Ec. Hist.*, **1** (Jan. 1928), 335–55. See also Clark (1235). Based in part on Backwell's ledgers, 1663–71.

1273 —— 'The "stop of the exchequer"', *Ec. Hist.*, **2** (Jan. 1930), 45–62. Cf. Browning (1233).

1274 Skeel, Caroline A. J. 'The Canary Company', *EHR*, **31** (Oct. 1916), 529–44. Covers 1665–7.

1275 Smith, Abbot E. 'Indentured servants: new light on some of America's "first families"', *Journal of Economic History*, **2** (May 1942), 40–53.

1276 Thirsk, Joan. 'The Restoration land settlement', *JMH*, **26** (Dec. 1954), 315–28.

1277 Usher, Abbott P. 'The growth of English shipping, 1572–1922', *Quarterly Journal of Economics*, **42** (May 1928), 465–78. Claims that the expansion of English commerce dates from the Protectorate or the Restoration rather than from the Elizabethan period.

1278 Viner, Jacob. 'English theories of foreign trade before Adam Smith', *Journal of Political Economy*, **38** (June, Aug. 1930), 249–301, 404–57. Footnotes contain valuable bibliographical information.

1279 Wilson, Charles H. 'Cloth production and international competition in the seventeenth century', *EcHR*, 2nd ser., **13** (Dec. 1960), 209–21.

1280 —— 'Economics and politics in the seventeenth century', *Hist. J.*, **5** (no. 1 1962), 80–92. A stimulating review of Hill (187).

1281 —— 'The other face of mercantilism', *TRHS*, 5th ser., **9** (1959), 81–101. Regards the 'profusion of welfare economics of 1649' as the basis for most of the economic thought in the following century.

IX AGRICULTURAL HISTORY

1 Printed Sources

1282 Baxter, Richard. *Reverend Richard Baxter's last treatise*, ed. Frederick J. Powicke. Manchester, 1926. 'The poor husbandman's advocate to rich racking landlords', written in 1691.

1283 Blagrave, Joseph. *The epitome of the art of husbandry*. 1669. A popular compilation, going through many eds. Based on Anthony Fitzherbert, *Book of husbandry* (1523).

1284 Houghton, John (ed.). *A collection of letters for the improvement of husbandry and trade*. 1681–3, 2 vols. A series of pamphlets published at intervals.

1285 McDonald, Donald. *Agricultural writers from Sir Walter of Henley to Arthur Young, 1200–1800. Reproductions in facsimile and extracts from their actual writings...to which is added an exhaustive bibliography*. 1908. Valuable.

1286 Worlidge, John. *Systema agriculturae, being the mystery of husbandry discovered*. 1669. The most systematic work on the subject at that time. Describes farm operations and implements, discusses crops, and has a dictionary of 'rustick terms'.

2 Surveys

1287 Ernle, Rowland E. Prothero, Baron. *English farming past and present*, with introductions by George E. Fussell and O. R. McGregor. 6th ed., 1961. The introductions bring this work, first published in 1912, up to date. Supersedes Prothero's *Pioneers and progress of English farming* (1888).

1288 Garnier, Russell M. *History of the British landed interest, its customs, laws, and agriculture*. 1892–3, 2 vols.

1289 Orwin, Charles S. *A history of English farming*. 1949.

1290 Trow-Smith, Robert. *English husbandry from the earliest times to the present day*. 1951.

3 Monographs

1291 Curtler, William H. R. *The enclosure and redistribution of our land*. Oxford, 1920. A good general treatment; contains one chapter on the seventeenth century.

1292 Darby, Henry C. *The draining of the fens*. Cambridge, 1940. A scholarly work covering the period 1500–1900.

1293 Fussell, George E. *The farmer's tools, 1500–1900: the history of British farm implements, tools, and machinery before the tractor came*. 1952.

1294 —— *Farming systems from Elizabethan to Victorian days in the North and East Ridings of Yorkshire*. York, 1944.

1295 —— *The old English farming books from Fitzherbert to Tull, 1523–1730*. 1947. See chap. 5, 'The age of Worlidge and Houghton, 1661–1700'.

1296 Gonner, Edward C. K. *Common land and enclosure*. New ed., 1966, with introduction by Gordon E. Mingay. A valuable work.

1297 Gras, Norman S. B. *The evolution of the English corn market from the twelfth to the eighteenth century*. Cambridge, Mass., 1926. A standard survey, supplementing Rogers (1200) on grain prices.

1298 Gray, Howard L. *English field systems* (Harvard Historical Studies, XXII). Cambridge Mass., 1915. Contains important material from seventeenth-century records.

1299 Hoskins, William G. *The Midland peasant: the economic and social history of a Leicestershire village*. 1957. Provides a detailed study of a village since 1066.

1300 Johnson, Arthur H. *The disappearance of the small landowner*. New ed. with introduction by Joan Thirsk. 1963. Ford Lectures; slight reference to the period.

1301 Kerridge, Eric. *The agricultural revolution*. 1967. Places the 'revolution' between 1590 and 1690.

1302 Orwin, Charles S. and Christabel S. *The open fields*. 3rd ed., Oxford, 1967. Useful in a general way, and more particularly for the treatment of Laxton, Nottinghamshire.

1303 Riches, Naomi. *The agricultural revolution in Norfolk*. 2nd ed., 1967. Includes a helpful bibliography.

1304 Seebohm, Mabel E. *The evolution of the English farm*. 2nd ed., rev., 1952. Chapter on 'The seventeenth century' contains some Restoration material.

1305 Thirsk, Joan. *English peasant farming: the agrarian history of Lincolnshire from Tudor to recent times*. 1957. A substantial contribution to agricultural history.

1306 Trow-Smith, Robert. *A history of British livestock husbandry to 1700*. 1957. An admirable survey of technical aspects of the subject.

4 Biographies

1307 Donaldson, John. *Agricultural biography, containing a notice of the life and writings of the British authors on agriculture, from the earliest date in 1480 to the present time*. 1854.

5 Articles

1308 Allison, Keith J. 'Flock management in the sixteenth and seventeenth centuries', *EcHR*, 2nd ser., **11** (Aug. 1958), 98–112.

1309 —— 'The sheep-corn husbandry of Norfolk in the sixteenth and seventeenth centuries', *AgHR*, **5** (pt. I, 1957), 12–30.

1310 Brandenburg, S. J., 'The place of agriculture in British national economy prior to Adam Smith', *Journal of Political Economy*, **39** (June 1931), 281–320.

1311 Chalklin, C. W. 'The rural economy of a Kentish wealden parish, 1650–1750', *AgHR*, **10** (pt. 1, 1962), 29–45. Studies the parish of Tonbridge.

1312 Fussell, George E. 'After the Restoration: Stuart squires, manors and farms', *Agriculture*, **58** (Sept. 1951), 264–7.

1313 —— 'Crop nutrition in the late Stuart age (1660–1714)', *Ann. Sci.*, **14** (Sept. 1958), 173–84. Interesting; focus is on the period. Shows gap existing between the thinking of the Royal Society and that of most farmers.

1314 —— 'Farmers' calendars from Tusser to Arthur Young', *Economic History*, **2** (Jan. 1933), 521–35. Includes references to Stevenson, Worlidge, and Blome.

1315 Gonner, Edward C. K. 'The progress of inclosure during the seventeenth century', *EHR*, **23** (July 1908), 477–501. Has map showing enclosed roads in 1675.

1316 Habakkuk, H. John. 'English landownership, 1680–1740', *EcHR*, **10** (Feb. 1940), 2–17. Mainly after the period, but of some relevance.

1317 Hoskins, William G. 'The Leicestershire farmer in the seventeenth century', *Agricultural History*, **25** (Jan. 1951), 9–20. Valuable for an understanding of the open-field system, though direct references to the period are scattered.

1318 John, Arthur H. 'The course of agricultural change, 1660–1760', in Leslie S. Pressnell (ed.), *Studies in the industrial revolution presented to T. S. Ashton*, 1960, pp. 125–55. Suggests that the failure of agriculture to respond to certain demands may have been a contributing factor in launching the industrial revolution.

1319 Jones, Eric L. 'Agricultural origins of industry', *PP*, no. 40 (July 1968), 58–71. Argues that developments in agricultural production were instrumental in bringing nations to the 'brink of industrialization'; little on the period.

1320 Lennard, Reginald. 'English agriculture under Charles II: the evidence of the Royal Society's "Enquiries"', *EcHR*, **4** (Oct. 1932), 23–45. A scholarly contribution.

1321 Leonard, E. M. 'The enclosure of common fields in the seventeenth century', *TRHS*, new ser., **19** (1905), 101–46. Some references to the period, though the emphasis is earlier.

1322 Thirsk, Joan. 'The content and sources of English agrarian history after 1500', *AgHR*, **3** (pt. 2, 1955), 66–79. A general discussion, and valuable as such, but not bearing to any extent on the period.

X SCIENCE AND TECHNOLOGY

1 Printed Sources

1323 Boyle, Robert. *The works of Robert Boyle*, ed. Thomas Birch. 1744, 5 vols.; later ed., 1772, 6 vols. The principal collected editions; a life is prefixed.

1324 Davy, Norman (ed.). *British scientific literature in the seventeenth century*. New York, 1953. Extracts from major scientific writers.

1325 Dewhurst, Kenneth E. 'Sydenham's original treatise on smallpox with a preface, and dedication to the earl of Shaftesbury, by John Locke', *Medical History*, **3** (Oct. 1959), 278–302.

1326 Hall, A. Rupert. 'Sir Isaac Newton's notebook, 1661–1665', *Camb. Hist. J.*, **9** (no. 2, 1948), 239–50.

1327 Halley, Edmond. *The correspondence and papers of Edmond Halley*, ed. Eugene F. MacPike. Oxford, 1932.

1328 Hodges, Nathaniel. *Loimologia, or an historical account of the plague in London in 1665*. 1720. Written by a physician who practised during the epidemic.

1329 Hooke, Robert. *The diary of Robert Hooke, 1672–80*, ed. Henry W. Robinson and Walter Adams. 1935.

1330 —— *The posthumous works of Robert Hooke*, published by Robert Waller, 1705. Contains life by Waller. See also Gunther (1369).

1331 Monconys, Balthasar de. *Journal des voyages*. Lyon, 1665–6, 3 pts. See pt. 2, pp. 1–84, 'Voyage d'Angleterre', made in 1663. Valuable, especially for science.

1332 Moxon, Joseph. *Mechanick exercises on the whole art of printing, 1683–4*, ed. Herbert Davis and Harry Carter. 1958. An important work by the best type maker of his day.

1333 Newton, Isaac. *The correspondence of Isaac Newton*, ed. Herbert W. Turnbull. Cambridge, 1959–. An admirable edition; vols. I–III cover 1661–94.

1334 —— *Papers and letters on natural philosophy*, ed. I. Bernard Cohen. Cambridge, Mass., 1958. Has a long introduction.

1335 —— *Sir Isaac Newton's mathematical principles of natural philosophy and his system of the world*, ed. T. R. Crawford. Andrew Motte's translation (1729), rev. by Florian Cajori. Berkeley, Calif., 1962, 2 vols. The standard edition of *Principia*.

1336 —— *Unpublished scientific papers of Isaac Newton*, ed. A. Rupert Hall and Marie Boas Hall. Cambridge, 1962. From the Portsmouth Collection in the University of Cambridge library.

1337 Oldenburg, Henry. *The correspondence of Henry Oldenburg*, ed. A. Rupert Hall and Marie Boas Hall. Madison, Wis., 1965–, 6 vols. Covers 1641–70. Important.

1338 Rigaud, Stephen P. (ed.). *Correspondence of scientific men of the seventeenth century, including letters of Barrow, Flamsteed, Wallis, and Newton*. Oxford, 1841–62, 2 vols.

1339 Royal Society of London. *Philosophical transactions*. 1665–. Vols. I–XVII cover the period. Basic for the activities of the Society. A general index by Paul H. Maty was published in 1787.

1340 Sprat, Thomas. *The history of the Royal Society*, ed. Jackson I. Cope and Howard W. Jones. St Louis, 1958. A facsimile of the first ed., 1667. The earliest history.

1341 Thayer, H. S. (ed.). *Newton's philosophy of nature*. New York, 1953. Selections from his writings and correspondence.

1342 Wallis, John. *A defence of the Royal Society and the Philosophical Transactions*. 1678.

2 Surveys

1343 Butterfield, Herbert. *The origins of modern science, 1300–1800*. 2nd ed., rev., 1957.

1344 Derry, Thomas K. and Trevor I. Williams. *A short history of technology from the earliest times to A.D. 1900*. Oxford, 1960. A first-rate survey, condensing Singer (1351).

1345 Forbes, Robert J. and Eduard J. Dijksterhuis. *A history of science and technology*, I: *Ancient times to the seventeenth century*. Harmondsworth, 1963.

1346 Hall, A. Rupert. *From Galileo to Newton, 1630–1720*. 1963.

1347 —— *The scientific revolution, 1500–1800: the formation of the modern scientific attitude*. 2nd ed., Boston, 1956.

1348 Kranzberg, Melvin and Carroll W. Pursell, Jr. (eds.). *Technology in western civilization*. New York, 1967, 2 vols. Vol. I goes to 1900.

1349 Osler, William. *The evolution of modern medicine*. New Haven, 1921.

1350 Schneer, Cecil. *The search for order: the development of the major ideas in the physical sciences from the earliest times to the present*. New York, 1960.

1351 Singer, Charles *et al.* (eds.). *A history of technology*, III: *From the renaissance to the industrial revolution, c. 1500 – c. 1750*. Oxford, 1957.

1352 Thorndike, Lynn. *A history of magic and experimental science*, VII and VIII: *The seventeenth century*. New York, 1958. Highly informative, excellent bibliographical coverage.

1353 Usher, Abbott P. *A history of mechanical inventions.* Rev. ed., Cambridge, Mass., 1966.

1354 Woolf, Abraham. *A history of science, technology, and philosophy in the sixteenth and seventeenth centuries,* rev. Douglas McKie. 1950.

3 Monographs

1355 Anderson, Paul R. *Science in defense of liberal religion: a study of Henry More's attempt to link seventeenth-century religion with science.* New York, 1933.

1356 Ball, Walter W. R. *An essay on Newton's Principia.* 1893. Includes Newton's correspondence with Hooke and Halley.

1357 —— *A history of the study of mathematics at Cambridge.* Cambridge, 1889.

1358 Birch, Thomas. *The history of the Royal Society of London for improving of natural knowledge, from its first rise.* 1756–7, 4 vols. More a defence than a history; contains papers presented to the Society which were not published in the *Philosophical Transactions* (1339).

1359 Cameron, H. Charles and Cecil Wall. *A history of the worshipful Society of Apothecaries of London,* I (1671–1815), ed. Edgar Ashworth Underwood. 1963. A scholarly work; chapter on the Revolution.

1360 Clark, George N. *A history of the Royal College of Physicians of London.* Oxford, 1964–6, 2 vols.

1361 —— *Science and social welfare in the age of Newton,* 2nd ed., Oxford, 1949. Largely lectures delivered at the University of London.

1362 Creighton, Charles. *A history of epidemics in Great Britain.* Cambridge, 1891–4, 2 vols. Should be supplemented with Mullett (1380).

1363 Crombie, Alistair C. *Oxford's contribution to the origins of modern science.* Oxford, 1954. A paper.

1364 Fisher, Mitchell S. *Robert Boyle, devout naturalist: a study in science and religion in the seventeenth century.* Philadelphia, 1945.

1365 Fordham, Herbert George. *Some notable surveyors and map-makers of the sixteenth, seventeenth, and eighteenth centuries, and their work.* Cambridge, 1929.

1366 Foster, Michael. *Lectures on the history of physiology during the sixteenth, seventeenth, and eighteenth centuries.* Cambridge, 1901. A broad coverage, but includes some Restoration figures.

1367 Gunther, Robert W. T. *Early British botanists and their gardens.* Oxford, 1922. Based on unpublished writings of Goodyer, Tradescant and others. Largely before 1660.

1368 —— *Early science in Cambridge.* Oxford, 1937. Topical treatment; astronomy mathematics, etc.

1369 —— *Early science in Oxford.* Oxford, 1923–45, 14 vols. Vols. I and II are vols. LXXVII and LXXVIII of Oxford Historical Society Publications. Vols. VI–VIII and X pertain to Hooke; they include the life by Waller and Hooke's lectures. Cf. Hooke (1330).

1370 Hall, A. Rupert and C. Donald O'Malley. *Scientific literature in sixteenth and seventeenth century England.* Los Angeles, 1961.

1371 Hall, Marie Boas. *Robert Boyle and seventeenth-century chemistry.* Cambridge, 1958. Probably the best treatment of his chemical work.

1372 Handover, Phyllis M. *Printing in London from 1476 to modern times: competitive practice and technical invention in the trade of book and Bible printing, periodical production, jobbing, etc.* 1960.

1373 Hartley, Harold (ed.). *The Royal Society: its origins and founders.* 1960. Essays by various authors.

1374 Herivel, John. *The background of Newton's Principia: a study of Newton's dynamical researches in the years 1664–84.* Oxford, 1965. A highly technical treatment.

1375 Jones, Richard F. *Ancients and moderns: a study of the rise of the scientific movement in seventeenth-century England.* 2nd ed., rev., St Louis, 1961. An important work; chapters VIII and IX bear directly on the period.

1376 Lyons, Henry G. *The Royal Society, 1660–1940: a history of its administration under its charters.* Cambridge, 1944. The first three chapters deal with the seventeenth century. Useful, though superseded for the earliest period by Purver (1386).

1377 Merton, Robert K. 'Science, technology, and society in seventeenth-century England', *Osiris*, 4 (1938), 360–632. A major study.

1378 Meyer, Gerald D. *The scientific lady in England, 1650–1760: an account of her rise, with emphasis on the major roles of the telescope and microscope* (University of California English Studies, no. 12). Berkeley, 1955. Has material on the duchess of Newcastle and other Restoration figures.

1379 Morison, Stanley. *The English newspaper: some account of the physical development of journals printed in London between 1622 and the present day.* Cambridge, 1932. Deals with format, printing.

1380 Mullett, Charles F. *The bubonic plague and England.* Lexington, Ky., 1956. An interesting treatment of social, economic, and medical interactions. Cf. Creighton (1362).

1381 —— *Public baths and health in England, 16th–18th century* (Bulletin of the History of Medicine Supplements, no. 5). Baltimore, 1946.

1382 Nicolson, Marjorie Hope. *Pepys' diary and the new science.* Charlottesville, Va., 1965. Three studies, elaborating lectures; goes considerably beyond Pepys.

1383 Nussbaum, Frederick L. *The triumph of science and reason, 1660–85.* New York, 1953. A good background work.

1384 Ornstein, Martha. *The role of scientific societies in the seventeenth century.* 3rd ed., Chicago, 1938. An important work, international in scope.

1385 Plomer, Henry R. *A short history of English printing, 1476–1898.* 1900.

1386 Purver, Margery. *The Royal Society: concept and creation.* 1967.

1387 Raven, Charles E. *English naturalists from Neckam to Ray: a study of the making of the modern world.* Cambridge, 1947.

1388 Scott, Joseph F. *The mathematical work of John Wallis, D.D., F.R.S., 1616–1703.* 1938.

1389 Snow, Adolph J. *Matter and gravity in Newton's physical philosophy: a study in the natural philosophy of Newton's time.* 1926. A doctoral dissertation.

1390 Stimson, Dorothy. *Scientists and amateurs: a history of the Royal Society.* 1949.

1391 Taylor, Eva G. R. *The mathematical practitioners of Tudor and Stuart England.* Cambridge, 1954.

1392 Underwood, Edgar Ashworth (ed.). *Science, medicine, and history.* 1953, 2 vols. A few essays deal with the period.

1393 Weld, Charles R. *A history of the Royal Society, with memoirs of the presidents.* 1848, 2 vols. The first real history, with emphasis on administration. Not entirely reliable, but still valuable.

1394 Westfall, Richard S. *Science and religion in seventeenth-century England* (Yale Historical Publications, Miscellany 67). New Haven, 1958. The work of a notable Newton scholar.

4 Biographies

1395 Andrade, Edward N. da C. *Sir Isaac Newton.* 1954. A good brief biography.

1396 Armitage, Angus. *Edmond Halley.* 1966.

1397 Barnett, Pamela R. *Theodore Haak, F.R.S., 1605–1690.* The Hague, 1962.

1398 Brewster, David. *The life of Sir Isaac Newton.* New ed., rev. by W. T. Lynn, 1875. Superseded by More (1410) and Manuel (1408).

1399 Brodetsky, Selig. *Sir Isaac Newton: a brief account of his life and work.* 1927. A useful summary.

1400 Calvert, E. M. and Robert T. *Sergeant surgeon John Knight, surgeon-general, 1664–1680.* 1940.

1401 Crowther, James G. *Founders of British science.* 1960. Includes Wilkins, Ray, Wren, Hooke, and Newton. Popular, informative.

1402 De Villamil, Richard. *Newton: the man.* 1931. Has foreword by Albert Einstein and a catalogue of Newton's library.

1403 Dewhurst, Kenneth E. *Dr. Thomas Sydenham (1624–1689): his life and original writings*. Berkeley, Calif., 1966.

1404 —— *John Locke, 1632–1704, physician and philosopher: a medical biography*. 1963. Includes medical notes from Locke's journals.

1405 Dircks, Henry. *The life, times, and scientific labours of the second marquis of Worcester*. 1865. Reprints the marquis's *Century of...inventions* (1663).

1406 'Espinasse, Margaret. *Robert Hooke*. 1956. Hooke's first modern biography.

1407 Hone, Campbell R. *The life of Dr. John Radcliffe, 1652–1714, benefactor of the University of Oxford*. 1950. Useful for early chapters dealing with his student days at Oxford and his career as a physician.

1408 Manuel, Frank E. *A portrait of Isaac Newton*. Cambridge, Mass., 1968. The leading biography, superseding More (1410).

1409 Montagu, M. F. Ashley. *Edward Tyson, M.D., F.R.S., 1650–1708, and the rise of human and comparative anatomy in England* (American Philosophical Society, Memoirs, xx). Philadelphia, 1943.

1410 More, Louis T. *Isaac Newton, 1642–1727: a biography*. New York, 1934. Long and scholarly, superseding previous lives; but see Manuel (1408).

1411 —— *The life and works of the honourable Robert Boyle*. New York, 1944. A valuable survey.

1412 Munk, William R. *The roll of the Royal College of Physicians of London, comprising biographical sketches of all the eminent physicians*. 1878, 3 vols. Considerable coverage of the period in vol. I.

1413 Payne, Joseph F. *Thomas Sydenham*. 1900. An excellent biography, but superseded by Dewhurst (1403).

1414 Raven, Charles E. *John Ray, naturalist: his life and works*. Cambridge, 1942.

1415 Royal Society of London. *The record of the Royal Society of London for the Promotion of Natural Knowledge*. 4th ed., rev., Edinburgh, 1940. Alphabetical list of Fellows, from the foundation.

1416 Shapiro, Barbara J. *John Wilkins, 1614–1672: an intellectual biography*. Berkeley, Calif., 1969.

1417 Sigerist, Henry E. *The great doctors: a biographical history of medicine*, trans. by Eden and Cedar Paul. New York, 1933. Contains chapters on eminent seventeenth-century English physicians.

1418 Sullivan, John W. N. *Isaac Newton, 1642–1727*. 1938.

1419 Symonds, Robert W. *Thomas Tompion: his life and work*. 1951. The great clock- and watch-maker of the period.

1420 Wright-Henderson, Patrick A. *The life and times of John Wilkins*. Edinburgh, 1910.

5 Articles

1421 Allen, Phyllis. 'Medical education in seventeenth-century England', *Journal of the History of Medicine and Allied Sciences*, I (Jan. 1946), 115–43.

1422 —— 'Scientific studies in the English universities of the seventeenth century', *JHI*, **10** (April 1949), 219–53.

1423 Andrade, Edward N. da C. 'The birth and early days of the *Philosophical Transactions*', *N. R. Roy. Soc.*, **20** (June 1965), 9–27.

1424 —— 'Newton and the science of his age', *Proceedings of the Royal Society of London*, ser. A, **181** (May 1943), 227–43. A useful survey.

1425 —— 'Robert Hooke', *Proceedings of the Royal Society of London*, ser. A, **201** (May 1950), 439–73. A competent survey, with helpful illustrations.

1426 —— 'Samuel Pepys and the Royal Society', *N. R. Roy. Soc.*, **18** (Dec. 1963), 82–93.

1427 Barnett, Pamela R. 'Theodore Haak and the early years of the Royal Society', *Ann. Sci.*, **13** (Dec. 1957), 205–18. Has some relevance, though largely before 1660.

1428 Bates, Thomas G. 'Thomas Willis and the epidemic fever of 1661: a commentary', *BHM*, **39** (Sept.–Oct. 1965), 393–414. Willis wrote in Latin an account of the epidemic, published in 1667.

1429 Boas, Marie and Rupert Hall, 'Newton's "Mechanical Principles"', *JHI*, **20** (April 1959), 167–78.

1430 Bredvold, Louis I. 'Dryden, Hobbes, and the Royal Society', *Mod. Phil.*, **25** (May 1928), 417–38.

1431 Broad, Charles D. 'Sir Isaac Newton', *Proceedings of the British Academy* (1927), 173–202.

1432 Browne, Charles A. 'Agricultural chemistry in the time of the early Royal Society', *Chronica Botanica*, **8** (no. 1, 1944), 54–96.

1433 Challinor, John. 'The early progress of British geology, I: From Leland to Woodward, 1558–1728', *Ann. Sci.*, **9** (June 1953), 124–53. Largely devoted to the period; extracts from original sources.

1434 Chalmers, Gordon K. 'Sir Thomas Browne, true scientist', *Osiris*, **2** (1936), 28–79.

1435 Chance, Burton. 'Charles Scarborough, an English educator and physician to three kings: a medical retrospect into the times of the Stuarts', *BHM*, **12** (July 1942), 274–303.

1436 Clark, George N. 'Social and economic aspects of science in the age of Newton', *Ec. Hist.*, **3** (Feb. 1937), 362–79.

1437 Cohen, I. Bernard. 'Newton in the light of recent scholarship', *Isis*, **51** (Dec. 1960), 489–514. Provides a conspectus of modern opinion.

1438 Colwell, Hector A. 'Gideon Harvey: sidelights on medical life from the Restoration to the end of the seventeenth century', *Annals of Medical History*, **3** (Fall 1921), 205–37. Focus is on the period.

1439 De Beer, Esmond S. 'The earliest fellows of the Royal Society', *BIHR*, **15** (Nov. 1937), 79–93. A list, with introductory comment.

1440 Denny, M. 'The early program of the Royal Society and John Evelyn', *Modern Language Quarterly*, **1** (1940), 240–65. Interesting on Evelyn's role.

1441 'Espinasse, Margaret. 'The decline and fall of Restoration science', *PP*, **14** (Nov. 1958), 71–89. Interesting, though mainly after 1689.

1442 Fisch, Harold. 'The scientist as priest: a note on Robert Boyle's natural theology', *Isis*, **44** (Sept. 1953), 252–65. Refers to *The usefulness of natural philosophy* (1663).

1443 Fulton, John F. 'Some aspects of medicine reflected in seventeenth-century literature, with special reference to the plague of 1665', in Richard F. Jones *et al.*, *The seventeenth century: studies in the history of English thought and literature from Bacon to Pope*, Stanford, Calif., 1951, pp. 198–208.

1444 Gillispie, Charles C. 'Physick and philosophy: a study of the influence of the College of Physicians of London upon the foundations of the Royal Society', *JHI*, **19** (Sept. 1947), 210–25.

1445 Greenstreet, William J. (ed.). *Isaac Newton: a memorial volume.* 1927. Contains valuable essays on Newton's thought, and a bibliography by H. Zeitlinger.

1446 Guerlac, Henry. 'The poets' nitre: studies in the chemistry of John Mayow, II', *Isis*, **45** (Sept. 1954), 243–55.

1447 Hall, Marie Boas. 'Oldenburg and the art of scientific communication', *British Journal for the History of Science*, **2** (Dec. 1965), 277–90. Deals with Oldenburg's network of scientific communication.

1448 —— 'Sources for the history of the Royal Society in the seventeenth century', *History of Science*, **5** (1966), 62–76. Of fundamental importance for a study of the subject.

1449 History of Science Society. *Sir Isaac Newton 1727–1927: a bicentenary evaluation of his work.* Baltimore, 1928. A series of papers.

1450 Hoff, Ebbe C. and Phebe M. 'The life and times of Richard Lower, physiologist and physician (1631–1691)', *Bulletin of the Institute of the History of Medicine*, **4** (Mar. 1936), 517–35.

1451 Hunter, Richard and Ida Macalpine. 'The diary of John Casaubon', *Hug. Soc. Proc.*, **21** (no. 1, 1966), 31–55. Based on the manuscript 'log' of a Canterbury surgeon.

1452 Jones, Gordon W. 'Robert Boyle as a medical man', *BHM*, **38** (Mar.–April 1964), 139–52. Based on Boyle's *Of the reconcilableness of specifick medicines to the corpuscular philosophy* (1685) and the accompanying *Discourse about the advantages of the use of simple medicines.*

1453 Keevil, John J. 'Sir Charles Scarburgh', *Ann. Sci.*, **8** (June 1952), 113–21. Cf. Chance (1435).

1454 Kuhn, Thomas S. 'Robert Boyle and structural chemistry in the seventeenth century', *Isis*, **43** (April 1952), 12–36. Technical.

1455 LeFanu, William R. 'Huguenot refugee doctors in England', *Hug. Soc. Proc.*, **19** (1956), 113–27.

1456 Lones, Thomas E. 'A precis of *Mettallum Martis* and an analysis of Dud Dudley's alleged invention', *Newcomen Society Transactions* (1939–40), **20** (1941), 17–28. Concerned with smelting iron with coal, 1665.

1457 McKie, Douglas. 'The arrest and imprisonment of Henry Oldenburg', *N. R. Roy. Soc.*, **6** (Dec. 1948), 28–47. A scholarly article dealing with the Dutch war as well as the Royal Society.

1458 —— 'James, duke of York, F.R.S.', *N. R. Roy. Soc.*, **13** (June 1958), 6–18. Provides an indication of the extent of James's scientific knowledge and his relations with the Royal Society.

1459 —— 'Men and books in English science (1600–1700)', *Science Progress*, **46** (Oct. 1958), 606–31. Considerable attention is paid to the period.

1460 —— 'The origins and foundations of the Royal Society of London', *N. R. Roy. Soc.*, **15** (1960), 1–37. Tercentenary number; contains biographies of Charles II and twenty of the earliest active members.

1461 —— 'Samuel Pepys, F.R.S.', *Discovery*, **13** (May, June, July 1952), 145–9, 184–9, 216–23. Pepys's interest in science.

1462 Merton, E. S. 'The botany of Sir Thomas Browne', *Isis*, **47** (June 1956), 161–71.

1463 Merton, Robert K. 'Science and the economy of seventeenth-century England', *Science and Society*, **3** (no. 1, 1939), 3–27.

1464 —— 'Some economic factors in seventeenth-century English science', *Scientia*, **62** (1937), 142–52.

1465 More, Louis T. 'Boyle as alchemist', *JHI*, **2** (Jan. 1941), 61–76. Represents Boyle's interest in alchemy as an obsession.

1466 Mullett, Charles F. 'Physician vs. apothecary, 1669–1671: an episode in an age-long controversy', *Scientific Monthly*, **49** (Dec. 1939), 558–65.

1467 —— 'Sir William Petty on the plague', *Isis*, **28** (Feb. 1938), 18–25.

1468 O'Malley, C. Donald. 'John Evelyn and medicine', *Medical History*, **12** (July 1968), 219–31.

1469 Partington, J. R. 'The life and work of John Mayow (1641–1679)', *Isis*, **47** (Sept., Dec. 1956), 217–30, 405–17.

1470 Prior, Moody E. 'Joseph Glanvill, witchcraft, and seventeenth-century science', *Mod. Phil.*, **30** (Nov. 1932), 167–93.

1471 Raven, Charles E. 'New light on John Ray', *Linnean Society of London, Proceedings*, 154th session (1941–2), pp. 3–10.

1472 Reilly, Conor. 'Jesuits and the Royal Society, 1665–1715', *Month*, **18** (Aug. 1957), 108–11. Relates to continental rather than English Jesuits.

1473 —— 'Robert Boyle and the Jesuits', *Dublin Review*, **229** (3rd quarter 1955), 288–98. Dealings of Robert Boyle with the English Jesuit scientist Francis Line.

1474 Rook, Arthur. 'Medicine at Cambridge, 1660–1760', *Medical History*, **13** (Apr. 1969), 107–22.

1475 Royal Society of London. *Newton tercentenary celebrations 15–19 July 1946*. Cambridge, 1947. Includes essays by E. N. Andrade, J. M. Keynes, N. Bohr, and others.

1476 Russell, K. F. 'John Browne, 1642–1702, a seventeenth-century surgeon, anatomist, and plagiarist', *BHM*, **33** (Sept.–Oct., Nov.–Dec. 1959), 393–414, 503–25. Browne was surgeon in ordinary to Charles II, James II, and William III.

1477 Schneer, Cecil. 'The rise of historical geology in the seventeenth century', *Isis*, **45** (Sept. 1954), 256–68.

1478 Scott, Joseph F. 'John Wallis as a historian of mathematics', *Ann. Sci.*, **1** (July 1936), 335–57.

1479 Scoville, Warren C. 'The Huguenots and the diffusion of technology', *Journal of Political Economy*, **60** (Aug., Oct. 1952), 294–311, 392–411. Argues that the English silk industry acquired a new vitality after the Huguenots introduced new patterns and processes.

1480 Shapiro, Barbara J. 'Latitudinarianism and science in seventeenth-century England', *PP*, no. 40 (July 1968), 16–41. Sees an intimate connection between religion and science, but 'hardly a simple cause-and-effect relation between Puritanism and scientific innovation'.

1481 Skinner, Quentin. 'Thomas Hobbes and the nature of the early Royal Society', *Hist. J.*, **12** (no. 2, 1969), 217–39. Why Hobbes was never made F.R.S.

1482 Stannard, Jerry. 'Materia medica in the Locke–Clarke correspondence', *BHM*, 37 (May–June 1963), 201–25. Interesting on pharmacological practices, particularly the utilization of medicinal plants.

1483 Stimson, Dorothy. 'Amateurs of science in seventeenth-century England', *Isis*, **31** (Nov. 1939), 32–47.

1484 —— 'The critical years of the Royal Society, 1672–1703', *Journal of the History of Medicine and Allied Sciences*, **2** (no. 1, 1947), 283–98.

1485 —— 'Dr. Wilkins and the Royal Society', *JMH*, **3** (Dec. 1931), 539–63.

1486 Strong, E. W. 'Newtonian explications of natural philosophy', *JHI*, **18** (Jan. 1957), 49–83.

1487 Syfert, R. H. 'Some early critics of the Royal Society', *N. R. Roy. Soc.*, **8** (Oct. 1950), 20–64. Includes Stubbes, Crosse, Casaubon.

1488 —— 'Some early reactions to the Royal Society', *N. R. Roy. Soc.*, 7 (April 1950), 207–58.

XI MILITARY AND NAVAL HISTORY

1 Printed Sources

1489 *An abridgment of the English military discipline, by his Majesty's special command for the use of his Majesty's forces*. 1678. The best contemporary manual.

1490 Allin, Thomas. *The journals of Thomas Allin, 1660–1678*, ed. Roger C. Anderson (Navy Records Society, LXXIX–LXXX), 1939–40. Fifteen naval journals, with letters in an appendix.

1491 Anderson, Roger C. (ed.). *Journals and narratives of the Third Dutch War* (Navy Records Society, LXXXVI). 1946. Contains miscellaneous pieces.

1492 —— (comp.). *Lists of men-of-war, 1650–1700*, pt. 1, *English ships, 1649–1720* (Society for Nautical Research, Occasional Publications, no. 5). Cambridge, 1935.

1493 —— 'Naval operations in the latter part of the year 1666' (Navy Records Society, LXIII, pp. 3–47). 1927.

1494 Barlow, Edward. *Barlow's journal of his life at sea in king's ships, East and West Indiamen, and other merchantmen, from 1659 to 1703*, ed. Basil Lubbock. 1934, 2 vols.

1495 Carleton, George. *Military memoirs*, ed. Arnold W. Lawrence. 1929. First published 1728; covers 1672–1713. Carleton's authorship has been questioned.

1496 Colenbrander, Herman T. (ed.). *Bescheiden uit vreemde archieven omtrent de groote Nederlandsche zeeoorlogen, 1652–1676*. The Hague, 1919, 2 vols. Important for the Anglo-Dutch wars; documents mainly from English and French archives, with a few from Swedish and Danish sources.

1497 Corbett, Julian S. (ed.). *Fighting instructions, 1530–1816* (Navy Records Society, XXIX). 1905. Parts 5 and 6 deal with the period. Extensive editorial comment; definitive.

1498 —— *A note on the drawings in the possession of the earl of Dartmouth illustrating the battle of Sole Bay...and the battle of the Texel* (Navy Records Society, XXXIV). 1908.

1499 Dalton, Charles. *English army lists and commission registers, 1661–1714*. 1892–1904, 6 vols.; repr. 1960, 3 vols. Invaluable for the personnel of the army.

1500 Davies, Godfrey. 'Letters on the administration of James II's army', *JSAHR*, **29** (Summer 1951), 69–84. Letters written by William Blathwayt, secretary at war, 1683–1704.

1501 —— 'The militia in 1685', *EHR*, **43** (Oct. 1928), 604–5. Presents letter containing a description of the militia at the time of Monmouth's Rebellion, confirming Macaulay's indictment.

1502 *Debates in the House of Commons in the late King James's reign, relating to the militia.* 1697. Covers 9–20 Nov. 1685.

1503 De Beer, Esmond S. 'Reports of Pepys' speech in the House of Commons, March 5th, 1688', *MM*, **14** (Jan. 1928), 55–8. Two versions of a speech defending the payment of seamen with tickets.

1504 'A discourse touching Tangier, in a letter to a person of quality', in *Harleian Miscellany* (480), VIII, 391–409. 1810. First published 1680. Appended is another piece, 'The interest of Tangier'.

1505 Firth, Charles H. (ed.). *Naval songs and ballads* (Navy Records Society, XXXIII). 1908. Has an interesting introduction.

1506 Hansen, Harold A. 'The opening phase of the Third Dutch War described by the Danish envoy in London, March–June, 1672', *JMH*, **21** (June 1949), 97–108.

1507 Historical Manuscripts Commission. *The manuscripts of J. Eliot Hodgkin, esq.* 15th rept., app. II. 1897. Has naval papers to and from Pepys *temp.* Charles II; includes Rupert's and Monck's reports on naval battles, 1665–7.

1508 —— *The manuscripts of the earl of Dartmouth.* 15th rept., app. I. 1887–96, 3 vols. Vol. I has papers relating to Tangier and to naval events of 1688; vol. III is useful for the Third Dutch War.

1509 Ingram, Bruce S. (ed.). *Three sea journals of Stuart times.* 1936. Includes journals of Jeremy Roch and Francis Rogers.

1510 James, duke of York. *Memoirs of the English affairs, chiefly naval, from... 1660 to 1673.* 1729. Orders and instructions issued by James as lord high admiral; a basic source.

1511 Laughton, John Knox (ed.). *Memoirs relating to the Lord Torrington* (Camden Society, new ser., XLVI). 1889. Gives an account of his sea service, 1678–1705.

1512 Luke, John. *Tangier at high tide: the journal of John Luke, 1670–1673*, ed. Helen A. Kaufman. Geneva, 1958. Luke was secretary to the governor and judge advocate; deals mostly with personalities.

1513 Marsden, Reginald G. (ed.). *Documents relating to law and custom of the sea*, vol. II, 1649–1767 (Navy Records Society, L). 1916. Concerned chiefly with prize courts.

1514 *The oeconomy of his Majesty's naval office.* 1717. Instructions for the Navy Board drawn up by Pepys and issued by the duke of York.

1515 Pepys, Samuel. *Further correspondence of Samuel Pepys, 1662–1679*, ed. Joseph R. Tanner. 1929. This and (1518) are from manuscripts in the Pepys–Cockerell collection, now dispersed.

1516 —— *Letters and the second diary of Samuel Pepys*, ed. Robert G. Howarth. 1932. Diary deals with the Tangier voyage; see also (1521).

1517 —— *Memoires relating to the state of the royal navy of England, 1679–88*, ed. Joseph R. Tanner. Oxford, 1906. First published 1690; deals with administration.

1518 —— *Private correspondence and miscellaneous papers of Samuel Pepys, 1679–1703*, ed. Joseph R. Tanner. 1926, 2 vols.

1519 —— *Samuel Pepys's naval minutes*, ed. Joseph R. Tanner (Navy Records Society, LX). 1926. Miscellaneous notes for Pepys's projected history of the navy.

1520 —— *Shorthand letters of Samuel Pepys*, ed. Edwin Chappell. Cambridge, 1933. 57 letters, 1664–76, but mainly 1665.

1521 —— *The Tangier papers of Samuel Pepys*, ed. Edwin Chappell (Navy Records Society, LXXIII). 1935. Some excisions, but valuable. Cf. (1516).

1522 Sandwich, Edward Montagu, earl of. *The journal of Edward Montagu, first earl of Sandwich, admiral and general at sea, 1659–1665*, ed. Roger C. Anderson (Navy Records Society, LXIV). 1929. Of some importance for diplomatic as well as naval history.

1523 Tanner, Joseph R. (ed.). *A descriptive catalogue of the naval manuscripts in the Pepysian library at Magdalene College, Cambridge* (Navy Records Society, XXVI–XXVII, XXXVI, LVII). 1903–23. Calendars or reproduces much valuable material.

1524 Teonge, Henry. *The diary of Henry Teonge 1675–1679*, ed. George E. Manwaring. 1927. By a naval chaplain; deals with life at sea during two Mediterranean voyages.

1525 Thompson, Edward M. 'Correspondence of Admiral Herbert during the Revolution', *EHR*, 1 (July 1886), 522–36.

1526 —— *Correspondence of the family of Haddock, 1657–1719* (Camden Miscellany, VIII, new ser., XXXI). 1883. Of maritime and naval interest.

1527 Wheeler, Adam. *Iter bellicosum: Adam Wheeler, his account of 1685*, ed. Henry E. Malden (Camden Miscellany, XII, pp. 153–66, 3rd ser., XVIII). 1910. A narrative of a soldier who fought against Monmouth.

1528 Whittle, John. *An exact diary of the late expedition of...the Prince of Orange ...from...The Hague to...his arrival at Whitehall.* 1689. A daily record of events by an army chaplain.

1529 Yonge, James. *The journal of James Yonge, 1647–1721*, ed. Frederick N. L. Poynter. 1963. Yonge was a navy surgeon and medical writer.

2 Surveys

1530 Clowes, William L. *et al. The royal navy: a history.* 1897–1903, 7 vols. Vol. II covers 1603–1714. A standard work but out of date.

1531 Cole, David H. and E. C. Priestley. *An outline of British military history, 1660–1936.* 1936.

1532 Fortescue, John W. *A history of the British army.* 1899–1930, 13 vols. Vol. I goes to 1713. A standard work; best for operations, but deals briefly with administration.

1533 Hannay, David. *A short history of the royal navy, 1217–1815.* 1898–1909, 2 vols. Vol. I goes to 1688. Long the standard shorter survey; should be supplemented with Marcus (1540).

1534 La Roncière, Charles G. Bourel de. *Histoire de la marine française*, vols. IV–VI. Paris, 1920–32. More useful than Clowes (1530) in following the course of the wars.

1535 Lediard, Thomas. *The naval history of England in all its branches.* 1735, 2 vols. Goes from 1066 to 1734. Account by a miscellaneous writer.

1536 Lewis, Michael. *The history of the British navy.* 1957. A brief survey.

1537 —— *The navy of Britain: a historical portrait.* 1948. More extensive than (1536); topical arrangement.

1538 Lloyd, Christopher. *The nation and the navy: a history of naval life and policy.* 1954. A short survey.

1539 Lloyd, Ernest M. *A review of the history of infantry.* 1908.

1540 Marcus, Geoffrey J. *A naval history of England*, I, *The formative centuries* (Naval History of England Series, no. 1). 1961. Standard work. Goes down to the late eighteenth century.

1541 Scott, Sibbald D. *The British army: its origin, progress, and equipment.* 1868–80, 3 vols. Vol. III covers 1660–89; an antiquarian work.

3 Monographs

1542 Albion, Robert G. *Forests and sea power: the timber problem of the royal navy, 1652–1862* (Harvard Economic Studies, XXIX). Cambridge, Mass., 1926.

1543 Atkinson, Christopher T. *History of the Royal Dragoons, 1661–1934.* Glasgow, 1934. Valuable and readable.

1544 —— *Marlborough and the rise of the British army.* New York, 1921.

1545 Buchan, John. *The history of the Royal Scots Fusiliers, 1678–1918.* 1925.

1546 Chappell, Edwin. *Samuel Pepys as a naval administrator.* Cambridge, 1933. A lecture.

1547 Charnock, John. *An history of marine architecture.* 1800–2, 3 vols. Still the best general work on the subject, though actually a survey of naval history, and often in error. Contains many documents.

1548 Clode, Charles M. *The military forces of the crown: their administration and government.* 1869, 2 vols. Laws and administrative orders relating to the army; a standard work, but in need of revision.

1549 Colliber, Samuel. *Columna rostrata, or a critical history of the English sea affairs, wherein all the remarkable actions of the English nation at sea are described.* 1727. A valuable quasi-contemporary account of the Anglo-Dutch Wars, making use of Dutch and French sources.

1550 Cooper, Leonard. *British regular cavalry, 1644–1914.* 1965. A popular work.

1551 Corbett, Julian S. *England in the Mediterranean: a study of the rise and influence of British power within the Straits, 1603–1713.* 1904, 2 vols. A brilliant work, valuable for British naval strategy.

1552 Cowper, Lionel I. (ed.). *The King's Own: the story of a royal regiment.* Oxford, 1939, 2 vols. Vol. I covers 1680–1814.

1553 Crump, Helen J. *Colonial admiralty jurisdiction in the seventeenth century* (Royal Empire Society, Imperial Studies, no. 5). 1931.

1554 Curtis, C. D. *Sedgemoor and the Bloody Assize: a history and guide.* 1930. Popular.

1555 Davies, Godfrey. *The early history of the Coldstream Guards.* Oxford, 1924. Contains appendices of documents.

1556 Davies, John. *History of the Second Queen's Royal Regiment.* 1887–1906, 6 vols. Vol. I deals entirely with Tangier. The most detailed regimental history for the Stuart era.

1557 De Watteville, Herman G. *The British soldier: his daily life from Tudor to modern times.* 1954.

1558 Fisher, Godfrey, *Barbary legend: war, trade, and piracy in North Africa, 1415–1830.* Oxford, 1957.

1559 Green, Emanuel. *The march of William of Orange through Somerset.* 1892. Cf. Whittle (1528).

1560 Groves, John Percy. *History of the 21st Royal Scots Fusiliers...1678–1895.* Edinburgh, 1895.

1561 Hannay, David. *Naval courts martial.* Cambridge, 1914. Covers 1680–1815.

1562 Hogg, Oliver F. G. *The royal arsenal: its background, origin, and subsequent history.* 1963, 2 vols. Scholarly and detailed; the early chapters of vol. I are useful for the period.

1563 Hutchinson, J. Robert. *The press-gang afloat and ashore.* 1913. A scholarly work dealing with legal, administrative, and humanitarian aspects of the subject.

1564 Keevil, John Joyce. *Medicine and the navy, 1200–1900*, vol. II, *1649–1714.* Edinburgh, 1958.

1565 Knight, Henry R. *Historical records of the Buffs.* 1905. Covers 1572–1704.

1566 Lewis, Michael. *England's sea officers: the story of the naval profession.* 1939. Deals with such topics as entry, rank, promotion; of particular interest for the period.

1567 Lord, Walter F. *England and France in the Mediterranean, 1660–1830.* 1901.

1568 Mackinnon, Daniel. *Origin and services of the Coldstream Guards.* 1833, 2 vols. Has six chapters in vol. I on the period; valuable documents.

1569 Mahan, Alfred T. *The influence of sea power upon history, 1660–1783.* Boston, Mass., 1890. A classic; of great importance, but it must be used with caution for details of operations.

1570 Petzet, Heinrich Wiegand. *Tangier und die britische Reichsbildung* (Schriften den geschichtliche Abteilung im historischen Seminar der Friedrich-Wilhelms-Universität, no. 23). Berlin, 1938. Deals with Tangier's importance, 1682–4.

1571 Pool, Bernard. *Navy Board contracts, 1660–1832.* 1966.

1572 Powley, Edward B. *The English navy in the Revolution of 1688.* Cambridge, 1928. Makes extensive use of authorities.

1573 Richmond, Herbert W. *The navy as an instrument of policy, 1558–1727.* Cambridge, 1953. An important work; includes chapters on the Second and Third Dutch Wars.

1574 Routh, Enid M. G. *Tangier: England's lost Atlantic outpost, 1661–1684*. 1912. A first-rate account, listing authorities.

1575 Seymour, William W. *On active service*. 1939. Includes Tangier military operations, 1681–4.

1576 Tanner, Joseph R. *Samuel Pepys and the Royal Navy*. Cambridge, 1920. Lectures.

1577 Tedder, Arthur W. *The navy of the Restoration, from the death of Cromwell to the Treaty of Breda*. Cambridge, 1916. Deals with operations of the Second Dutch War.

1578 Turner, Ernest S. *Gallant gentlemen: a portrait of the British officer, 1600–1956*. 1956.

1579 Walton, Clifford E. *History of the British standing army, 1660–1700*. 1894. A standard work, but not so useful for operations as for other matters.

4 Biographies

1580 Ashley, Maurice. *Marlborough*. 1939. A brief life, covering the essential features. Credits Marlborough with less far-sighted statesmanship than does Churchill (1586).

1581 Bryant, Arthur. *Samuel Pepys: the man in the making*. Cambridge, 1933. The first volume of an interesting, scholarly trilogy. See (1582) and (1583).

1582 —— *Samuel Pepys: the saviour of the navy*. Cambridge, 1938. Vol. III of the trilogy.

1583 —— *Samuel Pepys: the years of peril*. Cambridge, 1935. Vol. II of the trilogy.

1584 Campbell, John. *Lives of the admirals and other eminent British seamen*. 1812–17, 8 vols. First published 1742–4. Campbell's *Naval history of Great Britain*, 1818, 8 vols., is virtually another edition of this work.

1585 Charnock, John. *Biographia navalis, or impartial memoirs of the lives and characters of officers of the navy*. 1794–8, 6 vols. Goes from 1660 to date of publication. Long a standard work, but often erroneous.

1586 Churchill, Winston L. S. *Marlborough, his life and times*. 1933–8, 6 vols. A monumental biography; apologetic, but based on extensive research.

1587 Coxe, William. *Memoirs of John, duke of Marlborough*. 1818–19, 3 vols. Still useful for political affairs; incorporates important primary materials.

1588 Dyer, Florence E. *The life of Admiral Sir John Narbrough*. 1931.

1589 Fitzroy, Almeric W. *Henry, duke of Grafton, 1663–1690*. 1921. Of some military and naval interest.

1590 Harris, Frank R. *The life of Edward Mountagu, K.G., first earl of Sandwich (1625–1672)*. 1912, 2 vols. Uses family papers; important for diplomatic as well as naval affairs.

1591 Leake, Stephen Martin. *Life of Captain Stephen Martin, 1666–1740*, ed. Clements R. Markham (Navy Records Society, V). 1895. By his son; first published 1750. Appendix contains useful information on the state of the navy, 1688–98, lists of naval vessels, etc.

1592 —— *The life of Sir John Leake, Rear-Admiral of Great Britain*, ed. Geoffrey A. R. Callender (Navy Records Society, LII–LIII). 1920. Leake's service at sea covers 1673–1712. A panegyric by his nephew.

1593 Lediard, Thomas. *The life of John, duke of Marlborough*. 1736, 3 vols. A detailed work, containing many documents, all favourable to Marlborough. Not entirely superseded.

1594 Markham, Clements R. *Life of Robert Fairfax of Steeton, vice-admiral, alderman, and member for York...1666–1725*. 1885. Includes some letters.

1595 Penn, Granville. *Memorials of...Sir William Penn, Admiral and General of the Fleet, 1644 to 1670*. 1833, 2 vols. Important; contains many documents.

1596 Smith, John (ed.). *The life, journals, and correspondence of Samuel Pepys... including a narrative of his voyage to Tangier*. 1841, 2 vols. Includes letters to, as well as from, Pepys.

1597 Wolseley, Garnet Joseph, Viscount. *The life of John Churchill, duke of Marlborough, to the accession of Queen Anne*. 1894, 2 vols. Favourable; not entirely superseded.

5 Articles

1598 Atkinson, Christopher T. 'Charles II's regiments in France, 1672–1678', *JSAHR*, **24** (1946), in three parts.

1599 —— 'Two hundred and fifty years ago: James II and his army', *JSAHR*, **14** (Spring 1935), 1–11.

1600 Boxer, Charles R. 'Public opinion and the second Anglo-Dutch war, 1664–1667', *Hist. T.*, **16** (Sept. 1966), 618–26.

1601 —— 'The Tromps and the Anglo-Dutch wars, 1652–1674', *Hist. T.*, **3** (Dec. 1953), 836–45.

1602 Callender, Geoffrey A. R. 'Sir John Mennes', *MM*, **26** (July 1940), 276–85. Discusses Pepys's evaluation of Mennes, controller of the navy.

1603 Coox, Alvin D. 'The Dutch invasion of England, 1667', *Military Affairs*, **13** (Winter 1949), 223–33.

1604 Cowburn, P. M. 'Christopher Gunman and the wreck of the Gloucester', *MM*, **42** (May, Aug. 1956), 113–26, 219–29. The wreck (1682) was believed to have been deliberately arranged in order to kill the duke of York.

1605 Ehrman, John P. W. 'The official papers transferred by Pepys to the admiralty by 12 July 1689', *MM*, **34** (Oct. 1948), 255–70. A list of books and papers surrendered to Pepys's successor as Secretary of the Admiralty.

1606 —— 'Pepys's organization and the naval mobilizations of 1688', *MM*, **35** (July 1949), 203–39.

1607 Fielding, Xan. 'A seventeenth-century Atlantic outpost: the British occupation of Tangier', *Hist. T.*, **5** (July 1955), 463–72.

1608 Firth, Charles H. 'Royalist and Cromwellian armies in Flanders, 1657–1662', *TRHS*, new ser., **17** (1903), 67–119.

1609 Hardacre, Paul H. 'The English contingent in Portugal, 1662–1668', *JSAHR*, **38** (Sept. 1960), 112–25.

1610 James, G. F. and J. J. Sutherland Shaw. 'Admiralty administration and personnel, 1619–1714', *BIHR*, **14** (June 1936), 10–24; (Feb. 1937), 166–83. Lists important admiralty officials.

1611 Kitching, G. C. 'The loss and recapture of St. Helena, 1673', *MM*, **36** (Jan. 1950), 58–68. Appendix provides original material.

1612 McCully, Bruce T. 'From the North Riding to Morocco: the early years of Governor Francis Nicholson, 1655–1686', *William and Mary Quarterly*, 3rd ser., **19** (Oct. 1962), 534–56. Of some interest for his services in Tangier in the 1680s.

1613 McGuffie, Tom H. 'The last battle on English soil: Sedgemoor, 1685', *Hist. T.*, **5** (Jan. 1955), 54–60. Based on contemporary diaries.

1614 Murray, Oswyn. 'Papers on the history of the admiralty', *MM*, **23–4** (1937–8). Seven articles, as follows: vol. **23** (1937): pt. 1, Jan., pp. 13–35; pt. 2, Apr., pp. 129–47; pt. 3, July, pp. 316–31; vol. **24** (1938): pt. 4, Jan., pp. 101–8; pt. 5, Apr., pp. 204–25; pt. 6, July, pp. 329–52; pt. 7, Oct., pp. 458–78. Published posthumously; incomplete, but still the standard survey.

1615 Pool, Bernard. 'Samuel Pepys and navy contracts', *Hist. T.*, **13** (Sept. 1963), 633–41. Emphasizes Pepys's effectiveness. See also (1571).

1616 Reddaway, Thomas F. 'Sir Christopher Wren's navy office', *BIHR*, **30** (Nov. 1957), 175–88. Deals with facilities after the Great Fire.

1617 Robinson, Gregory. 'Admiralty and naval affairs, May 1660 to March 1674', *MM*, **36** (Jan. 1950), 12–40. Description of a folio volume among the papers of the Privy Council.

1618 Rose, John Holland. 'The influence of James II on the navy', *Fighting Forces*, **1** (1924), 211–21.

1619 Schoenfeld, Maxwell P. 'The Restoration seaman and his wages', *American Neptune*, **25** (Oct. 1965), 278–87. Deals with delays and dishonesty involved.

1620 Schoolcraft, Henry L. 'The capture of New Amsterdam', *EHR*, **22** (Oct. 1907), 674–93.

1621 Shaw, J. J. Sutherland. 'The commission of sick and wounded and prisoners, 1664–67', *MM*, **25** (July 1939), 306–27.

1622 Shelley, Roland J. A. 'The division of the English fleet in 1666', *MM*, **25** (Apr. 1939), 178–96.

1623 Swaine, Stephen A. 'English acquisition and loss of Dunkirk', *TRHS*, new ser., **1** (1883), 93–118.

1624 Sydenham, Michael J. 'The anxieties of an admiral: Lord Dartmouth and the Revolution of 1688', *Hist. T.*, **12** (Oct. 1962), 714–20. Discusses Dartmouth's fence-sitting.

1625 Tanner, Joseph R. 'The administration of the navy from the Restoration to the Revolution', *EHR*, **12** (Jan., Oct. 1897), 17–66, 679–710; **13** (Jan. 1898), 26–54; **14** (Jan. 1899), 47–70; **15** (Apr. 1899), 261–87. Based on manuscripts in Pepysian Library, Magdalene College, Cambridge; later expanded to form general introduction to (1523).

1626 —— 'Naval preparations of James II in 1688', *EHR*, **8** (Apr. 1893), 272–83.

1627 —— 'Samuel Pepys and the Trinity House', *EHR*, **44** (Oct. 1929), 573–87.

1628 —— 'Samuel Pepys as a naval official' in *Naval and military essays* (Cambridge Naval and Military Series, ed. Julian S. Corbett and Henry J. Edwards), Cambridge, 1914, pp. 55–82.

1629 —— and Christopher T. Atkinson. 'The Anglo-Dutch Wars' in *CMH*, v, chap. 8. Tanner deals with naval administration, Atkinson with the Second and Third Dutch Wars.

1630 Taylor, A. H. 'Galleon into ship of the line', *MM*, **44** (Nov. 1958), 267–85; **45** (Feb., May 1959), 14–24, 100–14.

1631 Vale, V. 'Clarendon, Coventry, and the sale of naval offices, 1660–8', *Camb. Hist. J.*, **12** (no. 2, 1956), 107–25.

1632 Wilson, Charles H. 'Who captured New Amsterdam?', *EHR*, **72** (July 1957), 469–74. Opposes idea that Capt. Robert Holmes was responsible.

XII RELIGIOUS HISTORY

1 Printed Sources

1633 Barrow, Isaac. *The theological works of Isaac Barrow*, ed. Alexander Napier. Cambridge, 1859, 9 vols. The standard edition.

1634 Barwick, Peter. *The life of the reverend John Barwick*, 1724. John Barwick (d. 1664) was dean of Durham and St Paul's. Peter Barwick was his brother.

1635 Baxter, Richard. *The autobiography of Richard Baxter*, ed. J. M. Lloyd Thomas. 1925. An abbreviation of *Reliquiae Baxterianae*.

1636 —— *The practical works of...Mr. Richard Baxter*, ed. William Orme. 1830, 23 vols. Includes a life.

1637 —— *Reliquiae Baxterianae, or Mr. Richard Baxter's narrative of the most memorable passages of his life and times*, ed. Matthew Sylvester. 1696. Very important. For abbreviated editions, see (1635) and Calamy (1641). Powicke (1884) serves to supplement it.

1638 Bowler, Hugh (ed.). *London sessions records, 1605–1685* (Catholic Record Society, XXXIV). 1934. Records of courts of criminal jurisdiction relating to Catholics; mostly in Latin.

1639 Bunyan, John. *Grace abounding to the chief of sinners, and, The Pilgrim's progress*, ed. Roger Sharrock. 1966. The former is Bunyan's autobiography; the latter the religious classic of the century.

1640 —— *The works of John Bunyan*, ed. George Offor. Glasgow, 1850–3, 3 vols.

1641 Calamy, Edmund. *An abridgement of Mr. Baxter's history of his life and times, with an account of many...ministers who were ejected after the Restoration.* 1702. Nearly half is devoted to the ejected ministers.

1642 —— *A continuation of the account of the ministers...who were ejected and silenced after the Restoration in 1660, by or before the Act for Uniformity.* 1727, 2 vols. Primarily emendations and replies to critics.

1643 —— *An historical account of my own life, with some reflections on the times I have lived in, 1671–1731*, ed. John T. Rutt. 1829, 2 vols.

1644 Cardwell, Edward (ed.). *Documentary annals of the reformed Church of England: being a collection of injunctions, declarations, orders, articles of inquiry, etc., from the year 1546 to the year 1716.* Oxford, 1844, 2 vols.

1645 —— *Enchiridion theologicum anti-Romanum: tracts on the points at issue between the churches of England and Rome.* Oxford, 1836–7, 3 vols. Includes writings of Taylor, Barrow, and others, written about 1686.

1646 —— *A history of the conferences and other proceedings connected with the revision of the Book of Common Prayer, from the year 1558 to the year 1690.* Oxford, 1849. A documentary history of the prayer book. The commentary is superseded by Procter and Frere (1810).

1647 —— *Synodalia: a collection of articles of religion, canons, and proceedings of convocations in the province of Canterbury from the year 1547 to the year 1717.* Oxford, 1842, 2 vols.

1648 Cartwright, Thomas. *The diary of Dr. Thomas Cartwright, bishop of Chester,* ed. Joseph Hunter (Camden Society, old ser., XXII). 1843. Useful for the background of the Revolution.

1649 Clarke, Samuel. *The lives of sundry eminent persons of this later age.* 1683. Characters, rather than biographies, of pious men and women, mostly divines.

1650 *A collection of letters and other writings relating to the horrid popish plot printed from originals in the hands of Sir George Treby.* 1681. Printed by order of the House of Commons. Treby was chairman of a committee of investigation.

1651 *A collection of the substance of several speeches and debates made in the House of Commons relating to the horrid popish plot.* 1681.

1652 Comber, Thomas. *The autobiographies and letters of Thomas Comber, sometime precentor of York and dean of Durham,* ed. Charles E. Whiting (Surtees Society, CLVI–CLVII). Durham, 1946–7.

1653 Compton, Henry. *Episcopalia, or letters of the right reverend...Henry lord bishop of London, to the clergy of his diocese,* ed. Sidney W. Cornish. Oxford, 1842. Includes a memoir; first published in 1686.

1654 Cope, Jackson I. '"The Cupri-cosmits": Glanvill on latitudinarian anti-enthusiasm', *HLQ*, **17** (May 1954), 269–86. Presents unpublished version of one of Joseph Glanvill's essays.

1655 Cosin, John. *The correspondence of John Cosin, D.D., lord bishop of Durham, together with other papers illustrative of his life and times,* pt. II, ed. George Ornsby (Surtees Society, LV). Durham, 1872. Covers 1660–71.

1656 Cuming, Geoffrey J. (ed.). *The Durham Book: being the first draft of the revision of the Book of Common Prayer in 1661.* 1961.

1657 Davis, Joseph (ed.). *A digest of legislative enactments relating to the Society of Friends, commonly called Quakers, in England.* Bristol, 1820.

1658 Duckett, George (ed.). *Penal laws and the Test Act: questions touching their repeal propounded in 1687–88 by James II.* 1882–3, 2 vols. Contains replies to three questions about the repeal of the Test Act, etc.

1659 Feiling, Keith G. 'A letter of Clarendon during the elections of 1661', *EHR*, **42** (July 1927), 407–8. Shows opposition to Presbyterians.

1660 Fox, George. *The journal of George Fox,* ed. John L. Nickalls. New York, 1952. Introduction by Geoffrey F. Nuttall; epilogue by Henry J. Cadbury. The standard edition.

1661 —— *A journal or historical account of the life of George Fox,* ed. Norman Penney. Cambridge, 1911, 2 vols. First to give the original manuscript *verbatim.* For *addenda* and *corrigenda,* see *JFHS*, **9–21** (1912–24).

1662 —— *The short journal and itinerary journals of George Fox,* ed. Norman Penney. Cambridge, 1925.

1663 —— *The works of George Fox.* Philadelphia, 1831, 8 vols. The fullest collection.

1664 Gee, Henry and William J. Hardy (eds.). *Documents illustrative of English church history.* 1896.

1665 Gibson, Edmund (ed.). *Codex juris ecclesiastici anglicani.* Oxford, 1761, 2 vols. A standard work. English abridgements are provided for Latin documents.

1666 Goodwin, Thomas. *The works of Thomas Goodwin.* Edinburgh, 1861–6, 12 vols. Writings of a prominent Independent divine; includes memoir by R. Halley.

1667 Gould, George (ed.). *Documents relating to the settlement of the Church of England by the Act of Uniformity of 1662.* 1862.

1668 Gutch, John (ed.). *Collectanea curiosa.* 1781, 2 vols. A miscellaneous selection of the papers of Archbishop Sancroft; useful for the reign of James II.

1669 Hale, Matthew. *The works, moral and religious, of Sir Matthew Hale,* ed. Thomas Thirlwall. 1805, 2 vols. Contains his life by Burnet.

1670 Hazlitt, William C. (ed.). *Fugitive tracts written in verse which illustrate the condition of religious and political feeling in England and the state of society there during two centuries. Second Series, 1600–1700.* 1875, 2 vols.

1671 Henry, Philip. *The diaries and letters of Philip Henry of Broad Oak, Flintshire,* ed. Matthew H. Lee. 1882. Written by a nonconformist divine; diary covers 1657–96, with gaps.

1672 Heywood, Oliver. *The rev. Oliver Heywood, B.A., 1630–1702: his autobiography, diaries, anecdote and event books,* ed. J. Horsfall Turner. Brighouse, 1881, 4 vols. Cf. (1673).

1673 —— *The whole works of the rev. Oliver Heywood.* Idle, 1825–7, 5 vols. Writings of a prominent nonconformist divine. Includes biographical memoir.

1674 Howard, Philip. 'Letters of Philip Howard, Fr. Thomas, O.P., in religion, later Cardinal Norfolk, 1645–1694', ed. Bede Jarrett (Catholic Record Society, XXV, pp. 1–94). 1925. 61 letters, 1660–90.

1675 James II. *Papers of devotion of James II,* ed. Godfrey Davies, Oxford, 1925. Provides little new historical information, but has some psychological interest.

1676 Jolly, Thomas. *The note book of the rev. Thomas Jolly, A.D. 1671–1693,* ed. Henry Fishwick (Chetham Society, new ser., XXXIII). Manchester, 1895. Spiritual reflections of a nonconformist.

1677 Josselin, Ralph. *The diary of the rev. Ralph Josselin, 1616–1683,* ed. E. Hockliffe (Camden Society, 3rd ser., XV). 1908. Short, occasional entries, illustrating the life of the rural clergy.

1678 Ken, Thomas. *The works of...Thomas Ken,* ed. W. Hawkins. 1721, 4 vols.

1679 Kidder, Richard. *The life of Richard Kidder, D.D., bishop of Bath and Wells,* ed. Amy E. Robinson (Somerset Record Society, XXXVII). 1924. Autobiography.

1680 Lake, Edward. *Diary of Dr. Edward Lake, archdeacon and prebendary of Exeter, chaplain and tutor to the princesses Mary and Anne...in the years 1677–78,* ed. George P. Elliott (Camden Miscellany, I, old ser., XLIX). 1847. An interesting brief diary.

1681 Le Neve, John. *Fasti ecclesiae anglicanae,* ed. Thomas D. Hardy. Oxford, 1854, 3 vols. First published 1716; based mostly on original research. A useful calendar of the principal ecclesiastical dignitaries.

1682 L'Estrange, Roger. *A brief history of the times.* 1687–8, 3 pts. A Tory history of the Popish Plot; concerned particularly with Godfrey.

1683 McGlothlin, William J. (ed.). *Baptist confessions of faith.* Philadelphia, 1911. Continental, English and American.

1684 Martindale, Adam. *The life of Adam Martindale, written by himself,* ed. Richard Parkinson (Chetham Society, IV). Manchester, 1845. Life of a Presbyterian divine.

1685 Mintz, Samuel I. 'Hobbes on the law of heresy: a new manuscript', *JHI,* **29** (July–Sept. 1968), 409–14. Prints unpublished manuscript in full.

1686 Moorman, John R. H. (ed.). *The curate of souls: being a collection of writings on the nature and work of a priest...1661–1760.* 1958.

1687 More, Paul E. and Frank L. Cross. *Anglicanism: the thought and practice of the Church of England, illustrated from the religious literature of the seventeenth century.* 1935. Source materials, topically arranged; considerable from the period.

1688 Mullett, Charles F. 'A letter on the Clarendon code', *HLQ,* **6** (Feb. 1943), 221–4. From Frances, widow of Sir John Hobart.

1689 Naish, Thomas. *The diary of Thomas Naish*, ed. M. Doreen Slatter (Wiltshire Archaeological and Natural History Society, XX). Devizes, 1965. Diary of the sub-dean of Salisbury, 1669–1728.

1690 Newcome, Henry. *The autobiography of Henry Newcome*, ed. Richard Parkinson (Chetham Society, XXVI–XXVII). Manchester, 1852. Life of a Lancashire minister; an abstract of a lost diary. Covers *c.* 1627–95.

1691 —— *The diary of the rev. Henry Newcome, from September 30, 1661, to September 29, 1663*, ed. Thomas Heywood (Chetham Society, XVIII). Manchester, 1849. Diary of a nonconformist clergyman.

1692 Newton, Isaac. *Sir Isaac Newton: theological manuscripts*, ed. Herbert McLachlan. Liverpool, 1950. A selection.

1693 Nye, Stephen. *Brief history of the Unitarians, called also Socinians*. 1687. Essentially an exposition of Unitarian belief, in the form of letters.

1694 Oates, Titus. *A true narrative of the horrid plot and conspiracy...against... his sacred Majesty, the government, and the Protestant religion*. 1679. Printed by order of Parliament.

1695 Owen, John. *The works of John Owen, D.D.*, ed. William H. Goold. 1850–5, 24 vols. With a life by A. Thompson.

1696 Patrick, Simon. *A brief account of the new sect of latitude-men*. ed. Thomas A. Birrell (Augustan Reprint Society, Publication no. 100; facsimile ed.). Los Angeles, 1963. First published in 1662.

1697 —— *The works of Symon Patrick, D.D., sometime bishop of Ely*, ed. Alexander Taylor. Oxford, 1858, 9 vols. Includes his autobiography, IX, 407–569. Well annotated.

1698 Pearson, John. *An exposition of the creed*. 1659. Many subsequent editions; the best by Temple Chevallier, rev. by Robert Sinker, Cambridge, 1882. A monumental work.

1699 —— *The minor theological works of John Pearson*, ed. Edward Churton. Oxford, 1844, 2 vols.

1700 Penn, William. *A collection of the works of William Penn*, ed. Joseph Besse. 1726, 2 vols. There are later editions; this one contains a life by Besse.

1701 Penney, Norman (ed.). *Extracts from state papers relating to Friends* (Friends' Historical Society). 1913.

1702 —— '*The first publishers of truth*', *being early records* (*now first printed*) *of the introduction of Quakerism into the counties of England and Wales*. 1907.

1703 Petti, Anthony G. (ed.). *Recusant documents from the Ellesmere manuscripts* (Catholic Record Society, LX). 1968.

1704 Pinney, John. *Letters of John Pinney, 1679–99*, ed. Geoffrey F. Nuttall. 1939. Written by a puritan minister, ejected after the Restoration.

1705 Pollen, John H. (ed.). *Memoir of Edmund Mathew...at St. Omers College, 1667* (Catholic Record Society, III, 59–81). 1906. Perhaps the earliest account of a Catholic boy of his years.

1706 Pomfret, John E. 'Robert Barclay and James II: Barclay's "Vindication", 1689', *Bulletin of the Friends' Historical Association*, **42** (Spring 1953), 33–40. Reprints Barclay's apology for his close relations with James II, with introduction.

1707 Pope, Walter. *The life of Seth* [*Ward*], *lord bishop of Salisbury*, ed. John B. Bamborough. Oxford, 1961. First published in 1697. Bamborough provides a biographical and critical introduction.

1708 Sharp, John. *The works of the most rev. Dr. John Sharpe*. 1754, 7 vols.

1709 Simon, Irène (ed.). *Three Restoration divines, Barrow, South, Tillotson: selected sermons*, I (Bibliothèque de la Faculté de Philosophie et Lettres de l'Université de Liège, CLXXXI). Paris, 1967. Contains sermons by Barrow and lengthy introduction.

1710 South, Robert. *Sermons preached upon several occasions*. Oxford, 1823, 7 vols.

1711 Stillingfleet, Edward. *The works of...Dr. Edward Stillingfleet*. 1707–10, 6 vols. Includes life by Richard Bentley.

1712 Taylor, Jeremy. *The whole works of the right rev. Jeremy Taylor...with a life of the author and a critical examination of his writings by Reginald Heber*. Rev. and corrected ed., Charles P. Eden, 1850–4, 10 vols. For his life, see also May (1875).

1713 Thorndike, Herbert. *The theological works of...Herbert Thorndike* (Library of Anglo-Catholic Theology). Oxford, 1844–56, 6 vols.

1714 Tillotson, John. *The works of the most reverend Dr. John Tillotson*, ed. Thomas Birch. 1752, 3 vols. The best edition; includes life by Birch.

1715 Turner, G. Lyon (ed.). *Original records of early nonconformity.* 1911, 3 vols. Vols. I and II provide documents relating to the persecution of nonconformists during the first half of Charles II's reign: vol. III is a commentary. See Nuttall (1949).

1716 Vernon, George. *The life of...Dr. Peter Heylyn.* 1682. Heylyn was a writer on religious subjects, and served as chaplain to Charles I and Charles II.

1717 Walker, Williston (ed.). *The creeds and platforms of Congregationalism.* New York, 1893.

1718 Ward, John. *Diary of the rev. John Ward, vicar of Stratford-upon-Avon*, ed. Charles Severn. 1839. Extracts from commonplace books; of some medical interest.

1719 Warner, John. *The history of English persecution of Catholics and the Presbyterian Plot*, pts. 1 and 2, ed. Thomas A. Birrell (Catholic Record Society, XLVII–XLVIII). Leeds, 1953–5. In Latin, with translation. Warner has been called the chief propagandist for the English Catholics at the time of the Popish Plot.

1720 Whitehead, George. *The Christian progress of that ancient servant and minister of Jesus Christ, George Whitehead.* 1725. Largely repr. in Samuel Tuke, *Memoirs of George Whitehead.* York, 1830, 2 vols.

1721 Whitley, William T. (ed.). *Minutes of the general assembly of the general Baptist churches in England, with kindred records.* 1909–10, 2 vols. Vol. I covers 1654–1728.

1722 Wilkins, David (ed.). *Concilia Magnae Britanniae et Hiberniae.* 1737, 4 vols. Extant records of convocations, 446–1717.

1723 Woodcock, Thomas. *Extracts from the papers of Thomas Woodcock, ob. 1695*, ed. George Charles Moore Smith (Camden Miscellany, XI, 3rd. ser., XIII), 49–89. 1907. Bits and pieces, mostly referring to persons, particularly clergymen, by an ejected minister.

2 Surveys

1724 Butler, Charles. *Historical memoirs respecting the English, Irish, and Scottish Catholics from the Reformation to the present time.* 1819–21, 4 vols. For a corrective, see Milner (1876).

1725 Carpenter, Spencer C. *The church in England, 597–1688.* 1954.

1726 Clark, Henry W. *History of English nonconformity from Wiclif to the close of the ninteenth century.* 1911–13, 2 vols. From a nonconformist point of view.

1727 Collier, Jeremy. *An ecclesiastical history of Great Britain from the first planting of Christianity to the end of the reign of King Charles II*, ed. Thomas Lathbury. 1852, 9 vols. First published 1708–14.

1728 Cragg, Gerald R. *The church and the age of reason, 1648–1789.* 1960 (Pelican History of the Church, vol. IV). Two useful chapters on the period.

1729 Crosby, Thomas. *The history of the English Baptists from the Reformation to the beginning of the reign of King George I.* 1738–40, 4 vols. An inferior work, but based on manuscript material at Dr Williams's Library and elsewhere.

1730 Dale, Robert W. *History of English Congregationalism*, ed. Alfred W. W. Dale. 1907. The best account, though not a work of profound research.

1731 Dodd, Charles (pseud. for Hugh Tootell). *The church history of England from ...1500 to...1688.* Brussels, 1737–42, 3 vols. The chief work for Catholic biography before Gillow (1858).

1732 Drysdale, Alexander H. *History of the Presbyterians in England: their rise, decline, and revival.* 1889. The best account.

1733 Emmott, Elizabeth B. *A short history of Quakerism.* 1923. Goes to 1725.

1734 Flanagan, Thomas. *History of the Church in England from the earliest period to the re-establishment of the hierarchy in 1850.* 1857, 2 vols. A history of the Roman Catholic church.

1735 Hutton, William H. *The English church from the accession of Charles I to the death of Anne, 1625–1714* (vol. VI of the *History of the English church*, ed. William R. W. Stephens and William Hunt). 1903. Anglican point of view.

1736 Hyamson, Albert M. *A history of the Jews in England.* 2nd ed., rev., 1928.

1737 Ivimey, Joseph. *A history of the English Baptists, including an investigation of the history of baptism in England.* 1811–30, 4 vols. Extends to 1820; inaccurate in detail.

1738 Jones, Robert Tudur. *Congregationalism in England, 1662–1962.* 1962.

1739 Mathew, David. *Catholicism in England, 1535–1935.* 2nd ed., 1948. A good, readable account.

1740 Moorman, John R. H. *A history of the church in England.* 2nd ed., 1967. A very good survey.

1741 Mott, Frederick B. *A short Unitarian history.* 1906.

1742 Neal, Daniel. *The history of the puritans or Protestant nonconformists from the Reformation to the Revolution*, ed. Joshua Toulmin. Bath, 1793–7, 5 vols. First published 1732–8; still valuable.

1743 Perry, George G. *The history of the Church of England from the death of Elizabeth to the present time.* 1861–4, 3 vols.

1744 Roth, Cecil. *A history of the Jews in England.* Oxford, 1941. A good textbook, with references to authorities.

1745 Routley, Erik. *English religious dissent.* Cambridge, 1960. Highly sympathetic, but a good introduction.

1746 Russell, Elbert. *The history of Quakerism.* New York, 1942.

1747 Sewel, Willem. *The history of the rise, increase, and progress of the Christian people called Quakers.* 1722. First published in Dutch, Amsterdam, 1717. Written to correct Gerard Croese, *General history of the Quakers* (1696).

1748 Stoughton, John. *History of religion in England from the opening of the Long Parliament to 1850.* 1901, 8 vols. Diffuse and antiquated, but useful in view of the absence of other works.

1749 Underwood, Alfred C. *A history of the English Baptists.* 1947. The best account.

1750 Vaughan, Robert. *The history of England.* 1840. Covers 1603–88. Chiefly religious history from the nonconformist point of view, as is his *Memorials of the Stuart dynasty*, 1831, 2 vols.

1751 Waddington, John. *Congregational history.* 1869–80, 5 vols. Vol. II covers 1567–1700.

1752 Wakeman, Henry O. *An introduction to the history of the Church of England from the earliest times to the present day.* 1896. Anglican point of view.

1753 Wand, John W. C. *A history of the modern church from 1500 to the present day.* 7th ed., 1952.

1754 Watkin, Edward I. *Roman Catholicism in England from the Reformation to 1950.* Oxford, 1957. A sound, readable survey.

1755 Whitley, William T. *History of British Baptists.* 2nd ed., 1932.

1756 Wilbur, Earl M. *A history of Unitarianism*, II, *In Transylvania, England, and America.* Cambridge, Mass., 1952.

1757 Wilkinson, John T. *1662 and after: three centuries of English nonconformity.* 1962. A scholarly work, with several chapters on the period.

3 Monographs

1758 Abernathy, George R., Jr. *The English Presbyterians and the Stuart restoration, 1648–1663* (American Philosophical Society, Transactions, new ser., LV, pt. 2). Philadelphia, 1965. Seeks to evaluate the influence of the Presbyterians and to explain their failure to implement their programme.

1759 Addleshaw, George W. O. *The high church tradition: a study in the liturgical thought of the seventeenth century.* 1941.

1760 Aveling, Hugh. *The Catholic recusants of the West Riding of Yorkshire, 1558–1790.* Leeds, 1963. This and the following studies by Aveling are valuable contributions to the history of Roman Catholicism.

1761 —— *Northern Catholics: the Catholic recusants of the North Riding of Yorkshire, 1558–1790.* 1966.

1762 Aveling, Hugh. *Post-Reformation Catholicism in East Yorkshire, 1558–1790* (East Yorkshire Local History Society, no. 11). York, 1960.

1763 Babington, Churchill. *Mr. Macaulay's character of the clergy in the latter part of the seventeenth century considered*. Cambridge, 1849. Corrects Macaulay to some extent; for other criticisms see Ditchfield (1074) and Churchill (1586).

1764 Bate, Frank. *The Declaration of Indulgence, 1672: a study in the rise of organised dissent*. 1908.

1765 Berington, Joseph. *History of the decline and fall of the Roman Catholic religion in England...from the reign of Elizabeth to the present*. 1813. Roman Catholic point of view; considerable emphasis on the structure of the church.

1766 Birrell, Thomas A. *Catholic allegiance and the Popish Plot: a study of some Catholic writers of the Restoration period*. Nijmegen. 1950.

1767 Bonet-Maury, Gaston. *Early sources of English Unitarian Christianity*. 1884. Has valuable introductory survey by J. Martineau, and appendix of documents.

1768 Bosher, Robert S. *The making of the Restoration settlement: the influence of the Laudians, 1649–1662*. New York, 1951.

1769 Boyer, Richard E. *English Declarations of Indulgence, 1687 and 1688*. The Hague, 1968. Deals rather generally with the reign of James II, despite title; sympathetic to James.

1770 Brady, William M. *The episcopal succession in England, Scotland, and Ireland, A.D. 1400–1875*. Rome, 1876–7, 3 vols. Important. Vol. III was separately reissued as *Annals of the Catholic hierarchy in England and Scotland, A.D. 1585–1876*, 1883.

1771 Brailsford, Mabel R. *Quaker women, 1650–90*. 1915. A readable account.

1772 Braithwaite, William C. *The second period of Quakerism*, 2nd ed. by Henry J. Cadbury. Cambridge, 1961. Covers 1660–1725, continuing his *Beginnings of Quakerism* (1912). The best account.

1773 Burn, John S. *The history of the French, Walloon, Dutch, and other foreign Protestant refugees settled in England, from the reign of Henry VIII to the revocation of the Edict of Nantes*. 1846.

1774 Carrel, Armand. *History of the counter-revolution in England for the re-establishment of popery under Charles II and James II*. 1846. First published in Paris (1827).

1775 Courson, Barbara F. M. de. *La persécution des Catholiques en Angleterre: un complot sous Charles II*. Paris, 1898. An English translation by Mrs R. Raymond-Barker appeared in 1899.

1776 Cragg, Gerald R. *From puritanism to the age of reason: a study of changes in religious thought within the Church of England, 1660 to 1700*. Cambridge, 1950.

1777 —— *Puritanism in the period of the great persecution, 1660–88*. Cambridge, 1957. The subject embraces Presbyterians, Independents, Baptists, and Quakers.

1778 Crinò, Anna Maria. *Il popish plot: nelle relazioni inedite dei residenti granducali alla corte di Londra, 1678–81*. Rome, 1954. Draws on despatches of the Grand Duke of Tuscany's residents in London.

1779 Foley, Henry. *Records of the English province of the Society of Jesus...in the sixteenth and seventeenth centuries*. 1875–83, 7 vols. The documents are valuable.

1780 George, Edward A. *Seventeenth-century men of latitude: forerunners of the new theology*. 1909.

1781 Green, Vivian H. H. *Religion at Oxford and Cambridge*. 1964. See chap. VI, 'Religion in the universities after the Restoration'.

1782 Griffiths, Olive M. *Religion and learning: a study in English Presbyterian thought from the Bartholomew ejections, 1662, to the foundation of the Unitarian movement*. Cambridge, 1955.

1783 Guilday, Peter K. *The English Catholic refugees on the continent*. 1914. Deals with English convents and colleges in the Low Countries; strong Catholic point of view.

1784 Gwatkin, Henry M. *Church and state in England to the death of Queen Anne*. 1917. Posthumous, lacking author's final revision.

1785 Hay, Malcolm V. *The Jesuits and the Popish Plot.* 1934. Maintains that John Sergeant, Roman Catholic controversialist, was associated with Oates in revealing the plot.

1786 Hemphill, Basil. *The early vicars apostolic of England, 1685–1700.* 1954.

1787 Henson, Herbert H. *The relation of the Church of England to the other reformed churches.* Edinburgh, 1911. Lecture; emphasis on seventeenth century.

1788 Hodgkin, Lucy V. *Quaker saint of Cornwall: Loveday Hambly and her guests.* 1927. Difficulties and dangers faced by early Quakers.

1789 Hunt, John. *Religious thought in England from the Reformation to the end of the last century: a contribution to the history of theology.* 1870–3, 3 vols.

1790 Kellaway, Charles William. *The New England Company, 1649–1776: missionary society to the American Indians.* 1961. Four chapters on Restoration period.

1791 Knox, Ronald A. *Enthusiasm: a chapter in the history of religion, with special reference to the seventeenth and eighteenth centuries.* Oxford, 1950. See chap. VIII, 'George Fox and seventeenth-century Protestantism'.

1792 Lathbury, Thomas. *A history of the convocation of the Church of England.* 1842. Goes to 1742.

1793 Legg, John Wickham. *English church life from the Restoration to the Tractarian movement.* 1914. Anglican point of view; valuable.

1794 Lindsey, Theophilus. *An historical view of the state of Unitarian doctrine and worship from the Reformation to our own times.* 1783. By an Anglican cleric, converted to Unitarianism.

1795 Luckock, Herbert M. *The bishops in the Tower: a record of stirring events affecting the church and nonconformists from the Restoration to the Revolution.* 1887. A series of lectures.

1796 McAdoo, Henry R. *The spirit of Anglicanism: a survey of Anglican theological method in the seventeenth century.* 1965. Lectures.

1797 McLachlan, Herbert. *The religious opinions of Milton, Locke, and Newton* (University of Manchester Publications, Theological ser., no. 6). Manchester, 1941.

1798 —— *Socinianism in seventeenth-century England.* 1951.

1799 Madden, Richard R. *The history of the penal laws enacted against Roman Catholics.* 1847.

1800 Makower, Felix. *The constitutional history and constitution of the Church of England.* 1895. Still the best work of its kind.

1801 Martin, Hugh. *Puritanism and Richard Baxter.* 1954. Baptist lectures.

1802 Matthews, Arnold G. *Mr. Pepys and nonconformity.* 1954.

1803 Morgan, Irvonwy. *The nonconformity of Richard Baxter.* 1946. A doctoral dissertation.

1804 Overton, John H. *Life in the English church, 1660–1714.* 1885. Still very useful.

1805 Pawson, Geoffrey P. H. *The Cambridge Platonists and their place in religious thought.* 1930. A prize essay.

1806 Plum, Harry G. *Restoration puritanism: a study of the growth of English liberty.* Chapel Hill, 1943. Emphasizes importance of puritanism; somewhat inaccurate.

1807 Pollock, John. *The Popish Plot: a study in the history of the reign of Charles II.* New ed., Cambridge, 1944. First published 1903. Still the most substantial work on the subject, but not entirely convincing.

1808 Poole, Reginald L. *A history of the Huguenots of the dispersion at the recall of the Edict of Nantes.* 1880. Exhaustive documentation, but not much on the period.

1809 Portus, Garnet V. *Caritas anglicana, or an historical inquiry into those religious and philanthropical societies that flourished in England between the years 1678 and 1740.* 1912. Extends beyond activities of the Church of England; cf. Owen (1012).

1810 Procter, Francis and Walter H. Frere. *A new history of the Book of Common Prayer.* 1914. The best history of the subject.

1811 Raistrick, Arthur. *Quakers in science and industry.* 1950. Scattered references to the period.

1812 Ramsey, Michael *et al. The English Prayer Book, 1549–1662.* 1963. Five addresses commemorating the 1662 version.

1813 Ratcliff, Edward C. *The Book of Common Prayer of the Church of England: its making and revisions, M.D.XLIX–M.D.CLXI.* 1949.

1814 Rees, Thomas Mardy. *History of Protestant nonconformity in Wales.* 1861. Biased, but valuable.

1815 Richards, Thomas. *Religious developments in Wales, 1654–62.* 1923. The fullest account.

1816 —— *Wales under the indulgence, 1672–75.* 1928.

1817 —— *Wales under the penal code, 1662–87.* 1925.

1818 Richardson, Caroline F. *English preachers and preaching, 1640–1670.* New York. 1928. A substantial work with a good bibliography.

1819 Rogers, Philip G. *The Fifth Monarchy men.* 1966. Has chapter on the rising of 1661.

1820 St John, Wallace. *The contest for liberty of conscience in England.* Chicago, 1900. Brief treatment of later Stuart period. A doctoral dissertation, with original source materials arranged chronologically.

1821 Schickler, Fernand D. G. de, Baron. *Les églises du refuge en Angleterre.* Paris, 1892, 3 vols. Chap. 3 in vol. II deals with the period; concerned only with French-speaking religious bodies.

1822 Schlatter, Richard B. *The social ideas of religious leaders, 1660–88.* Oxford, 1940. Shows how much the churches were in agreement on some matters.

1823 Seaton, Alexander A. *The theory of toleration under the later Stuarts.* Cambridge, 1911.

1824 Simon, Walter G. *The Restoration episcopate.* New York, 1965. An analysis of the episcopal bench. Of political and social, as well as religious, interest.

1825 Smiles, Samuel. *The Huguenots: their settlements, churches, and industries in England and Ireland.* 1867.

1826 Smith, Hugh F. Russell. *The theory of religious liberty in the reigns of Charles II and James II.* Cambridge, 1911.

1827 Sykes, Norman. *The Church of England and non-episcopal churches in the sixteenth and seventeenth centuries: an essay towards an historical interpretation of the Anglican tradition from Whitgift to Wake.* 1948.

1828 —— *From Sheldon to Secker: aspects of English church history, 1660–1768.* Cambridge, 1959. Ford Lectures, 1958.

1829 —— *Old priest and new presbyter.* Cambridge, 1956. Particularly chap. 5, 'The parting of the ways'. Lectures.

1830 Taunton, Ethelred L. *The history of the Jesuits in England, 1580–1773.* 1901. By a secular priest; for Protestant replies, see Grose (32), no. 1520.

1831 Thaddeus, Father. *Franciscans in England, 1600–1850.* 1898. Valuable for citations from contemporary accounts. His list of friars is largely superseded by lists published by the Catholic Record Society.

1832 Tindall, William Y. *John Bunyan: mechanick preacher.* New York, 1934; repr. 1964. A study of aspects of Bunyan's work, rather than a biography.

1833 Tulloch, John. *English puritanism and its leaders: Cromwell, Milton, Baxter, Bunyan.* Edinburgh, 1861. The work of a prominent Scottish theologian.

1834 Weiss, Charles. *History of the French Protestant refugees.* New York, 1854. Begins in 1685.

1835 Whiting, Charles E. *Studies in English puritanism from the Restoration to the Revolution.* 1931. Learned but unsympathetic; of little interpretive value.

1836 Whitley, William T. *The Baptists of London, 1612–1928: their fellowship, their expansion, with notes on their 850 churches,* 1928.

1837 Williamson, Hugh Ross. *Jeremy Taylor.* 1952. A study of Taylor's writings in relation to his background.

1838 Wilson, Walter. *The history and antiquities of dissenting churches and meeting houses in London, Westminster, and Southwark, including the lives of their ministers.* 1808–14, 4 vols.

1839 Wood, Alfred H. *Church unity without uniformity: a study of seventeenth-century English church movements and of Richard Baxter's proposals for a comprehensive church.* 1963. Valuable; extensive documentation and bibliography.

4 Biographies

1840 Agnew, David C. A. *Protestant exiles from France in the reign of Louis XIV*. 2nd ed., 1871, 3 vols. Short biographical sketches of Huguenots and their descendants in Great Britain and Ireland.

1841 Batten, Joseph M. *John Dury: advocate of Christian reunion*. Chicago, 1944.

1842 Besse, Joseph. *Collection of the sufferings of the people called Quakers*. 1753, 2 vols. Useful for biographical information; covers 1650–89.

1843 Brailsford, Mabel R. *The making of William Penn*. 1930. Includes a few letters.

1844 Brook, Benjamin. *The lives of the puritans, containing a biographical account of those divines who distinguished themselves in the cause of religious liberty*. 1813, 3 vols. Extends from Elizabeth I to 1662.

1845 Brown, John. *John Bunyan: his life, times, and work*, rev. ed. by Frank M. Harrison. 1928. First published 1885; widely regarded as the best life.

1846 Calamy, Edmund. *Memoirs of the life of the late reverend Mr. John Howe*. 1724.

1847 Carpenter, Edward F. *Thomas Tenison, archbishop of Canterbury: his life and times* (Church Historical Society). 1948.

1848 Challoner, Richard. *Memoirs of missionary priests and other Catholics of both sexes that have suffered death in England upon religious accounts, from the year 1577 to 1684, carefully collected from the accounts of eye-witnesses*, ed. J. H. Pollen. 1924. First published in 2 vols., 1741–2. Valuable; strong Roman Catholic point of view.

1849 Clarke, Thomas E. S. and Helen C. Foxcroft. *A life of Gilbert Burnet, bishop of Salisbury*. Cambridge, 1907. A good biography.

1850 Clarkson, Thomas. *Memoirs of the private and public life of William Penn*. 1813, 2 vols.

1851 Collins, William E. (ed.). *Typical English churchmen from Parker to Maurice: a series of lectures* (Church Historical Society, LXV, LXXVIII). 1902–9. Includes Taylor and Burnet.

1852 Comfort, William W. *William Penn, 1644–1718: a tercentenary estimate*. Philadelphia, 1944.

1853 Cope, Jackson I. *Joseph Glanvill: Anglican apologist* (Washington University Studies). St Louis, 1956.

1854 Culross, James. *Hanserd Knollys, 'a minister and witness of Jesus Christ', 1598–1691*. 1895. A sympathetic biography of the prominent Baptist divine.

1855 Dobrée, Bonamy. *William Penn, Quaker and pioneer*. 1932.

1856 D'Oyly, George. *The life of William Sancroft, archbishop of Canterbury*. 1821, 2 vols. An adequate life, based on Bodleian Library manuscripts.

1857 Froude, James A. *Bunyan*. New York, 1880.

1858 Gillow, Joseph. *A literary and biographical history, or biographical dictionary, of the English Catholics from the breach with Rome in 1534 to the present time*. 1885–1902, 5 vols. Valuable, and fairly complete through the letter P.

1859 Gosse, Edmund W. *Jeremy Taylor*. 1904. A brief life.

1860 Graham, John W. *William Penn, founder of Pennsylvania*. Rev. ed., 1918. A good popular life, including a few letters.

1861 Harrison, George B. *John Bunyan: a study in personality*. 1928. An attempt to trace the development of Bunyan's mind and personality from his writings.

1862 Hart, Arthur Tindal. *The life and times of John Sharp, archbishop of York* (Church Historical Society). 1949. Reflects extensive research in unpublished sources.

1863 —— *William Lloyd, 1627–1717: bishop, politician, author, and prophet* (Church Historical Society). 1952. An illuminating study.

1864 Hennessy, George (comp.). *Novum repertorium ecclesiasticum parochiale Londinense, or London diocesan clergy succession from the earliest time to the year 1898*. 1898.

1865 Hodgkin, Thomas. *George Fox*. 1896. A good short life.

1866 Hook, Walter F. *Lives of the archbishops of Canterbury*. 1860–76, 12 vols. Extends only through Juxon.

1867 Hull, William I. *Eight first biographies of William Penn, in seven languages and seven lands* (Swarthmore College Monographs on Quaker history, no. 3). Philadelphia, 1936. Translations of excerpts.

1868 —— *William Penn: a topical biography*. 1937.

1869 Hunter, Joseph. *The rise of the old dissent, exemplified in the life of Oliver Heywood*. 1842. Cf. Heywood (1672).

1870 Lacey, Thomas A. *Herbert Thorndike, 1598–1672* (English Theologians ser.). 1929.

1871 Longden, Henry I. *Northamptonshire and Rutland clergy from 1500*. Northampton, 1938–52, 16 vols. Short biographical notices of hundreds of clergymen.

1872 Manners, Emily. 'Elizabeth Hooton, first Quaker woman preacher (1600–72)' (*JFHS*, suppl. 12). 1914. A 90-page essay dealing with her experiences in New England as well as England.

1873 Marah, William H. *Memoirs of Archbishop Juxon and his times, with a sketch of the archbishop's parish, Little Compton*. Oxford, 1869.

1874 Matthews, Arnold G. *Calamy revised, being a revision of Edmund Calamy's account of the ministers and others ejected and silenced, 1660–2*. Oxford, 1934. Amplifies Calamy (1641). A valuable work, particularly for its statistical conclusions.

1875 May, E. H. *A dissertation on the life, theology, and times of...Jeremy Taylor*. 1892.

1876 Milner, John. *Supplementary memoirs of English Catholics*. 1820. Serves to correct Butler (1724).

1877 Nankivell, James W. H. *Edward Stillingfleet, bishop of Worcester, 1689–99*. Worcester, 1946.

1878 Nightingale, Benjamin. *The ejected of 1662 in Cumberland and Westmorland*. 1911, 2 vols. Arrangement by communities: many documents.

1879 Noble, Vernon. *The man in the leather breeches: the life and times of George Fox*. 1953.

1880 Nuttall, Geoffrey F. *Richard Baxter*. 1965. A readable short life.

1881 Osmond, Percy H. *Isaac Barrow: his life and times*. 1944. The fullest account.

1882 —— *A life of John Cosin, bishop of Durham, 1660–1672*. 1913. Provides some documents. Cf. Cosin (1655).

1883 Plumptre, Edward H. *The life of Thomas Ken...bishop of Bath and Wells*. Rev. ed., 1890, 2 vols. A detailed work, providing many letters. Valuable for the Anglo-Catholic point of view.

1884 Powicke, Frederick J. *A life of the reverend Richard Baxter, 1615–1691*. 1924. Presents new material from Baxter MSS in Dr Williams's Library.

1885 —— *The reverend Richard Baxter under the cross, 1662–1691*. 1927.

1886 Rice, Hugh A. L. *Thomas Ken: bishop and non-juror*. 1958.

1887 Ross, Isabel. *Margaret Fell, mother of Quakerism*. 1949. Prints some letters.

1888 Salmon, Nathaniel. *The lives of the English bishops from the Restauration to the Revolution*. 1733. A useful compilation, presenting 74 lives. Non-juring bias.

1889 Sharrock, Roger. *John Bunyan*. New ed., 1968.

1890 Staley, Vernon. *The life and times of Gilbert Sheldon, sometime warden of All Souls College, Oxford, bishop of London, archbishop of Canterbury, and chancellor of the University of Oxford*. 1913. An adequate account.

1891 Stranks, Charles J. *The life and writings of Jeremy Taylor*. 1952.

1892 Strickland, Agnes. *The lives of the seven bishops committed to the Tower in 1688*. 1866. Includes some letters.

1893 Sykes, Norman. *William Wake, archbishop of Canterbury, 1657–1737*. Cambridge, 1957, 2 vols.

1894 Wallace, Robert. *Antitrinitarian biography...to which is prefixed a history of Unitarianism in England*. 1850, 3 vols. The biographies go to 1700; the history to 1800.

1895 Wildes, Harry E. *Voice of the Lord: a biography of George Fox*. Philadelphia, 1965.

1896 Williamson, George C. *Lodowick Muggleton*. 1919. Founder of the Muggletonian sect.

1897 Winslow, Ola E. *John Bunyan*. New York, 1961.

1898 Wordsworth, Christopher (ed.). *Ecclesiastical biography, or lives of eminent men connected with the history of religion in England*. 1853, 4 vols. First published in 1810. Goes from the Reformation to the Revolution; includes many lives reprinted or extracted from earlier works.

5 Articles

1899 Abernathy, George R., Jr. 'Clarendon and the Declaration of Indulgence', *JEH*, **11** (Apr. 1960), 55–73. The conclusions have not been entirely accepted.

1900 Acton, John E. E. Dalberg, Baron. 'Secret history of Charles II', in his *Historical essays and studies*, New York, 1967, pp. 85–122. First published 1907; deals with Charles's Catholicism and James de Cloche. Cf. Simon (1957).

1901 Barnes, Arthur S. 'Charles II and reunion with Rome', *Monthly Review*, **13** (Dec. 1903), 140–55. Concerned with Richard Bellings's mission to Rome, 1662; includes some documents.

1902 Bennett, J. Harry. 'English bishops and imperial jurisdiction, 1660–1725', *Historical Magazine of the Protestant Episcopal Church*, **32** (Sept. 1963), 175–88. Shows that Compton established the tradition that the colonies were subject to the jurisdiction of the bishop of London; article includes comments by Anthony H. Forbes.

1903 Blundell, Margaret. 'William Blundell, junior', *Dublin Review*, **206** (1940), 367–78. Extracts from family letters; of some interest for condition of Catholics.

1904 Bolam, C. Gordon. 'The ejection of 1662 and its consequences for the Presbyterians in England', *Hibbert Journal*, **60** (Apr. 1962), 184–95.

1905 Braithwaite, Alfred W. 'Early Friends' experience with juries', *JFHS*, **50** (no. 4, 1964), 217–27. Shows some reluctance to convict Quakers.

1906 —— 'Early tithe prosecutions: Friends as outlaws', *JFHS*, **49** (Autumn 1960), 148–56. Claims that early Friends suffered less from deliberate religious persecution than from the unwieldiness of legal procedure.

1907 Brauer, Jerald C. 'Puritan mysticism and the development of liberalism', *Church Hist.*, **19** (Sept. 1950), 151–70. Full documentation.

1908 Brown, Lawrence L. 'Henry Compton, 1632–1713, bishop of London, 1675–1713: pioneer leader in the expansion of the Anglican communion', *Historical Magazine of the Protestant Episcopal Church*, **25** (Mar. 1956), 7–71.

1909 Brown, Louise F. 'Religious factors in the Convention Parliament', *EHR*, **22** (Jan. 1907), 51–63.

1910 Bussby, F. 'George Morley: bishop of Winchester, 1662–1684', *CQR*, **168** (Oct.–Dec. 1967), 433–42. Morley's career as bishop.

1911 —— 'George Morley: Caroline divine', *CQR*, **165** (Apr.–June 1964), 185–97.

1912 Carter, Alice C. 'The ministry of the English churches in the Netherlands in the seventeenth century', *BIHR*, **32** (Nov. 1960), 166–79.

1913 Cuming, Geoffrey J. 'The grand debate', *CQR*, **163** (Jan.–Mar. 1962), 29–39. On the Savoy Conference, 1661.

1914 —— 'The Prayer Book in convocation, November 1661', *JEH*, **8** (Oct. 1957), 182–92.

1915 Day, E. Hermitage. 'The country clergy of the Restoration period', *Theology*, **35** (Dec. 1937), 354–60. A discussion and criticism of Macaulay's third chapter.

1916 De Pauley, William C. 'Richard Baxter surveyed', *CQR*, **164** (Jan.–Mar. 1963), 32–43. Baxter's religious position.

1917 Dudley, Albert C. 'Nonconformity under the "Clarendon code"', *AHR*, **18** (Oct. 1913), 65–78. Based on Quaker records. Opposes idea that Clarendon launched a persecution of religious dissent.

1918 Dwyer, J. J. 'The Popish Plot', *Month*, new ser., **13** (May 1955), 281–91.

1919 Feiling, Keith G. 'Clarendon and the Act of Uniformity, 1662–3', *EHR*, **44** (Apr. 1929), 289–91.

1920 Firth, Charles H. 'John Bunyan', in his *Essays historical and literary*, Oxford, 1938, pp. 129–73.

1921 Fletcher, Charles R. L. 'Some troubles of Archbishop Sancroft', *Hug. Soc. Proc.*, **13** (no. 3, 1929), 209–59. Concerned mainly with the year 1685.

1922 Fletcher, James M. J. 'Seth Ward, bishop of Salisbury, 1667–1689', *Wiltshire Archaeological and Natural History Magazine*, **49** (June 1940), 1–16.

1923 Foster, Herbert D. 'International Calvinism through Locke and the Revolution of 1688', *AHR*, **32** (Apr. 1927), 475–99. Provides comment on Locke's religious and political inheritance.

1924 Furley, O. W. 'The pope-burning processions of the late seventeenth century', *Hist.*, **44** (Feb. 1959), 16–23. Cf. Williams (1969).

1925 Gee, Henry. 'The Derwentdale plot, 1663', *TRHS*, 3rd ser., **11** (1917), 125–42. Related to the Clarendon code. Cf. Walker (1964).

1926 Giffin, Frederick C. 'John Locke and religious toleration', *Journal of Church and State*, **9** (no. 3, 1967), 378–90. Importance of Locke in summing up what had been written on the subject.

1927 Grose, Clyde L. 'The religion of Restoration England', *Church History*, **6** (Sept. 1937), 223–32. A brief survey of the subject.

1928 Gwatkin, Henry M. 'Religious toleration in England', in *CMH*, v, 324–37. The best short introduction to the subject.

1929 Higham, Florence. 'A note on Gilbert Sheldon', *JEH*, **14** (Oct. 1963), 209–12. Discredits alleged violent statement on Roman Catholicism.

1930 Horwitz, Henry. 'Protestant reconciliation in the exclusion crisis', *JEH*, **15** (Oct. 1964), 201–17. Deals with unsuccessful parliamentary attempts to effect religious concord and advance Protestant unity.

1931 Huelin, Gordon. '"The delight of the English nation": William Juxon (1582–1663)', *CQR*, **164** (July–Sept. 1963), 311–21. Adds little, if anything, to what was known.

1932 —— 'Leaves from a seventeenth-century parson', *CQR*, **159** (Apr.–June 1958), 246–55. Based on the diary of John Wade, an Anglican clergyman sympathetic to Presbyterianism.

1933 Jones, G. F. Trevallyn. 'The Bristol affair, 1663', *Journal of Religious History*, **5** (June 1968), 16–30. Deals with the Earl of Bristol's attempt to impeach Clarendon; of some interest with regard to religious toleration.

1934 —— 'The composition and leadership of the Presbyterian party in the Convention', *EHR*, **79** (Apr. 1964), 307–30. Concerned with the Convention of 1660.

1935 Kaufmann, Moritz. 'Latitudinarianism and pietism', in *CMH*, v, 742–63.

1936 Kimball, Howard E. 'The Anglican church in British North America: ecclesiastical government before 1688', in Samuel C. McCulloch (ed.), *British humanitarianism: essays honoring Frank J. Klingberg*, Philadelphia, 1950, pp. 84–99. Considerable attention to Compton and the jurisdiction of the bishop of London.

1937 Kirby, Ethyn Williams. 'The Quakers' efforts to secure civil and religious liberty', *JMH*, **7** (Dec. 1935), 401–21.

1938 —— 'The reconcilers and the Restoration, 1660–1662', in *Essays in modern English history in honor of Wilbur Cortez Abbott*, Cambridge, Mass., 1941, pp. 49–79. Deals with the activities of clergymen, including Baxter, in connection with the religious settlement.

1939 Legg, John Wickham. 'The degradation of the rev. Samuel Johnson in 1686', *EHR*, **29** (Oct. 1914), 723–42. Discusses proceedings against a well-known Whig clergyman.

1940 Maclear, James F. 'The birth of the Free Church tradition', *Church Hist.*, **26** (June 1957), 99–131. Has little bearing directly on the period, but there is a useful discussion of puritanism.

1941 Maddocks, M. H. St J. 'Bishop Ken', *CQR*, **164** (Apr.–June 1963), 173–80. Highly sympathetic, adding little to our knowledge.

1942 Moens, William J. C. 'On the registers of the French and Walloon churches established in England, and other sources of Huguenot knowledge', *Hug. Soc. Proc.*, **1** (no. 1, 1887), 17–56.

1943 Mullett, Charles F. 'Protestant dissent as crime (1660–1828)', *Review of Religion*, **13** (May 1949), 339–53.

1944 —— 'Some seventeenth-century manuscript sermon memoranda', *HLQ*, **2** (Apr. 1939), 305–8. Based on notes of sermons by the earl of Huntingdon (1650–1701).

1945 —— 'Toleration and persecution in England, 1660–89', *Church Hist.*, **18** (Mar. 1949), 18–43.

1946 Norling, Bernard. 'Contemporary English Catholics and the policies of James II', *Mid-America*, **26** (Oct. 1955), 215–28. Deals with the reactions of various groups of Catholics.

1947 Nuttall, Geoffrey F. 'Dissenting churches in Kent before 1700', *JEH*, **14** (Oct. 1963), 175–89.

1948 —— 'The first Nonconformists', in Owen Chadwick and Geoffrey F, Nuttall (eds.), *From uniformity to unity, 1662–1962*, 1962, pp. 149–87.

1949 —— 'Lyon Turner's *Original Records:* notes and identifications', *Congregational Historical Society Transactions*, **14** (1940–3), 14–24, 112–20, 122, 181–7; **15** (May 1945), 41–7. Elucidates Turner (1715).

1950 —— 'Richard Baxter's correspondence: a preliminary survey', *JEH*, **1** (no. 1, 1950), 85–95.

1951 Peyton, Sidney A. 'The religious census of 1676', *EHR*, **48** (Jan. 1933), 99–104.

1952 Plum, Harry G. 'The English religious restoration, 1660–1665', in Baldwin Maxwell *et al.* (eds.), *Renaissance studies in honor of Hardin Craig*, Palo Alto, Calif., 1941, pp. 324–34. Also in *Philological Quarterly*, **20** (July 1941), 516–26.

1953 Ratcliff, Edward C. 'The Savoy Conference and the revision of the Book of Common Prayer', in Owen Chadwick and Geoffrey F. Nuttall (eds.), *From uniformity to unity, 1662–1962*, 1962, pp. 89–148.

1954 Robbins, Caroline. 'Marvell's religion: was he a new methodist?', *JHI*, **23** (Apr.–June 1962), 268–72.

1955 Shideler, Emerson W. 'The concept of the church in seventeenth-century Quakerism (part 1)', *Bulletin of the Friends' Historical Association*, **45** (Autumn 1956), 67–81. Highly theological in treatment.

1956 Simon, Walter G. 'Comprehension in the age of Charles II', *Church Hist.*, **31** (Dec. 1962), 440–8. Largely devoted to Bishop Wilkins.

1957 —— 'Lord Acton and the religion of Charles II', *Anglican Theological Review*, **40** (July 1958), 203–8. An answer to Acton (1900).

1958 —— 'The Restoration episcopate and the Popish Plot', *Anglican Theological Review*, **39** (Apr. 1957), 139–47.

1959 Slatter, M. Doreen. 'The records of the court of arches', *JEH*, **4** (Oct. 1953), 139–53. Deals with the chief ecclesiastical court of the province of Canterbury.

1960 Spalding, James C. 'The demise of English Presbyterianism, 1660–1760', *Church Hist.*, **28** (Mar. 1959), 63–83.

1961 Tanner, Joseph R. 'Pepys and the Popish Plot', *EHR*, **7** (Apr. 1892), 281–90.

1962 Thomas, Roger. 'Comprehension and indulgence', in Owen Chadwick and Geoffrey F. Nuttall (eds.), *From uniformity to unity, 1662–1962*, 1962, pp. 189–253.

1963 Trevor-Roper, Hugh R. 'The restoration of the church, 1660', *Hist. T.*, **2** (Aug. 1952), 539–43. A brief commentary for the general reader.

1964 Walker, James. 'The Yorkshire plot, 1663', *Yorkshire Archaeological Journal*, **31** (1934), 348–59, Cf. Gee (1925).

1965 West, Francis H. 'A Nottinghamshire parson in the seventeenth century', *CQR*, **151** (Oct.–Dec. 1950), 1–14. Concerned with William Sampson, rector of Clayworth (1672–1703), a Whig.

1966 Whiteman, Anne O. 'The re-establishment of the Church of England, 1660–1663', *TRHS*, 5th ser., **5** (1955), 111–31. Draws on the records of various dioceses to illustrate the structure and character of the restored episcopal administration.

1967 Whiteman, Anne O. 'The restoration of the Church of England', in Owen Chadwick and Geoffrey F. Nuttall (eds.), *From uniformity to unity, 1662–1962*, 1962, pp. 60–72. Cf. Bosher (1768), with whom her views conflict.

1968 Whitley, William T. 'The great raid of 1670 on certain London churches under the new Conventicle Act', *Baptist Quarterly*, **9** (Oct. 1938), 247–51.

1969 Williams, Sheila. 'The pope-burning processions of 1679, 1680, and 1681', *Journal of the Warburg and Courtauld Institutes*, **21** (1958), 104–18. Cf. Furley (1924).

1970 Wolf, Lucien. 'The Jewry of the Restoration, 1660–1664', *Transactions of the Jewish Historical Society*, **5** (1908), 5–33.

1971 —— 'The status of the Jews in England after the resettlement', *Transactions of the Jewish Historical Society*, **4** (1903), 177–93.

XIII HISTORY OF THE FINE ARTS

1 Printed Sources

1972 Campbell, Colin. *Vitruvius britannicus, or the British architect.* 1715, 2 vols. Provides invaluable illustrations for most of the important British buildings of the latter part of the seventeenth century.

1973 Gunther, Robert W. T. (ed.). *The architecture of Sir Robert Pratt, Charles II's commissioner for the rebuilding of London after the Great Fire.* Oxford, 1928. Printed from his notebooks.

1974 Lafontaine, Henry C. de. *The king's musick: a transcript of records relating to music and musicians (1460–1700).* 1909. From the Lord Chamberlain's records in the PRO.

1975 *Musica britannica.* 1951–. A collection of British music, from the middle ages through the eighteenth century.

1976 Palladio, Andrea. *Architecture...in four books...to which are added several notes and observations made by Inigo Jones*, trans. N. du Bois. 1715–20, 15 pts. Part I appeared in England in 1663; the first ed., in Italian, was published in 1573. One of the most influential works on the subject.

1977 Wren Society. *Publications*, ed. Arthur T. Bolton and H. D. Hendry. Oxford, 1924–. Designed to provide a complete view of Wren's work; replete with drawings, plans, elevations, etc.

2 Surveys

1978 Baker, Charles H. C. *British painting.* 1933. A good short history.

1979 Blom, Eric W. *Music in England.* Harmondsworth, 1942.

1980 Burney, Charles. *A general history of music from the earliest ages to the present period*, ed. Frank Mercer. 1935, 2 vols. Originally published 1776–89.

1981 Davey, Henry. *History of English music.* 2nd ed., 1921. See chap. 7: 'The period of foreign influence, and of dramatic music (1660–1700)'.

1982 Edwards, Ralph and L. G. G. Ramsey (eds.). *The Stuart period, 1603–1714* (Connoisseur Period Guides). 1957. A survey of architecture, painting, sculpture, furniture, etc., with essays by various authors.

1983 Fuller-Maitland, John. *The age of Bach and Handel* (Oxford History of Music, IV). Oxford, 1902. Valuable; not confined to England.

1984 Grove, George. *Dictionary of music and musicians.* 5th ed. by Eric Blom, 1954, 9 vols. Indispensable.

1985 Leroy, Alfred. *Histoire de la peinture anglaise, 800–1938: son évolution et ses maîtres.* Paris, 1939.

1986 MacQuoid, Percy. *A history of English furniture.* 1904–8, 4 vols. Vol. II covers 1660–1700. Plates in colour.

1987 MacQuoid, Percy and R. Edwards. *The dictionary of English furniture.* 2nd ed. rev. 1954, 3 vols. Extends from middle ages to late Georgian period; profusely illustrated.

1988 Nagel, Wilibald. *Geschichte der Musik in England.* Strassburg, 1894–7, 2 vols. An important work; ends with Purcell.

1989 Parry, Charles Hubert Hastings. *The music of the seventeenth century* (Oxford history of music, III). 2nd ed., rev. by Edward J. Dent, 1938. See chap. 7, 'English music after the Commonwealth'.

1990 Pevsner, Nikolaus *et al. The buildings of England.* Harmondsworth, 1951–. 41 vols. A very useful regional survey.

1991 Summerson, John N. *Architecture in Britain, 1530 to 1830.* 5th ed. rev., 1969. An excellent work, well illustrated, in Pelican History of Art. See especially pt. 3, 'Wren and the baroque (1660–1710)'.

1992 Walker, Ernest. *A history of music in England,* 3rd ed., rev. by Jack A. Westrup. Oxford, 1952. The standard survey; see especially chap. 6, 'Purcell and his contemporaries.'

1993 Walpole, Horace. *Anecdotes of painting in England, with some account of the principal artists and incidental notes on other arts, collected by the late Mr. George Vertue.* Strawberry Hill, 1762–71, 4 vols. Vertue (1684–1756) had collected materials for a history of art.

1994 Waterhouse, Ellis K. *Painting in Britain, 1530–1790* (Pelican History of Art). 2nd ed., 1962. Pt. 2, 'Painting under the Stuarts, up to the Revolution of 1688'; illustrations.

1995 Whinney, Margaret D. *Sculpture in Britain, 1530–1830* (Pelican History of Art). 1964. A valuable survey, profusely illustrated.

1996 Whinney, Margaret D. and Oliver Millar. *English art, 1625–1714* (Oxford History of English Art, VIII). Oxford, 1957. The standard survey of the fine arts in general.

1997 Young, Percy M. *A history of British music.* 1967. See chap. 7, 'English baroque'.

3 Monographs

1998 Addleshaw, George W. O. and Frederick Etchells. *The architectural setting of Anglican worship.* 2nd ed., 1956. Portions, especially chap. 5, are of some use for the period.

1999 Baker, Charles H. C. *Lely and the Stuart portrait painters: a study of English portraiture before and after Van Dyke.* 1912. The best conspectus of the subject, though in part conjectural; over 200 reproductions.

2000 —— and William G. Constable. *English painting of the sixteenth and seventeenth centuries.* New York, 1930. A scholarly study with good reproductions and a valuable bibliography.

2001 Birch, George H. *London churches of the seventeenth and eighteenth centuries.* 1896. Deals with churches built between 1630 and 1730, from designs of Jones, Wren, Hawksmoor and Gibbs.

2002 Blomfield, Reginald T. *A history of renaissance architecture in England, 1500–1800.* 1897, 2 vols. A standard work.

2003 Buckley, Francis. *A history of old English glass.* 1925.

2004 Chappell, William. *Old English popular music,* ed. Harry E. Woolridge. 1893, 2 vols. Useful for folk music.

2005 Colvin, Sidney. *Early engraving and engravers in England, 1545–1695.* 1905.

2006 Crawford and Balcarres, David A. E. Lindsay, earl of (ed.). *Historical monuments of Great Britain.* 1955–. A survey of existing buildings of archaeological or historical significance, with illustrations.

2007 Croft-Murray, Edward. *Decorative painting in England, 1537–1837,* I: *Early Tudor to Sir James Thornhill.* 1962. Two chapters on the period; illustrated.

2008 Crossley, Frederick H. *Timber building in England from early times to the end of the seventeenth century.* 1951.

2009 Davies, David W. *Dutch influences on English culture, 1558–1725.* Ithaca, N.Y., 1964. Useful for trade, religion, etc., but particularly for the fine arts.

2010 Day, Cyrus L. and Eleanore B. Murrie. *English song-books, 1651–1702, and their publishers.* 1936. Chiefly concerns publishers.

2011 Dent, Edward J. *Foundations of English opera: a study of musical drama in England during the seventeenth century.* Cambridge, 1928.

2012 Downes, Kerry. *English baroque architecture.* 1966. A handsome folio vol., profusely illustrated.

2013 Dutton, Ralph. *The age of Wren.* 1951. Includes comment on Wren's contemporaries; profusely illustrated.

2014 —— *The English interior, 1500 to 1900.* 1948.

2015 Esdaile, Katharine A. *English church monuments, 1510–1840.* 1946.

2016 —— *English monumental sculpture since the renaissance.* 1927. A pioneer work, now somewhat out of date. Scattered Restoration material.

2017 Field, Horace and Michael Bunney. *English domestic architecture of the seventeenth and eighteenth centuries.* New, rev. ed., 1928. Examples of smaller buildings, measured, drawn, and photographed; brief introductory comment.

2018 Furst, Viktor. *The architecture of Sir Christopher Wren.* 1956. A detailed study, with many architectural drawings.

2019 Gloag, John. *Georgian grace: a social history of design from 1660–1830.* 1956. Of some use for the period, despite emphasis on later times.

2020 Grant, Maurice H. *A chronological history of the old English landscape painters (in oil), from the sixteenth century to the nineteenth century.* 1926–47, 3 vols.

2021 Hayes, Gerald R. *Musical instruments and their music, 1500–1700.* 1928–30, 2 vols.

2022 Hill, Oliver and John Cornforth. *English country houses: Caroline, 1625–1685.* 1966. Over 500 photographs.

2023 Hind, Arthur M. *Wenceslaus Hollar and his views of London and Windsor in the seventeenth century.* 1922. Many reproductions.

2024 Holst, Imogen (ed.). *Henry Purcell, 1659–1695: essays on his music.* 1959. Musical rather than historical emphasis.

2025 Hughes, George B. *English, Scottish, and Irish table glass from the sixteenth century to 1820.* 1956.

2026 Jenkins, Frank. *Architect and patron: a survey of professional relations and practice in England from the sixteenth century to the present day.* 1961. Especially for chap. 4 on the architectural profession, and chap. 5 on patronage and taste.

2027 Jourdain, Margaret. *English interior decoration, 1500–1830.* 1950.

2028 Killanin, Michael M. *Sir Godfrey Kneller and his times, 1646–1723, being a review of English portraiture of the period.* 1948.

2029 Lang, Jane. *Rebuilding St Paul's after the Great Fire of London.* 1956.

2030 Lenygon, Francis H. *The decoration and furniture of English mansions during the seventeenth and eighteenth centuries.* 1909. A handsome work, profusely illustrated.

2031 —— *Decoration in England from 1600 to 1770.* 2nd ed., rev., 1927.

2032 —— *Furniture in England from 1660 to 1770.* 2nd ed., rev., 1924.

2033 Loftie, William J. *Inigo Jones and Wren, or the rise and decline of modern architecture in England.* 1893.

2034 Mackerness, Eric D. *A social history of English music.* 1964. A study of the musical tastes of Englishmen from the middle ages to the present.

2035 Meyer, Ernst H. *English chamber music: the history of a great art from the middle ages to Purcell.* 1946. Gives musical examples.

2036 Moore, Robert E. *Henry Purcell and the Restoration theatre.* Cambridge, Mass., 1961. A study of Purcell's operas.

2037 Mulliner, Herbert H. *The decorative arts in England during the late seventeenth and eighteenth centuries.* 1923. Primarily illustrations, with accompanying comment.

2038 North, Roger. *Memoires of musick,* ed. Edward F. Rimbauld. 1846. Written *c.* 1728; chiefly valuable for seventeenth century.

2039 Ogden, Henry V. S. and Margaret S. *English taste in landscape in the seventeenth century.* Ann Arbor, Mich., 1955.

2040 Oman, Charles C. *English domestic silver.* 4th ed., 1959. Profusely illustrated.

2041 Papworth, Wyat. *The renaissance and Italian styles of architecture in Great Britain.* 1883. Covers 1450–1700.

2042 Reynolds, Graham. *English portrait miniatures.* 1952. Two chapters on the period.

2043 Richardson, Albert E. and C. Lovett Gill. *London houses from 1660 to 1820*. 1911.
2044 Richardson, Albert E. and H. Donaldson Eberlein. *The smaller English house of the later renaissance, 1660–1830*. 1925.
2045 Rosenberg, Louis C. *Cottages, farmhouses, and other minor buildings in England of the sixteenth, seventeenth, and eighteenth centuries*. New York, 1923.
2046 Rostenberg, Leona. *English publishers in the graphic arts, 1599–1700*. New York, 1963. Deals with printsellers and publishers of engravings, manuals on art and architecture, etc.
2047 Salaman, Malcolm C. *The old engravers of England in relation to contemporary life and art, 1540–1800*. 1907. One chapter on seventeenth-century engravers.
2048 Sekler, Eduard F. *Wren and his place in European architecture*. New York, 1956. An interesting study, with many illustrations and an excellent bibliography.
2049 Simpson, Claude M. *The British broadside ballad and its music*. New Brunswick, N.J., 1966.
2050 Sitwell, Sacheverell. *British architects and craftsmen: a survey of taste, design, and style during three centuries, 1600 to 1830*. 3rd ed., rev., 1947. A very interesting and readable account.
2051 Small, Tunstall and Christopher Woodbridge. *Houses of the Wren and early Georgian periods*. 1928. Almost entirely drawings and photographs.
2052 Stratton, Arthur J. *The English interior: a review of the decoration of English houses from Tudor times to the nineteenth century*. 1920.
2053 Symonds, Robert W. *English furniture from Charles II to George II*. 1929. Extensively illustrated.
2054 —— *Masterpieces of English furniture and clocks: a study of walnut and mahogany furniture*. 1940.
2055 Tipping, Henry A. *English homes, period IV...late Stuart, 1649–1714*, vol. I. 1920.
2056 —— *Grinling Gibbons and the woodwork of his age (1648–1720)*. 1914.
2057 Whiffen, Marcus. *Stuart and Georgian churches: the architecture of the Church of England outside London, 1603–1837*. 1948.
2058 White, Eric W. *The rise of English opera*. 1951. Only the first chapter relates to the period.
2059 Woodward, John. *Tudor and Stuart drawings*. 1951.

4 Biographies

2060 Arundell, Dennis D. *Henry Purcell*. 1927.
2061 Baker, Charles H. C. *Lely and Kneller* (in *British artists*, ed. S. C. Kaines Smith). 1922.
2062 Beckett, Ronald B. P. *Lely*. 1951. Reproductions, with an introductory essay.
2063 Briggs, Martin S. *Wren the incomparable*. 1953. Many illustrations of Wren's buildings.
2064 Colvin, Edward M. *A biographical dictionary of English architects, 1660–1840*. 1954.
2065 Elmes, James. *Memoirs of the life and works of Sir Christopher Wren*. Rev. ed., 1852, 3 pts. An old standard work, with documents, but inaccurate.
2066 Faber, Harald. *Caius Gabriel Cibber, 1630–1700: his life and work*. Oxford, 1926. Life of the sculptor.
2067 Grant, Maurice H. *A dictionary of British sculptors from the thirteenth century to the twentieth century*. 1953. Very brief notices.
2068 Green, David B. *Grinling Gibbons: his work as carver and statuary, 1648–1721*. 1964.
2069 Gunnis, Rupert. *Dictionary of British sculptors, 1660–1851*. 1953. A standard work of reference.
2070 Holland, Arthur K. *Henry Purcell: the English musical tradition*. 1932.
2071 Parthey, Gustav F. *Wenzel Hollar*. Berlin, 1853. A study of the engraver.
2072 Pulver, Jeffrey. *A biographical dictionary of old English music*. 1927. A handy reference work.

2073 Summerson, John. *Sir Christopher Wren.* New York, 1953. A good short life.
2074 Webb, Geoffrey. *Wren.* 1937.
2075 Westrup, Jack A. *Purcell.* 3rd ed., 1947.
2076 Whitaker-Wilson, Cecil. *Sir Christopher Wren: his life and times.* 1932.
2077 Williamson, Hugh R. *Four Stuart portraits.* 1949. Includes Sir Balthazar Gerbier (d. 1667), painter and courtier.
2078 Zimmerman, Franklin B. *Henry Purcell, 1659–1695.* 1967.

5 Articles

2079 Allen, Derek. 'Thomas Simon's sketch-book' (Walpole Society, XXVII, 13–54). 1939. Profusely illustrated; includes some examples of his work in the 1660s.
2080 Baker, Charles H. C. 'Lely's financial relations with Charles II', *Burlington Magazine*, **20** (1911–12), 43–5.
2081 —— 'Notes on Edmund Ashfield' (Walpole Society, III, 83–7). 1914. Discusses examples of this pastellist; illustrations of some of his portraits.
2082 Batten, Marjorie I. 'The architecture of Dr. Robert Hooke, F.R.S.' (Walpole Society, XXV, 83–113). 1937. A good treatment of this phase of Hooke's career.
2083 Bell, Charles F. 'English seventeenth-century portrait drawings in Oxford collections' (Walpole Society, V, 1–18). 1917. Continued by Bell and Mrs Reginald L. Poole in Walpole Society, XIV, 43–80 (1926).
2084 Bradac, Joseph. 'The art of Wenceslas Hollar', *Hist. T.*, **15** (Oct. 1965), 706–12.
2085 Burdon, Gerald. 'Sir Thomas Isham: an English collector in Rome in 1677–8', *Italian Studies*, **15** (1960), 1–25. An interesting sidelight on the grand tour.
2086 Emslie, Macdonald. 'Pepys songs and songbooks in the diary period', *Lib.*, 3rd ser., **12** (Dec. 1957), 240–55. Comments on songs mentioned in the diary, and attempts to identify songbooks.
2087 Esdaile, Katharine A. 'John Bushnell, sculptor' (Walpole Society, XV, 21–45). 1927. Deals with Restoration artist strongly influenced by Bernini.
2088 Gladding, Bessie A. 'Music as a social force during the English Commonwealth and the Restoration (1649–1700)', *Musical Quarterly*, **15** (Oct. 1929), 506–21.
2089 Hart, Eric F. 'The Restoration catch', *Music and Letters*, **34** (Oct. 1953), 288–305.
2090 Hill, Ralph. 'Henry Purcell', in Alfred L. Bacharach (ed.), *Lives of the great composers*, I, Harmondsworth, 1942, pp. 167–76.
2091 Hulton, Paul H. 'Drawings of England in the seventeenth century by Willem Schellinks, Jacob Esselens, and Lambert Doomer' (Walpole Society, XXXV, 2 pts.). 1959. Interesting for drawings providing views of seventeenth-century England. Part 1 is introduction and catalogue, part 2 plates.
2092 Knowles, John A. 'Henry Gyles, glass-painter of York' (Walpole Society, VIII, 47–72). 1923. Has illustrations of some of his Restoration windows.
2093 Lawrence, W. J. 'Foreign singers and musicians at the court of Charles II', *Musical Quarterly*, **9** (Apr. 1923), 217–25.
2094 Mackerness, Eric D. 'A speculative dilettante', *Music and Letters*, **34** (July 1953), 236–42. Discusses Roger North's comments on Restoration music; see North (2038).
2095 Murdock, W. G. Blaikie. 'Charles the Second: his connection with arts and letters', *Scottish Historical Review*, **3** (Oct. 1905), 41–52.
2096 Poole, Rachael E. 'Edward Pierce, the sculptor' (Walpole Society, VIII, 33–44). 1923.
2097 —— 'An outline of the history of the de Critz family of painters' (Walpole Society, II, 45–68). 1913. Contains material on Emmanuel de Critz, a court painter in the 1660s.
2098 Thomas, A. H. 'The rebuilding of London after the Great Fire', *Hist.*, **25** (Sept. 1940), 97–112.

2099 Tristram, Ernest W. 'A painted room of the seventeenth century' (Walpole Society, III, 75–81). 1914. Describes room decorated in 1669.

2100 Westrup, Jack A. 'Domestic music under the Stuarts', *Proceedings of the Musical Association*, **68** (1941–2), 19–53.

2101 —— 'Foreign musicians in Stuart England', *Musical Quarterly*, **27** (Jan. 1941), 70–89. Well documented.

XIV INTELLECTUAL HISTORY

1 Printed Sources

2102 Ashmole, Elias. *Autobiographical and historical notes, his correspondence, and other contemporary sources relating to his life and work*, ed. Conrad H. Josten. Oxford, 1967, 5 vols. An illuminating, well-edited work.

2103 Baskerville, Thomas. *Thomas Baskerville's account of Oxford*, c. *1670–1700*, ed. Humphrey Baskerville (Oxford Historical Society, XLVII, 179–225). Oxford, 1905. Describes the university and comments on figures of the time.

2104 Baxter, Richard. *Richard Baxter and puritan politics*, ed. Richard B. Schlatter. New Brunswick, N.J., 1957. Selections from his political writings, some hitherto unpublished.

2105 Brockbank, Thomas. *The diary and letter book of the rev. Thomas Brockbank, 1671–1709*, ed. Richard Trappes-Lomax (Chetham Society, new ser., LXXXIX). Manchester, 1930. Mostly after 1689, but has some interesting comment on his student days at Oxford.

2106 Browne, Thomas. *The works of Thomas Browne*, ed. Geoffrey L. Keynes. New ed., 1964, 4 vols.

2107 Burnet, Gilbert. *Some passages of the life and death of the right honourable John earl of Rochester . . . written by his own direction on his death-bed*. 1680. There is a facsimile ed. by Lord Ronald Gower (1875).

2108 Butler, Samuel. *Hudibras*, ed. John Wilders. Oxford, 1967.

2109 Campagnac, Ernest T. (ed.). *The Cambridge Platonists*. Oxford, 1901. Selections from their writings.

2110 Cragg, Gerald R. (ed.). *The Cambridge Platonists*. New York, 1968. Selections from their writings.

2111 Dryden, John. *The works of John Dryden*, ed. Edward N. Hooker *et al.* Berkeley, Calif., 1956–. One volume of the poems and two volumes of the plays have appeared to date.

2112 —— *The works of John Dryden*, ed. Walter Scott. 1808, 18 vols. Revised by George Saintsbury, Edinburgh, 1892–3, 18 vols. Now being superseded by (2111).

2113 Dugdale, William. *The life, diary, and correspondence of Sir William Dugdale*, ed. William Hamper. 1827. Diary covers 1643–86; correspondence 1635–86.

2114 Dunton, John. *The life and errors of John Dunton . . . with the lives and characters of more than a thousand contemporary divines and other persons of literary eminence*, ed. John B. Nichols. 1818, 2 vols. First published in 1705.

2115 Evelyn, John. *Miscellaneous writings, now first collected, with occasional notes*, ed. William Upcott. 1825.

2116 Filmer, Robert. *Patriarcha and other political works*, ed. Peter Laslett. Oxford, 1949. The best ed. of *Patriarcha.*

2117 Forster, Thomas (ed.). *Original letters of Locke, Algernon Sidney, and Anthony Lord Shaftesbury, author of the 'Characteristics'*. 1830.

2118 Halifax, George Savile, marquess of. *The complete works of George Savile, first marquess of Halifax*, ed. Walter Raleigh. Oxford, 1912.

2119 —— *Halifax: complete works*, ed. John P. Kenyon. Harmondsworth, 1969.

2120 Harrison, John and Peter Laslett. *The library of John Locke* (Oxford Bibliographical Society). Oxford, 1965. A catalogue of Locke's books, with interesting introductory comment.

2121 Hobbes, Thomas. *The English works of Thomas Hobbes*, ed. William Molesworth. 1839–45, 11 vols.

2122 Holdsworth, William S. 'Sir Matthew Hale on Hobbes', *LQR*, **37** (July 1921), 274–303. Three unpublished tracts.

2123 Hoole, Charles. *A new discovery of the old art of teaching school, in four small treatises*, ed. Ernest T. Campagnac. Liverpool, 1913. First published 1660.

2124 Lawrence, William. *The diary of William Lawrence, covering periods between 1662 and 1681*, ed. Gerald E. Aylmer. Beaminster, 1961. Mainly two letters by the minor poet, one in the form of a journal, 1675 and 1679.

2125 Locke, John. *The educational writings of John Locke*, ed. James L. Axtell. Cambridge, 1968. Primarily a critical ed. of *Some thoughts on education* (1693); also prints Locke's letters to Clarke on education, 1684–91.

2126 —— *Essays on the law of nature*, ed. W. von Leyden. Oxford, 1954. Contains hitherto unpublished writings.

2127 —— *Lettres inédites de John Locke*, ed. Henry Ollion. The Hague, 1912. Letters to Thoynard, van Limborch, and Clarke.

2128 —— *Two tracts on government*, ed. Philip Abrams. Cambridge, 1967.

2129 —— *Two treatises of government*, ed. Peter Laslett. Cambridge, 1960.

2130 —— *The works of John Locke*, ed. Edmund Law. New Ed., corrected, 1823, 10 vols.

2131 Lord, George de F. *et al.* (eds.). *Poems on affairs of state: Augustan satirical verse, 1660–1714*. New Haven, 1963–. Six vols. now in print. Vols. I–IV cover 1660–88.

2132 Marvell, Andrew. *Complete works in prose and verse*, ed. Alexander B. Grosart. 1872–5, 4 vols. Vol. II consists for the most part of letters describing parliamentary proceedings, 1660–78.

2133 —— *Poems and letters*, ed. Herschel M. Margoliouth. Oxford, 2nd ed., 1952. The standard edition. The correspondence (1653–78) is mainly of political interest.

2134 Milton, John. *Complete prose works of John Milton*, ed. Don M. Wolfe *et al.* New Haven, 1953–. The four volumes which have been published cover 1624–55. A full-scale critical edition with elaborate commentary.

2135 —— *The works of John Milton*, ed. Frank A. Patterson. New York, 1931–8, 18 vols. Vols. VI, X–XII, and XVIII are relevant for the period.

2136 Mintz, Samuel I. 'Hobbes on the law of heresy: a new manuscript', *JHI*, **29** (July–Sept. 1968), 409–14. The manuscript is dated 1673; opposes punishment for heresy.

2137 Nalson, John. *The common interest of king and people: showing the original antiquity and excellency of monarchy compared with aristocracy and democracy, and particularly of our English monarchy*. 1678.

2138 Nicolson, Marjorie Hope (ed.). *Conway letters: the correspondence of Anne, Viscountess Conway, Henry More, and their friends, 1642–1684*. New Haven, 1930. Also valuable for social and religious history.

2139 Poole, Dorothy L. 'Some unpublished letters of George Savile, Lord Halifax, to Gilbert Burnet', *EHR*, **26** (July 1911), 535–42. Ten letters, dated 1680–1.

2140 Rand, Benjamin (ed.). *The correspondence of John Locke and Edward Clarke*. 1927. Over 200 hitherto unpublished letters (1682–1704) illustrating various aspects of Locke's life and thought.

2141 Robbins, Caroline (ed.). *Two English republican tracts*. Cambridge, 1969. One is Henry Neville's *Plato redivivus* (1681), suggesting a republican solution to the problem of the Exclusion Controversy.

2142 Robinson, Matthew. *Autobiography of Matthew Robinson*, ed. John E. B. Mayor. Cambridge, 1856. Autobiography of an Anglican vicar and Cambridge don.

2143 Shadwell, Lionel L. (ed.). *Enactments in parliament specially concerning the universities of Oxford and Cambridge, the colleges and halls therein, and the colleges of Winchester, Eton, and Westminster* (Oxford Historical Society, LVII). Oxford, 1912. This volume covers the years from Edward III's reign to that of Anne.

2144 Sidney, Algernon. *Discourses concerning government published from an original manuscript*, ed. John Toland. 1698. Written during the early 1680s and published posthumously; an answer to Filmer (2116).

2145 —— *The works of Algernon Sidney*, ed. J. Robertson. 1772. Contains letters as well as philosophical works.

2146 Skinner, Quentin. 'Hobbes on sovereignty: an unknown discussion', *Political Studies*, **13** (no. 2, 1965), 213–18. A hitherto unpublished fragment.

2147 S[tarkey], G[eorge]. *The dignity of kingship asserted*, ed. William R. Parker (Facsimile Text Society, no. 54). New York, 1942. Originally published 1660; a reply to Milton's *Ready and easy way to establish a free commonwealth*.

2148 Temple, William. 'An essay upon the original and nature of government', ed. Robert C. Steensma (Augustan Reprint Society, no. 109). Los Angeles, 1964. Written in 1672; first published 1680.

2149 Varley, Frederick J. 'The Restoration visitation of the university of Oxford and its colleges' (Camden Miscellany, XVIII, 3rd ser., LXXIX). 1948.

2150 Walker, Obadiah. *Of education, especially of young gentlemen*. Oxford, 1673.

2151 Ward, Charles E. (ed.). *The letters of John Dryden, with letters addressed to him*. Durham, N.C., 1942.

2152 Whichcot, Benjamin. *The works of the learned Benjamin Whichcot*. Aberdeen, 1751, 4 vols. Writings of a prominent Cambridge Platonist.

2153 Wood, Anthony à. *Athenae oxonienses: an exact history of all the writers and bishops who have had their education in the... University of Oxford*, ed. Philip Bliss. 1813–20, 4 vols. First published 1691–2. Short biographies; valuable but in need of revision.

2154 Worthington, John. *The diary and correspondence of Dr. John Worthington, master of Jesus College, Cambridge*, ed. James Crossley and Richard C. Christie (Chetham Society, XIII, XXXVI). Manchester, 1847–55. Covers 1617–67. The Restoration terminated Worthington's academic career; thereafter he held various church livings.

2 Surveys

2155 Carré, Meyrick H. *Phases of thought in England*. Oxford, 1949.

2156 Dunning, William A. *A history of political theories from Luther to Montesquieu*. New York, 1905.

2157 Gooch, George P. *Political thought in England from Bacon to Halifax*. 1915.

2158 Hearnshaw, Fossey J. C. (ed.). *The social and political ideas of some English thinkers of the Augustan age, A.D. 1650–1750*. 1928. Lectures by various persons.

2159 Laski, Harold J. *Political thought in England from Locke to Bentham*. 1920.

2160 Sabine, George H. *A history of political theory*. 3rd ed., New York, 1961. Useful brief treatments of leading political thinkers, including Hobbes, Halifax, and Locke.

2161 Sutherland, James. *English literature of the late seventeenth century* (Oxford History of English Literature, VI). Oxford, 1969. A valuable survey; has detailed bibliographical sections useful for students of social and intellectual history.

2162 Ward, Adolphus W. and Alfred R. Waller (eds.). *The Cambridge history of English literature*, VIII, *The age of Dryden*. 1912. Contains useful chapters on various subjects, including early Quakers, political and ecclesiastical satire, memoir- and letter-writers, Platonists and latitudinarians.

3 Monographs

2163 Aaron, Richard I. *John Locke*. 2nd ed., corrected, Oxford, 1963. Primarily an analysis of Locke's philosophy, but contains a short biographical essay.

2164 Adamson, John W. *Pioneers of modern education, 1600–1700*. 1905.

2165 Allen, Beverly Sprague. *Tides in English taste (1619–1800): a background for the study of literature*. Cambridge, Mass., 1937, 2 vols. Deals mostly with the eighteenth century, but vol. I is of some use for the period.

2166 Armytage, Walter H. G. *Four hundred years of English education*. Cambridge, 1965.

2167 Bastide, Charles. *John Locke: ses théories politiques et leur influence en Angleterre*. Paris, 1907. Part 1 is a biography.

2168 Beales, Arthur C. F. *Education under penalty: English Catholic education from the Reformation to the fall of James II, 1547–1689*. 1963.

2169 Beatty, Edward C. O. *William Penn as a social philosopher*. New York, 1939. The title notwithstanding, this is primarily useful in describing Penn's activities as a colony-founder.

2170 Beljame, Alexandre. *Men of letters and the English public in the eighteenth century, 1660–1744: Dryden, Addison, Pope*, ed. Bonamy Dobrée. 1948. A translation of a work originally published in Paris, 1881.

2171 Bense, Johan F. *The Anglo-Dutch relations from the earliest times to the death of William the Third*. The Hague, 1924. Deals mostly with cultural, social, and economic relations.

2172 Bonno, Gabriel D. *Les relations intellectuelles de Locke avec la France, d'après des documents inédits* (University of California Publications in Modern Philology, XXXVIII, no. 2). Berkeley, 1955. Includes an extensive bibliography.

2173 Bowle, John. *Hobbes and his critics: a study in seventeenth-century constitutionalism*. 1951.

2174 Brauer, George C., Jr. *The education of a gentleman: theories of gentlemanly education in England, 1660–1775*. New York, 1959.

2175 Bredvold, Louis I. *The intellectual milieu of John Dryden: studies in some aspects of seventeenth-century thought*. Ann Arbor, Mich., 1934. Interesting for science, Roman Catholic apologetics, and Toryism, among other things. The principal thesis, on Dryden's religious scepticism, is opposed by Harth (2200).

2176 Cassirer, Ernst. *Die platonische Renaissance in England und die Schule von Cambridge*. Leipzig, 1932. English trans., James P. Pettegrove, 1953.

2177 Clarke, Martin L. *Classical education in Britain, 1500–1900*. Cambridge, 1959.

2178 Cox, Richard H. *Locke on war and peace*. Oxford, 1960. An interpretation of Locke's theory of natural law and political society.

2179 Curtis, Stanley J. *History of education in Great Britain*. 7th ed., 1967.

2180 De Boer, John J. *The theory of knowledge of the Cambridge Platonists*. Madras, 1931. A doctoral dissertation.

2181 De Pauley, William C. *The candle of the Lord: studies in the Cambridge Platonists* (Church Historical Society Publications, new ser., no. 28). 1937. Treats nine figures, including Whichcote, More, Cudworth, and Stillingfleet.

2182 Douglas, David C. *English scholars, 1660–1730*. 2nd ed., rev., 1951. Deals with work in England on English medieval history.

2183 Dunn, John M. *The political thought of John Locke: an historical account of the argument of the 'Two treatises of government'*. Cambridge, 1969.

2184 Figgis, John N. *The theory of the divine right of kings*, ed. Geoffrey R. Elton. New York, 1965. Originally published in 1896; still an important monograph.

2185 Fink, Zera S. *The classical republicans: an essay in the recovery of a pattern of thought in seventeenth-century England* (Northwestern University Studies in the Humanities, no. 9). Evanston, Ill., 1945. An illuminating study, with an excellent bibliography.

2186 Fox, Levi (ed.). *English historical scholarship in the sixteenth and seventeenth centuries*. 1956. A collection of papers by prominent scholars.

2187 Frantz, Ray W. *The English traveller and the movement of ideas, 1660–1732* (University of Nebraska Studies, XXXII–XXXIII). Lincoln, 1934; paperback ed., 1967. Mainly concerned with natural science, religion, ethics, and politics.

2188 Gardiner, Dorothy. *English girlhood at school: a study of women's education through twelve centuries*. 1929.

2189 Gibson, James. *Locke's theory of knowledge and its historical relations.* Cambridge, 1917.

2190 Gillett, Charles R. *Burned books: neglected chapters in British history and literature.* New York, 1932, 2 vols. Vol. II provides considerable information on the period.

2191 Goldsmith, Maurice M. *Hobbes's science of politics.* 1966. Argues that Hobbes sought to create a philosophical system encompassing both natural and political science.

2192 Gooch, George P. *English democratic ideas in the seventeenth century*, 2nd ed., with notes by Harold J. Laski. Cambridge, 1927. A useful introduction to the subject.

2193 —— *Hobbes.* 1940. A lecture.

2194 Gough, John W. *John Locke's political philosophy: eight studies.* Oxford, 1950.

2195 —— *The social contract: a critical study of its development.* Oxford, 1936. Important for the development and application of the theory.

2196 Greenleaf, William H. *Order, empiricism, and politics: two traditions of English political thought, 1500–1700.* 1964. Has chapters on Harrington and Sir William Petty.

2197 Greenslet, Ferris. *Joseph Glanvill: a study of English thought and letters of the seventeenth century* (Columbia University Studies in English). New York, 1900.

2198 Gunn, John A. W. *Politics and the public interest in the seventeenth century.* 1969.

2199 Harris, Brice. *Charles Sackville, sixth earl of Dorset: patron and poet of the Restoration* (Illinois Studies in Language and Literature, XVI, nos. 3–4). Urbana, 1940.

2200 Harth, Philip. *Contexts of Dryden's thought.* Chicago, 1968. Deals primarily with religious thought. Cf. Bredvold (2175).

2201 Higgons, Bevill. *Historical and critical remarks on Bishop Burnet's History of his own time.* 1725. A reply to Burnet.

2202 Hodgkin, Robert H. *Six centuries of an Oxford college: a history of the Queen's College, 1340–1940.* Oxford, 1949.

2203 Hood, Francis C. *The divine politics of Thomas Hobbes.* Oxford, 1964. An interpretation of *Leviathan.*

2204 Hutchinson, Francis E. *Milton and the English mind.* 1946. Useful for Milton's ideas, social, religious, and political.

2205 James, David G. *The life of reason: Hobbes, Locke, Bolingbroke.* 1949. Primarily concerned with literary and religious consequences of their writings. Excellent on Locke.

2206 Kendall, Willmoore. *John Locke and the doctrine of majority rule* (Illinois Studies in the Social Sciences, XXVI, no. 2). Urbana, 1941.

2207 Lambley, Katherine. *The teaching and cultivation of the French language in England during Tudor and Stuart times.* 1920. An excellent piece of research. Includes chapter on Gallomania after the Restoration.

2208 Lamprecht, Sterling P. *The moral and political philosophy of John Locke.* New York, 1918.

2209 Laurie, Simon S. *Studies in the history of educational opinion from the Renaissance.* Cambridge, 1903. Includes treatment of Comenius, Milton, and Locke.

2210 Leeuwen, Henry G. van. *The problem of certainty in English thought, 1630–1690.* The Hague, 1963. Deals with attempts to develop a theory of knowledge justifying scientific investigation.

2211 McLachlan, Herbert. *English education under the Test Acts, being the history of the nonconformist academies, 1662–1820.* Manchester, 1931.

2212 Macpherson, Crawford B. *The political theory of possessive individualism, Hobbes to Locke.* Oxford, 1962. Seeks a consistent pattern in the speculations of seventeenth-century political thinkers; Marxist assumptions.

2213 Mallet, Charles E. *A history of the University of Oxford*, II, *The sixteenth and seventeenth centuries.* 1924. The standard history, with a chapter on 'The Oxford of Anthony Wood'.

2214 Manuel, Frank E. *Isaac Newton, historian.* Cambridge, Mass., 1963. An excellent study, though mostly after the period.

2215 Mintz, Samuel I. *The hunting of Leviathan: seventeenth-century reactions to the materialism and moral philosophy of Thomas Hobbes*. Cambridge, 1962.

2216 Morris, Charles R. *Locke, Berkeley, Hume*. Oxford, 1931. Individual treatments, under headings of life, theory of knowledge, and moral, political and economic theory.

2217 Mullinger, James B. *The University of Cambridge*. Cambridge, 1873–1911, 3 vols. The standard work. Vol. III covers 1626 to *c*. 1670.

2218 Parker, Irene. *Dissenting academies in England: their rise and progress, and their place among the educational systems of the country*. Cambridge, 1914. Appendix gives list of academies.

2219 Pocock, John G. A. *The ancient constitution and the feudal law: a study of English historical thought in the seventeenth century*. Cambridge, 1957. Substantial; the last three chapters deal with the period.

2220 Powicke, Frederick J. *The Cambridge Platonists: a study*. 1926. Supersedes Tulloch (2235).

2221 Raab, Felix. *The English face of Machiavelli: a changing interpretation, 1500–1700*. 1964. Mostly pre-1660, but has an interesting chapter on the period.

2222 Reynolds, Myra. *The learned lady in England, 1650–1760*. Boston, Mass., 1920. Valuable for the education of women; good bibliography.

2223 Robbins, Caroline. *The eighteenth-century commonwealthsman: studies in the transition, development, and circumstance of English liberal thought from the restoration of Charles II until the war with the thirteen colonies*. Cambridge, Mass., 1959. Thorough scholarship, based on wide research; two chapters on seventeenth-century thinkers, notably Harrington and Locke.

2224 Roberts, Sydney C. *A history of the Cambridge University Press, 1521–1921*. Cambridge, 1921.

2225 Rostenberg. Leona. *Literary, political, scientific, religious, and legal publishing, printing, and bookselling in England, 1551–1700: twelve studies*. New York, 1965, 2 vols. Vol. II has two chapters on the period. There is an index of booksellers.

2226 Sandys, John E. *A history of classical scholarship*, II, *From the revival of learning to the end of the eighteenth century*. Repr. 1967. Deals with France, Italy, and the Netherlands, as well as England.

2227 Seliger, Martin. *The liberal politics of John Locke*. 1968.

2228 Sensabaugh, George F. *That grand Whig, Milton*. Stanford, Calif., 1952. Milton's importance in inspiring Whig theories of government.

2229 Smith, Joe William Ashley. *The birth of modern education: the contribution of the dissenting academies, 1660–1800*. 1954.

2230 Stauffer, Donald A. *English biography before 1700*. Cambridge, Mass., 1930. A historical and critical treatment. Good bibliography, including a list of about sixty of the 'most important' English biographies, 1660–1700.

2231 Stephen, Leslie. *History of English thought in the eighteenth century*. 1876, 2 vols. Begins with writers of the Restoration era.

2232 Straka, Gerald M. *Anglican reaction to the Revolution of 1688*. Madison, Wis. 1962. An interesting investigation of divine right and its relation to the Revolution.

2233 Strauss, Leo. *The political philosophy of Hobbes: its basis and its genesis*. Oxford, 1936.

2234 Tawney, Richard H. *Religion and the rise of capitalism*. 1926.

2235 Tulloch, John. *Rational theology and Christian philosophy in England in the seventeenth century*. Edinburgh, 1872, 2 vols. Superseded by Powicke (2220).

2236 Vaughan, Charles E. *Studies in the history of political philosophy before and after Rousseau*, ed. Andrew G. Little. Manchester, 1925, 2 vols. Hobbes and Locke are treated in vol. I, which is primarily concerned with the social contract.

2237 *Victoria county history of Oxford*, III: *The University of Oxford*, ed. Herbert E. Salter and Mary D. Lobel. 1954. Contributions by various writers; profusely illustrated.

2238 Wagner, Anthony R. *Heralds of England: a history of the office and College of Arms*. 1967. Demonstrates, among other things, the association between heraldry and antiquarian scholarship, as promoted by Dugdale and Ashmole.

2239 Wallace, John M. *Destiny his choice: the loyalism of Andrew Marvell*. 1968. An attempt to resolve the problem of shifting allegiances.

2240 Warrender, Howard. *The political philosophy of Hobbes*. Oxford, 1957.

2241 Watkins, J. W. N. *Hobbes's system of ideas: a study in the political significance of philosophical theories*. 1965. A clear introductory survey, of value to historians.

2242 Wedgwood, Cicely V. *Poetry and politics under the Stuarts*, Cambridge, 1960. Lectures.

2243 Willey, Basil. *The seventeenth century background: studies in the thought of the age in relation to poetry and religion*. 1934. A stimulating work.

2244 Wormald, Francis and Cyril E. Wright (eds.). *The English library before 1700*. 1958.

2245 Wright, Luella M. *Literary life of the early Friends* (Columbia University Studies). New York, 1932.

2246 —— *Literature and education in early Quakerism* (University of Iowa Studies, Humanistic Series, v, no. 2). Iowa City, 1933.

2247 Yolton, John W. (ed.). *John Locke: problems and perspectives, a collection of new essays*. Cambridge, 1969. Thirteen essays on various aspects of Locke's thought.

4 Biographies

2248 Bourne, Henry Richard Fox. *Life of John Locke*. 1876, 2 vols. Based on extensive research.

2249 Cranston, Maurice W. *John Locke: a biography*. New York, 1957. The standard life. Uses important Locke papers in the Bodleian.

2250 Foster, Joseph (comp.). *Alumni oxonienses: the members of the University of Oxford, 1500–1714*. Oxford, 1891–2, 4 vols. Comprised of very brief notices.

2251 Heal, Ambrose. *The English writing-masters and their copy-books, 1570–1800: a biographical dictionary and a bibliography*. Cambridge, 1931. With an introduction by Stanley Morison on the development of handwriting.

2252 Hiscock, Walter G. *Henry Aldrich of Christ Church, 1648–1710*. Oxford, 1960.

2253 King, Peter, Baron. *The life of John Locke, with extracts from his correspondence, journals, and common-place books*. 1829. King was a descendant of Locke's executor.

2254 Legouis, Pierre A. *Marvell: poète, puritain, patriote, 1621–1678*. 1928. Also an English translation, 2nd ed., Oxford, 1968, with minor corrections and additional material, chiefly bibliographical.

2255 Marburg, Clara. *Sir William Temple: a seventeenth-century 'libertin'*. New Haven, 1932. Temple as philosopher, historian, and critic.

2256 Masson, David. *The life of John Milton, narrated in connection with the political, ecclesiastical, and literary history of his time*. 1859–94, 7 vols. Valuable and well-nigh exhaustive.

2257 Parker, William R. *Milton: a biography*. Oxford, 1968, 2 vols.

2258 Petersson, Robert T. *Sir Kenelm Digby: the ornament of England, 1603–1665*. Cambridge, Mass., 1956. A detailed account of the life of a virtuoso, but little on the period.

2259 Pinto, Vivian de S. *English biography in the seventeenth century: selected short lives*. 1951. Includes Aubrey (846) on Boyle, Hobbes, Marvell, and Milton.

2260 Ponsonby, Arthur P., Baron. *John Evelyn*. 1933. Discusses Evelyn's interests and activities.

2261 Saurat, Denis. *Milton: man and thinker*. Rev. ed., 1944.

2262 Stephen, Leslie. *Hobbes*. 1904.

2263 Venn, John and John A. (comps.). *Alumni cantabrigienses: a biographical list of all known students, graduates, and holders of office at the University of Cambridge*, pt. 1, *From the earliest times to 1751*. 1922–7, 4 vols. Short notices, but superior to Foster (2250).

2264 Ward, Charles E. *The life of John Dryden*. Chapel Hill, N.C., 1961. A valuable, comprehensive treatment.

2265 Ward, John. *The lives of the professors of Gresham College*. 1740. Includes interesting sketches on Hooke and Wren.

2266 Woodbridge, Homer E. *Sir William Temple: the man and his work* (Modern Language Association of America, Monograph Series, XII). New York, 1940.

5 Articles

2267 Adamson, John W. 'Education', in Adolphus W. Ward and Alfred R. Waller (eds.), *The Cambridge history of English literature*, IX (1912), chap. 15. Covers *c.* 1660–1760; has useful bibliography.

2268 Ashcraft, Richard. 'Locke's state of nature: historical fact or moral fiction', *American Political Science Review*, **52** (Sept. 1968), 898–915.

2269 Axtell, James L. 'The mechanics of opposition: Restoration Cambridge *v.* Daniel Scargill', *BIHR*, **38** (May 1965), 102–11. Scargill was convicted of atheism.

2270 Behrens, Betty. 'The Whig theory of the constitution in the reign of Charles II', *Camb. Hist. J.*, **7** (no. 1, 1941), 42–71.

2271 Butt, John. 'The facilities for antiquarian study in the seventeenth century', *Essays and Studies by Members of the English Association*, **24** (1939), 64–79.

2272 Cherry, George L. 'The legal and philosophical position of the Jacobites, 1688–1689', *JMH*, **22** (Dec. 1950), 309–21.

2273 Colie, Rosalie L. 'Spinoza and the early English deists', *JHI*, **20** (Jan. 1959), 23–46.

2274 —— 'Spinoza in England, 1665–1730', *Proceedings of the American Philosophical Society*, **107** (1963), 183–219. Contains some hitherto unpublished writings of Robert Boyle relating to Spinoza and the subject of miracles.

2275 Cope, Jackson I. 'Joseph Glanvill, Anglican apologist: old ideas and new style in the Restoration', *Publications of the Modern Language Association*, **69** (Mar. 1954), 223–50. An examination of Glanvill's thought with regard to certain aspects of late seventeenth-century intellectual developments.

2276 Corson, James C. 'Resistance no rebellion', *Juridical Review*, **42** (Sept. 1930), 245–56. Discusses juridical aspects of the Whig interpretation of the Revolution of 1688.

2277 Cronne, H. A. 'The study and use of charters by English scholars in the seventeenth century', in Levi Fox (ed.), *English historical scholarship in the sixteenth and seventeenth centuries*, Oxford, 1956, pp. 73–91. See (2186). Deals with Henry Spelman and Sir William Dugdale.

2278 Davies, Godfrey. 'The conclusion of Dryden's *Absalom and Achitophel*', *HLQ*, **10** (Nov. 1946), 69–82. Advances idea that Dryden was influenced by Charles II.

2279 —— 'Milton in 1660', *HLQ*, **18** (Aug. 1955), 351–63. How Milton fared.

2280 Dickins, Bruce. 'Henry Gostling's library: a young don's books in 1674', *Transactions of the Cambridge Bibliographical Society*, **3** (no. 3, 1961), 216–24.

2281 Douglas, David C. 'The development of English medieval scholarship between 1660 and 1730', *TRHS*, 4th ser., **21** (1939), 21–39. See also (2182).

2282 —— 'William Dugdale, the "grand plagiary"', *Hist.*, **20** (Dec. 1935), 193–210. A sympathetic discussion of the charge of plagiarism.

2283 Duncan, James L. 'The end and aim of law, II: legal theories in the sixteenth and seventeenth centuries', *Juridical Review*, **50** (Sept. 1938), 257–81. Important.

2284 —— 'The end and aim of law, III: the Revolution of 1688 and eighteenth-century theories of law', *Juridical Review*, **50** (Dec. 1938), 404–38. Important.

2285 —— 'Juristic theories of the British revolution of 1688', *Juridical Review*, **44** (Mar. 1932), 30–8. Emphasis on Locke.

2286 Dunn, John M. 'Consent in the political theory of John Locke', *Hist. J.*, **10** (no. 2, 1967), 153–82.

2287 —— 'Justice and the interpretation of Locke's political theory', *Political Studies*, **16** (Feb. 1968), 68–87.

2288 Fink, Zera S. 'King and doge: a chapter in Anglo-Venetian political and literary relations', *English Studies Today*, 4th ser., **4** (1966), 212–33. Deals with project for reducing royal power to that of the doge.

2289 Firth, Charles H. 'Burnet as an historian', in his *Essays historical and literary*, Oxford, 1938, pp. 174–209. Reprinted from the introduction to Clarke and Foxcroft (1849).

2290 —— 'The development of the study of seventeenth-century history', *TRHS*, 3rd ser., **7** (1913), 25–48. How historical knowledge of the period was acquired.

2291 Foxcroft, Helen C. 'The works of George Savile, first marquis of Halifax', *EHR*, **11** (Oct. 1896), 703–30.

2292 Fulton, John F. 'Robert Boyle and his influence on thought in the seventeenth century', *Isis*, **18** (1932), 77–102.

2293 Gooch, George P. 'Burnet and the Stuart kings', in his *Courts and cabinets*, 1944, pp. 70–85.

2294 Greene, Robert A. 'Henry More and Robert Boyle: on the spirit of nature', *JHI*, **23** (Oct.–Dec. 1962), 451–74. Focus is on second half of the seventeenth century.

2295 Greenleaf, William H. 'Filmer's patriarchal history', *Hist. J.*, **9** (no. 2, 1966), 157–71.

2296 Gunn, John A. W. '"Interest will not lie": a seventeenth-century political maxim', *JHI*, **29** (Oct.–Dec. 1968), 551–64.

2297 Ham, Roswell S. 'Dryden as historiographer-royal: the authorship of *His Majesties declaration defended*, 1681', *Review of English Studies*, **11** (July 1935), 284–98.

2298 Hardacre, Paul H. 'Portrait of a bibliophile: Edward Hyde, earl of Clarendon, 1609–1674', *Book Collector*, **7** (Winter 1958), 361–8.

2299 Hinton, Raymond W. K. 'Husbands, fathers, and conquerors, I: Filmer and the logic of patriarchalism', *Political Studies*, **15** (no. 3, 1967), 291–300.

2300 —— 'Husbands, fathers, and conquerors, II: Patriarchalism in Hobbes and Locke', *Political Studies*, **16** (no. 1, 1968), 55–67.

2301 Hoppen, K. Theodore. 'Sir William Petty, polymath, 1623–1687', *Hist. T.*, **15** (Jan. 1965), 126–34. A general assessment.

2302 Houghton, Walter E., Jr. 'The English virtuoso in the seventeenth century', *JHI*, **3** (Jan., Apr. 1942), 51–73, 190–219.

2303 Kaufmann, Moritz. 'Latitudinarianism and pietism', in *CMH*, v, 742–63. 1908.

2304 Krook, Dorothea. 'Two Baconians: Robert Boyle and Joseph Glanvill', *HLQ*, **18** (May 1955), 261–78.

2305 Lamprecht, Sterling P. 'Hobbes and Hobbism', *American Political Science Review*, **34** (Feb. 1940), 31–53.

2306 —— 'Innate ideas in the Cambridge Platonists', *Philosophical Review*, **35** (Nov. 1926), 553–73. Deals with the period 1650–90, prior to the publication of Locke's *Essay concerning humane understanding*.

2307 —— 'The role of Descartes in seventeenth-century England', *Studies in the History of Ideas*, III, 181–240. New York, 1935. Stresses widespread and consequential influence of Descartes, 1640–1700.

2308 Laslett, Peter. 'The English revolution and Locke's *Two treatises of government*', *Camb. Hist. J.*, **12** (no. 1, 1956), 40–55. Maintains that Locke wrote the treatises by *c.* 1681, and not in 1688. Important.

2309 Linnell, Charles L. S. 'Daniel Scargill: "a penitent Hobbist"', *CQR*, **156** (July–Sept. 1955), 256–65. See also Axtell (2269).

2310 Lord, George de F. 'Satire and sedition: the life and work of John Ayloffe', *HLQ*, **29** (May 1966), 255–73.

2311 Lough, John. 'Locke's reading during his stay in France (1675–79)', *Lib.*, 5th ser., **8** (Dec. 1953), 229–58. A list, compiled from Bodleian Library manuscripts.

2312 MacLean, A. H. 'George Lawson and John Locke', *Camb. Hist. J.*, **9** (no. 1, 1947), 69–77. Lawson's works, according to MacLean, show that the major concepts in Locke's second *Treatise* had been expressed in England by 1660.

2313 Macpherson, Crawford B. 'Sir William Temple, political scientist?', *Canadian Journal of Economics and Political Science*, **9** (Feb. 1943), 39–54.

2314 —— 'The social bearing of Locke's political theory', *Western Political Quarterly*, **7** (Mar. 1954), 1–22.

2315 Madan, Falconer, 'The Oxford Press, 1650–75: the struggle for a place in the sun', *Lib.*, 4th ser., **6** (Sept. 1925), 113–47.

2316 Mosse, George L. 'Thomas Hobbes: jurisprudence at the crossroads', *University of Toronto Quarterly*, **15** (July 1946), 346–55. Maintains that Hobbes's criticism of the common law demonstrates a growing divergence between legal practice and political thought.

2317 Mullinger, James B. 'Platonists and latitudinarians', *CMH*, VIII, chap. 11. 1912. Includes some Restoration writers and their works; bibliography.

2318 Nicolson, Marjorie Hope. 'Christ's College and the latitude-men', *Mod. Phil.*, **27** (Aug. 1929), 35–53. Largely pre-1660.

2319 Nobbs, Douglas. 'Philip Nye on church and state', *Camb. Hist. J.*, **5** (no. 1, 1935), 41–59. Deals with the writings of a prominent independent divine.

2320 O'Neil, Charles J. 'Is Locke's state the secular state?', *New Scholasticism*, **26** (Oct. 1952), 424–40. Maintains that Locke paved the way for the modern secular state.

2321 Parks, George B. 'The decline and fall of the English renaissance admiration of Italy', *HLQ*, **31** (Aug. 1968), 341–57. Sees the decline spreading from France to England during the Restoration years.

2322 Pocock, John G. A. 'Robert Brady, 1627–1700: a Cambridge historian of the Restoration', *Camb. Hist. J.*, **10** (no. 2, 1951), 186–204. See Brady (212).

2323 Pollard, Alfred W. 'English book sales, 1676–1680, 1681–1686', *Bibliographica*, **1** (1895), 373–84; **2** (1896), 112–26.

2324 Quintana, Ricardo. 'Notes on English educational opinion during the seventeenth century', *Studies in Philology*, **27** (Apr. 1930), 265–92. Scattered references to the period.

2325 Randall, Helen W. 'The rise and fall of a martyrology: sermons on Charles I', *HLQ*, **10** (Feb. 1947), 135–67. Traces anniversary sermons on Charles I's death, from 1649 to the nineteenth century.

2326 Robbins, Caroline. 'Algernon Sidney's *Discourses concerning government:* textbook of revolution', *William and Mary Quarterly*, 3rd ser., **4** (July 1947), 267–96.

2327 Rogers, C. A. G. 'Boyle, Locke, and reason', *JHI*, **27** (Apr.–June 1966), 205–16.

2328 Romanell, Patrick. 'Locke's aphorisms on education and health', *JHI*, **22** (Oct.–Dec. 1961), 549–54. Discusses *Some thoughts concerning education.* Based on letters from Locke to Edward Clarke. See also Rand (2140).

2329 —— 'Robert Scott: Restoration stationer and importer', *Papers of the Bibliographical Society of America*, **48** (1st quarter 1954), 49–76. An account of a versatile man, regarded at the time as the greatest librarian in Europe.

2330 —— 'Robert Stephens, messenger of the press: an episode in seventeenth-century censorship', *Papers of the Bibliographical Society of America*, **49** (2nd quarter 1955), 131–52. Interesting on the suppression of anti-royalist sentiment.

2331 Rowen, Herbert H. 'A second thought on Locke's *First treatise*', *JHI*, **17** (Jan. 1956), 130–2. Regards the treatise as essential for Locke's total argument for the social compact state.

2332 Schwoerer, Lois G. 'Roger North and his notes on legal education', *HLQ*, **22** (Aug. 1959), 323–43.

2333 Sensabaugh, George F. 'Milton and the attempted Whig revolution', in Richard F. Jones *et al.*, *The seventeenth century: studies in the history of English thought and literature from Bacon to Pope*, Stanford, Calif., 1951, pp. 291–305.

2334 Sensabaugh, George F. 'Milton and the doctrine of passive obedience', *HLQ*, **13** (Nov. 1949), 19–54.

2335 —— 'Milton and the Revolution settlement', *HLQ*, **9** (Feb. 1946), 175–208. The influence of Milton's ideas.

2336 Simon, Walter M. 'John Locke: philosophy and political theory', *American Political Science Review*, **45** (June 1951), 386–99. Essentially a comparison of the *Essay concerning humane understanding* with the *Second treatise of civil government*.

2337 Skinner, Quentin. 'History and ideology in the English revolution', *Hist. J.*, **8** (no. 2, 1965), 151–78. Investigates various historical and ideological attitudes in the seventeenth century.

2338 —— 'The ideological context of Hobbes's political thought', *Hist. J.*, **9** (no. 3, 1966), 286–317.

2339 Smith, Donal. 'The political beliefs of Andrew Marvell', *University of Toronto Quarterly*, **36** (Oct. 1966), 55–67.

2340 Smith, John Harrington. 'Some sources of Dryden's toryism, 1682–1684', *HLQ*, **20** (May 1957), 233–44.

2341 Snow, Vernon F. 'The concept of revolution in seventeenth-century England', *Hist. J.*, **5** (no. 2, 1962), 167–74.

2342 Stapleton, Laurence. 'Halifax and Raleigh', *JHI*, **2** (Apr. 1941), 211–24. Maintains that they display a 'surprising' similarity of opinions.

2343 Stewart, Herbert L. 'The personality of Thomas Hobbes', *Hibbert Journal*, **47** (Jan. 1949), 123–31.

2344 Upham, Alfred H. 'English *femmes savantes* at the end of the seventeenth century', *Journal of English and Germanic Philology*, **12** (1913), 262–76.

2345 Wagner, Fritz. 'Church history and secular history as reflected by Newton and his time', *History and Theory*, no. 1 (1969), 97–111.

2346 Westfall, Richard S. 'Isaac Newton: religious rationalist or mystic?', *Review of Religion*, **22** (Mar. 1958), 155–70.

2347 Whiting, Charles E. 'The study of the classics in England during the Restoration period', *Durham University Journal*, **26** (1928–30), 255–69, 339–48.

2348 Whitley, William T. 'Private schools, 1660–1689: a study based on Matthews' *Calamy revised*', *Congregational History Society Transactions*, **12** (Sept. 1934), 172–85.

2349 Wood, Thomas. 'A great English casuist', *CQR*, **147** (Oct.–Dec. 1948), 29–45. Deals with Robert Sanderson, bishop of Lincoln (1660–3).

2350 Yolton, John W. 'Locke and the seventeenth-century logic of ideas', *JHI*, **16** (Oct. 1955), 431–52.

INDEX OF AUTHORS, EDITORS, AND TRANSLATORS

[*Numbers are entry numbers*]